SONG OF A SPARROW

by

C. S. Ragsdale

authorHOUSE™

Bloomington   London

First published by AuthorHouse 07/29/05

ISBN: 1-4208-2440-6 (sc)
ISBN: 1-4208-2439-2 (dj)

Printed in the United States of America
Bloomington, Indiana

This book is printed on acid-free paper.

This book is based on a true story.
Fictitious names are used for all characters except
family members and historical figures.
Interviews with and the diary of Benny Lipman
provide documentation.

Cover Artist Christopher Oppegard
is a high school senior and will attend
Mary Hardin Baylor University where he will
major in advertising/graphic design.

AUTHOR'S NOTE

When I reflect on the moments that have most influenced my life, I call them God's winks -- flashes of intuition that may have been lost forever had I not acknowledged them. I am thankful I recognized the "moment clues" that led me to one of the most remarkable experiences of my life.

In early 1994 a former teacher handed me Benny Lipman's diary to read and asked me to consider writing a book based on his struggle to survive the bloodbath of European World War II. Because of my many years researching the Holocaust, I was comfortable with the historical perspective, but when I read his diary, the task seemed daunting. How could I put into words this boy's battle with loss and fear, as well as his physical and mental abuse?

Little did I know that a remarkable experience was awaiting me. I spent considerable time preparing for the series of interviews. As an historian I had a number of questions about facts -- dates and documented incidents. I made timelines and maps -- one set based on Benny's diary and the other on secondary documented sources.

Further, I made a list of typical interview questions, and a separate list, which I called "my intuitive questions." The latter dealt with the things I sensed as I read the diary.

During our initial interview, Benny and I discussed the maps and the timelines to determine their accuracy. I told him I would ask two different sets of questions, and I started with the general ones. Toward the end of the first day of interviews, I tried one of the "intuitive questions." I explained that I would act out a scene, after which I would ask for his response. As I concluded the first scene, his eyes began to tear. With trembling voice, he asked, "How do you know my soul? How is it that you know? I have never told anyone." Without waiting for an answer, he looked toward the ceiling and said, "Thank you, God, for sending this woman to me."

Each time I presented a scene, Benny appeared overwhelmed, and I have to admit, I was stunned. This was just the beginning of a bond that empowered both of us.

Throughout the writing of the book, the intuition became stronger. At one point, I went to see a rabbi and explained what was happening. His answer was quick, "You are guided by God. You must listen, for a book written by a Gentile about a Jew will be ten times more powerful."

Driven, I climbed daily the ladder to my attic writing room and there, I wrote feverishly. With each scene that recorded Benny's astonishing escapes, his bravery, perseverance, and sagacity to survive the many uncertainties he faced, I too gained strength. As I wrote, I listened to Mozart and other favorites of the Lipman family. When I had unexpected surgery and could not climb to the attic room or sit to type, I dictated scenes to a friend who typed them for me.

By late summer 1995, I sent the first draft to Benny. Within days he telephoned. Between the sobs, he said to me, "There is absolutely no way anyone can convince me you were not with me during those horrible times. I sleep with this manuscript next to my heart."

Benny's life story is an amazing account of courage. This book is based on our interviews and the diary he wrote after his liberation. The dialogue is constructed not only from Benny's diary but also from our intensive talks. Substantial documentation collaborates his diary and validates the circumstances of Jewish life during the war. The published diaries of Adam Czerniakow and Chaim A. Kaplan -- Jews caught up in the Holocaust that ravaged Warsaw, Poland -- enrich Benny's story with data the boy would not have known or remembered. Czerniakow, Jewish Judenrat Chairman, was a personal friend of Benny's family, and Kaplan was a teacher who once lived near the Lipmans.

Song of a Sparrow gives a unique perspective of the Holocaust. From Benny's perseverance we learn that within each of us is the instinct to survive; the knowledge that hope and dreams need not be stifled, for the human spirit can rise above hate.

Research for this kind of book is extensive and sources are invaluable. I wish to thank the following sources: Sicgie Izakson, President of the Houston Council of Jewish Survivors; Rabbi Leo Heim, survivor; Rabbi Ernesto Yattah, who aided me in the philosophy of Judaism; Susan Ganc and Edith Minceberg, language specialists; Dr. Charles S. Hausmann, Professor of Music, University of Houston; William Adams, Fort Bend Boys Choir Director; and Dr. Irene Corbit, psychotherapist and researcher of prisoner trauma.

Thanks to the staff of the United States Holocaust Museum in Washington, and in Houston the Holocaust Education Center, Congregation Beth Yeshurun Synagogue Library, and the Jewish Community Center.

Good guides are essential to the finished product. Thanks to reviewers Ellen M. Roberts, Joan Upton Hall, and Carolyn Boyd. I am especially grateful to editor Susan McKenzie for lending her special talent to the fine-tuning of this work.

My family and friends have been generous. I include among those Bill and Betsy Lipman and Ruth Lipman Kummings.

La Fawn Biddle, I am honored to count you among my friends.

I sing because I'm happy,
I sing because I'm free.
His eye is on the sparrow,
And I know He watches me

ONE

Józefów na Wisla, Poland 1940

IT TOOK ALMOST AN HOUR to bury him. Each shovel of earth placed in the hole muffled Moses' cry from the grave. As the acid taste of bile burned his throat, Benny shoveled frantically, trying to cover the terrible screams of his friend being buried alive. The twelve-year-old fought tears, his eyes on fire. Nausea swept his small frame. He swallowed hard, trying to keep his insides from erupting. If he failed, the guards would not hesitate to make his fate that of Moses, who lay in his earthen bed, blanketed forever by dirt and stones. The boy shoveled faster and faster trying to block the horror of the moment. . . .

—◆ ☼ ◆—

Warsaw, Poland 1938

The sun passed behind the western horizon just as the street lights began their flickering dance to the mid-September nightfall, casting shadows over the Georgian terrace-houses on Ogrodowa Street. Bright lights shone through the tall, arched windows of number sixteen, where strains of Schubert's "Serenade" drifted through the open windows.

Inside, ten-year-old Benny Lipman stood singing by an ebony grand piano, a German-made Blutner, one of the finest in Europe.

1

Finely carved claw-foot legs held the beautiful instrument. As Benny sang, he watched his father closely, who sat at the piano bench, long fingers caressing the keys. The youth smiled inwardly and sang more confidently. Even the room appeared majestic in its beauty.

At one end of the room stood a massive fireplace crafted from the best of Pyrenees marble. Above it hung a large mirror, a late baroque gold leaf and beveled glass. On each side of the fireplace ivory colored built-in cabinets, topped by carved modillion-lock fretwork, displayed a collection of eighteenth century Chelsea porcelain.

Softly tinted blue walls rose high, separated from the ceiling by a wide sculptured molding, painted ivory. A chandelier with hundreds of small, delicately shaped crystal prisms cast reflections of light onto the nearby writing desk where a Ming vase held long-stemmed red roses. Festoon curtains with swag cornices, slightly billowed inward, caught by the breeze at the open windows.

Several guests sat in the parlor listening to Benny's melody. His soon-to-be brother-in-law, Natan sat on the window seat leaning forward, his handsome face smiling as he listened. Occasionally his hand smoothed strands of curly black hair from his forehead. Natan once told Benny his treble voice sounded pure and clear, a rich resonance. Benny hoped that was what he was thinking now.

He glanced toward the man in a wing chair near Natan. Silver-haired Mr. Rosenberg was dressed in a tweed jacket and brown bow tie, looking every bit like the editor he was. His head rested on the back of the chair, his eyes closed, a smile on his face, and his fingers tapped the rose-colored brocade arm. Benny was glad to see Mr. Rosenberg's right foot move in rhythm to the music, pushing softly at the Persian Herati that partially covered the oak floor.

The fastidious, portly man, slightly balding, who sat on the eighteenth century Biedermeier sofa, was Adam Czerniakow, one of his father's closest friends. Sharing the settee with him was Josef Pernowski, a square-faced, blond man in his thirties. The man looked up at Benny and smiled and Benny nodded his head. Pernowski reached toward the tea table and lifted a crystal decanter, pouring himself another glass of Schnapps. He held the decanter toward Czerniakow, who shook his head, declining the drink.

"Softly through the night," Benny sang, "my songs entreat you. Come to me beloved. . . ." He stood, now with his eyes closed, his body swaying with the melody.

When he finished, silence filled the room. Rosenberg wiped his eyes. Benny was thrilled his singing brought joy. He loved to sing.

It was all right that his audience did not applaud. It would have shattered the moment.

The boy smiled broadly, squaring his shoulders. He looked at his father, who sat quietly at the piano bench and nodded his head in approval.

"Sing another," said Natan from the window seat.

"Please do," echoed one of the men on the sofa.

"Well, how about it, son?" asked his father.

"What would you like to hear?" the young singer asked his enthusiastic audience.

"You had better choose something I can play," teased his father.

Benny leaned over and whispered in his father's ear, "Why don't we do 'Silvia'?" Then turning to his audience he said, "We're going to do 'An Silvia'?"

"'Who is Silvia?' Ah, that is my favorite, Benny," remarked Rosenberg from the wing chair. "Aaron, can you play it?"

"I think I can handle this one, Michal. If I remember correctly, Schubert wrote it for a neophyte pianist such as I." Aaron looked at his friends and rolled his eyes. "At least my son did not put me to the test with Mendelssohn."

The guests chuckled, familiar with Aaron's good humor.

"I need only to maintain Schubert's rhythm. Correct, Benick?"

"Yes, Father, and I will try not to hurt Shakespeare's words."

Affectionately he watched Father shift his weight on the piano bench and replace his fingers on the keys. He may not have been the best pianist in the world, but he was a striking figure at six-feet-four-inches, and he wore a light blue, pin-stripped and double-breasted suit, clothing of his own design. The wide collar of his white shirt held a burgundy bow tie. Strands of gray at his temples highlighted his dark hair. His brown eyes held a steady gaze on the piano keys while his mouth creased into a smile. Benny thought his father was very handsome.

"Is she kind as well as fair? O Song, resound to Sylvia. . . ." The notes dipped and rose.

When he had finished, one of the men called, "Bravo!"

Benny smiled and bowed, receiving the applause and the compliments with great pride.

"Did you take lessons from Master Ernest Lough?" asked Pernowski, straight-faced.

"No sir, Mr. Pernowski. I've never been to London." When Benny realized the man was teasing, he blushed.

"I heard you sing recently with the synagogue choir, young man," noted Rosenberg. "*Mazel tov*! You are quite good. Such a small boy -- such a big talent."

"Thank you," Benny answered. "I do like singing."

"Aaron, you have a bright son; very adult for his age. I could use him one day in the newspaper business."

Benny beamed. He knew his father was proud of him, for he had told him so many times. At ten years old, he was proficient in five languages and was an honor student. His mother and father believed in a "well-rounded" education for both their children. Benny attended public school by day and a private school in the evening. His sister, Sala, four years older, was an advanced student, waiting entry into nursing studies.

Taken by a sudden flash of embarrassment from his father's bragging, Benny smiled shyly.

Adam Czerniakow, sitting with Pernowski on the sofa, winked at Benny who winked back.

"Ah, my friend," said Czerniakow watching Aaron move from the piano to the fireplace. "I remember some delightful evenings sharing your love of music."

"You are right. It has been too long."

"It certainly has, Mr. Czerniakow," said Benny.

The older man grinned. Patting the chair next to him, he said, "Come sit by me."

Benny remembered proudly how Czerniakow compared him to his own son Jas, who was older than Benny. "How mature you are!" he had said, "Such a bright boy!"

The boy loved the engineer's easy manner with young people, a trait that made Czerniakow popular when he taught in the Jewish vocational schools. Now that his time was spent working with Jewish craftsmen in Warsaw and in the provinces, he no longer had the opportunity to share his humorous fables.

"Are you still playing sports, Benny?" asked Czerniakow.

"Yes."

"Well, that answers why you have those muscles." Benny ducked his chin, the blush instantaneous. "And your sister, how is she?"

"Sala's well. She and Mother are at the theatre this evening. Oh! Have you heard? Sala and Natan are engaged," he announced proudly.

"Is that right?" said the engineer, looking toward the window seat. "Congratulations, Epstein."

"Thank you," answered Natan, a smile creasing his handsome face.

"Tell me, Benny," continued Czerniakow, "do you still have dreams of being an astronomer?"

Avoiding his father's eyes, the young man answered, "Yes. I still would like to be one."

"What young boy does not have his head in the stars," remarked Aaron. "Benny will come around."

His father talked often about him taking over the family business someday. Benny knew that Father had made Aaron Lipman a name to be remembered in Warsaw. Everyone thought he was an excellent tailor and fashion designer. He often designed clothes for the wives of his friends and business acquaintances. Mrs. Czerniakow -- Felicja -- wore a number of his father's dress designs and one of his beautifully crafted furs.

"Michal, what is happening today in the newspaper business?" asked Aaron as he settled into his favorite chair.

The lean, craggy-faced newspaper publisher shook his head. "Well, Aaron, it is busy in the office, the usual. As far as the incoming world news, I am depressed at what is happening in Europe. This expropriation of Jewish property and German restrictions on Jews bothers me, and not just because I am a Jew."

"I agree," responded Josef Pernowski, a successful Polish lawyer and a business acquaintance. "A Jewish friend has practiced law in Germany his entire career. He no longer is allowed to do so."

"What will he do?" asked Rosenberg.

"He and his family are considering moving to the United States."

"I think it would be wise for him to do so," responded Czerniakow.

Benny looked quickly at his father, wanting reassurance they would not leave the place he loved so much.

"Why do you say that, Adam?" asked Benny's father.

"I believe it is obvious. The handwriting is there."

"Things will settle in."

"I do not think so," interjected Rosenberg. "I think it is only the beginning. Do you recollect what I told you this past summer about the limitations placed on German Jewish physicians?"

"I do," said Natan, directing his remarks to Aaron, "Their patients must be Jewish."

Agitated by the memory, Rosenberg's voice elevated. "The reports were sinister all summer. Then came the unbelievable news about the Nazi order to destroy the Great Synagogue in Munich."

"I, too, believe it is only the beginning," said Czerniakow. "As a matter of fact, I think every Jew living in Europe should consider moving."

Surprised by his friend's remark, Benny turned toward his father.

"Moving?" questioned Aaron, his voice elevated in disbelief. "Leaving our homes and our businesses?"

"Yes! I spoke with German General Hans Frank not long ago. You remember Hans and I attended university studies together. He hinted that I leave Poland soon. He even offered to help me. If any of you consider leaving, I will be glad to speak in your behalf."

"Adam, you cannot be serious." Aaron leaned forward, looking intently at Czerniakow. "Warsaw is not affected."

"Not yet!"

"The Germans would not ignore the fact that we are successful, well-known business leaders."

"Perhaps."

"It would be foolish not to use our knowledge and experience as well as our wealth. My God, they would not commit economic suicide!"

"Aaron, my friend, look at what is happening here in Warsaw. Gangs roam the streets, violence is an everyday occurrence, and prejudice escalates against Jews."

Benny knew Pernowski loved his Jewish friend, but the frown on the Slav's face showed doubt about his father's theory. The boy believed his father was open-minded and did not harbor concerns about political matters. He was a businessman.

"Aaron, do you remember the police response to the tear and stink bombs thrown at your fabric warehouse?" probed Natan.

"Yes," interjected Benny, agreeing with his future brother-in-law. He rolled his brown eyes, mocking the manner in which the police had neglected to respond to Lipman's call. "What can we do? By tomorrow, it might be worse."

"Young Benny is right," remarked Rosenberg. "Where are the police in all of this? And the issues of *Falana* do not help. I believe The People's Union publishes that damn bigotry trash just to stir up trouble between the Poles and the Jews in this community."

"Look," said Aaron taking a cigarette from the silver canister on the table next to his chair. "Jews have been persecuted throughout history." He lit the cigarette, slowly blowing smoke into the air. "We are strong people. Our businessmen and our craftsmen helped build a strong middle class in Poland."

"That is true, Aaron, but . . . ."

"Why would the Germans want to destroy that? Destroy the Jew; destroy the Gentile." Aaron's voice lowered to almost a whisper. "That does not make sense."

Benny looked to the others for agreement. He noticed Natan's frown. The boy knew Natan admired Aaron's head for business. He had said so many times, but Benny sensed that Natan did not agree with Father on this subject.

"I fear, Aaron," said Natan, "you may be in denial of the possible danger. The Germans have already occupied Austria. Look what they are doing in Hungary, cutting the Jewish economic activities to only twenty percent. How much protection can we get from the leadership of Poland?"

"That is a good question," said Pernowski, his mouth forming a cynical smirk. "Not being a Jew, I certainly have no concerns, though I think you should since the largest population of Jews in Europe is right here in Poland."

"But that will be our strength," argued Aaron.

Benny, torn between fear and bravery, waited for Pernowski's answer.

"Your strength? You cannot do it by yourself. Believe me, Aaron, as a Pole I have to take an honest look at Polish history, and when I do I have grave concerns."

"All nations have experienced declines and even dictatorships."

"True, Aaron, but I am not sure how many have been wiped off a map."

"Or made enemies of their next-door neighbors," said Rosenberg. "We did not make Russia too happy after World War I when we extended our borders to take in the Baltic Sea."

"Do you think Russia will ally with Germany?" asked Natan.

"Who knows," answered Pernowski. "Maybe Pilsudski could have prevented the coalition. I personally believe he was the most capable and visionary Polish leader in recent history."

"I love the story of Pilsudski's revolt!"

The adults turned toward the young voice.

Pernowski laughed. "A historian as well as a singer, huh?"

The warm flush tickled Benny's neck.

"What do the school books say nowadays?"

"He was a soldier -- in the 1920s, I think. He led a revolt, stopped a peasant uprising, and took over the government."

"Correct, and he became a benevolent dictator."

"Are you being facetious, Josef?" Czerniakow looked closely at Pernowski. "I think some will remember him in sympathy with Mussolini and Hitler."

"Do you think so, Adam?" asked Rosenberg. "If you review his speeches and writings, you will find it was he who first saw the danger in Hitler's rise to power. I once heard him refer to the Nuremberg Laws of '35 as a warning for all Jews, not just Jews who had to disclaim their citizenship in Germany."

"If they come, we will fight them," said Benny with adolescent zeal.

"We will not have to fight them, Benny," answered his father.

Czerniakow patted the naive young Jew on the shoulder and smiled. Benny felt the comfort of the touch, but his friend's smile seemed flimsy.

Was Mr. Czerniakow really that worried? Surely Father knows what he is doing. Everyone says that he is a shrewd businessman. The boy wondered if he should be more concerned. *How could they survive if this were really true?*

Without warning, a clap of thunder with a sharp lightning strike interrupted the conversation.

Standing, Natan reached over and closed the window behind him then moved to the other window and closed it. The rain began to spatter against the glass as he turned to the others. "It sounds like an oncoming September storm. Please excuse me. I need to leave before it becomes heavy."

Benny noticed the look on his future brother-in-law's face. *Had the evening's conversation worried him that much?* The boy decided to ignore the troubled look. Eager to learn, he enjoyed being included in adult conversation. It was exciting to see history in the making.

TWO

THE GERMANS BOMBED POLAND on September 1, 1939. Within days the German Luftwaffe blackened the skies of Warsaw, dropping leaflets that demanded surrender and warned of death and destruction if Poland chose to fight.

In response to the leaflets, officials ordered the citizens of Warsaw to dig shelter trenches and build barricades. The inhabitants prayed they would not have to use them.

The unprepared Polish forces expected assistance from England under the terms of an existing treaty. It did not come. The signing of the Nazi-Soviet Pact in August of 1939 had opened the door for the Germans to enter Poland.

Three hundred fifty-one days after the conversation in the Lipman living room, Benny was eleven years old, less than two years from his bar mitzvah. At the moment the first air raid sirens shrieked their warning of impending danger to Warsaw, Benny was upstairs dressing. As the alert sounded, he heard his mother's voice calling from the stairwell.

"Benny, get your sister! The shelter! Hurry!"

Sala entered the kitchen first. "Where's Father?"

"He is at the main warehouse. Do you remember a shelter near there?"

"I don't." Sala moved quickly to the stairwell. "Benny, come now. We must hurry!"

Benny ran down the stairs. "Where's Father?"

"Mother says he's gone to the warehouse. We must move to the shelter immediately."

As the three reached the street, heavy bombers droned overhead deafening those below. The strikes came faster than the people had anticipated. The first bomb exploded in the next block, a thunderous vibration, shaking the ground and rattling the windows.

Benny and the two women quickly joined the crowd of people scurrying toward the shelter, frantically trying to find a hiding place. They were almost there when the second bomb hit. Before their eyes, the shelter folded like a piece of cardboard, trapping inside those it should have housed in protection. The sounds of crumbling bricks and screams of terror pierced the air, sending chills through those who watched helplessly.

"Oh, my God, my God!" cried Mirla. "No!"

"Mother, let's go back home."

"Benny, it is not safe," she argued.

"We have no choice! Hurry!" He grabbed each by the hand and began to run. The three-story stone structure would have to serve as their shelter.

The boy led the two women along the center of the street away from the flames that torched the buildings. Loose stones and bricks covering their path hampered a fast progress toward their home. Neighbors lay dying among the debris. Others fled, desperate to find safety.

Benny and his family were almost to their front steps when an incendiary bomb struck the house several doors away. An inferno of flames burst forth, generating a heat so intense the walls of the Lipman house felt hot to the touch. The windowpanes rattled violently. One shattered. The three Lipmans moved quickly inside and down the stairs to the basement.

They did not come out of their home shelter until late afternoon. A deadly silence awaited them. The odor of burning wood and smoke hung heavy over the city. The Lipman home still stood.

Benny headed for the front door.

"Benny, where are you going?" his mother called.

"To find Father. I'll be back as soon as I can."

Sala called after him. "Do you want me to go with you?"

"No. You stay with Mother."

Benny ran toward his father's business on Zlota Street. Bombs had cut a wide path of destruction through the city, and flames lashed from the buildings. People sat in the street crying or moaning, some holding the dead in their arms. Trying hard not to be afraid, Benny ran past them.

As he ran toward his father's warehouses, a sudden spasm gripped his stomach. The boy had stopped to catch his breath when a hand reached out from the rubble and touched his leg. "For God's sake, help me!" wailed a voice.

Torn between fear and disgust, Benny ran for his life, but he could not outrun the mayhem. Near the warehouses, he came upon a small blackened and burned little girl, no more than four years old, tears and soot smearing her face. She sat beside the lifeless body of a woman. The child reached over and touched the woman, but quickly withdrew her hand and stared at the blood on her fingers.

"Mama! Mama!" she screamed, jumping to her feet, her body shaking. She looked frantically in all directions, her eyes searching. Then she stumbled toward the remaining shell of a house and tried to climb the broken stairs. Unable to do so, she ran back into the street and stood there sobbing.

Benny watched as long as he dared. He turned away finally, his heart in his throat. Panic threatened to swallow his courage completely.

Ultimately he reached his father's warehouse. Fire, shooting flames skyward, consumed the entire building; its light reflected the fear in the boy's eyes.

Benny saw the car parked near the warehouse, a 1935 blue Chevrolet, one of a kind in Warsaw. It was Aaron's pride and joy. A piece of flaming debris had fallen on the roof of the car, and the blaze crept toward the gas tank. He recognized his father behind the wheel.

Benny ran toward the car, as he prayed silently, "*Dear God, let him be alive.*"

He yelled, "Father! Father!"

No response. Benny moved quickly to the driver's side and grabbed the door handle, but instantly yanked his hand from the stinging heat. Undaunted, he frantically fumbled again with the handle, at last opening the door. Horror shaped his father's look into a taciturn stare, his dark eyes void. Perspiration dripped from his face.

"Father!"

When his father did not respond, panic gripped the boy. He reached out and touched his father's temple. Startled, the man jerked away.

"Get out, Father! Get out of the car now!"

The flames spread quickly, threatening to engulf the car.

"Benny, my son. It was awful . . . awful!"

"Father, get out of the car!" The boy began pulling at him.

Aaron moved slowly, mumbling, "It is gone . . . it is gone."

"Come, Father. Hurry!"

Benny tugged on his father's arm, as he forced him to run with him from the burning car.

A thundering noise punched the air, knocking them both to the ground. Benny gasped for breath, the heat from the asphalt street sucking at his body. His heart raced and his nose burned from the acid stench. When he could catch his breath, he looked at his father lying beside him, his body covered in sweat and soot.

"Father." His voice was hoarse, barely audible.

Aaron rolled over slowly looking up at the sky, now nearly obstructed by the black smoke.

Silence.

After a moment, Aaron slowly pulled himself to a sitting position and stared at the burning car. Grabbing his knees, he rocked back and forth, tears streaming down his cheeks. Benny crawled to his father and wrapped his arms around the shaking body. "Shh, shh," said the little boy.

"I heard him cry out, Benny."

"Who, Father?"

"Abrachman!"

"Your bookkeeper . . . he was in there?"

"The flames were too much. I heard Abrachman cry out, but I could not get to him." Aaron looked toward the heavens and cried, "Lord, Lord, why?"

———*———

Polish soldiers from surrounding cities came to save Warsaw. It was a utopian gesture. They had no guns or rations, not even clothing for the on-coming winter. Though Mayor Starzynski made an appeal to the civilian population for arms and ammunition, they were unable to respond.

The ill-equipped Polish defenses and populace proved to be ineffective. Patriotism could not compete with the massive German attack that produced widespread devastation. What better means to procure the surrender of the Polish nation than to seriously cripple its capitol and its mammoth population?

Droning constantly overhead, the heavy bombers of the German Luftwaffe glutted the sky. They dropped their payload, and death and destruction claimed the city and its inhabitants. As the explosives hit, the city buildings crumbled, causing gigantic clouds of fine powdery dust to float above the rubble. Incendiary bombs set off hundreds of fires. More than a hundred people hiding in the Jewish cemetery burned to death. The city reeked of noxious smoke.

Terrified by the fusillade, men, women, and children huddled in the streets and cellars of the city. Each time the air raid sirens whined their warning, they prayed that God would have mercy and spare their lives. No mercy existed. A crippled city and violated populace -- mangled or dead -- affirmed that the forces of darkness had invaded the area.

As the bombing continued, thousands fled Warsaw. Others decided to stay and ride out the ordeal. Night and day death prevailed. The inflammable bombs dropped into the night's stillness mutilated and killed many more, while others met death buried alive under the weight of rubble left after each bombing.

The explosives heavily damaged the large city's water and electrical utilities. Water became contaminated and supplies limited. Money was practically worthless for items such as food. The small amount available was not enough to go around. Bombardment continued for weeks as the populace prayed, cried, and sought places to hide.

Later the Warsaw masses would refer to the explosive barrage that rumbled day and night throughout the city as "the days of hell." What followed the blistering attack took them farther into Hades' bowels.

Following the initial invasion, the Lipman family remained close to home. They considered safety illusory anywhere. In the daylight, between bombings, they reorganized their daily life and prayed for respite. When deafening bombs broke the silence of night, they huddled in the basement.

Their house sat among similar structures and apartments lining Orgrodowa Street. The first floor consisted of three rooms and a bath; the second, two bedrooms and a bath; and the small attic was Benny's. A basement served as a storage area.

In order to conserve the short supply of coal, they no longer used the larger rooms on the first floor. Pieces of cardboard sealed heating vents. The bigger pieces of furniture in the living room barricaded windows, warding off the cold. A board covered the shattered window. Most of the furniture and accessories remained in place, hoarded until the very last minute. The kitchen served not only as a place for their meals but also as a reading and conversation area.

The constant barrage of the city had resulted in a critical food deficit. Bread was in short supply and milk non-existent at any price. The family separated their possessions to use for food bartering. Clothing and utensils for cooking and eating were good trading pieces. The larger items and luxury pieces would be of no use for exchanging, but the family hoped to preserve them for use after the occupation. The safe, hidden in the basement, temporarily held the gold and silver items.

Benny was worried about Father. Mother had tried to console Aaron, but he had drifted into long periods of silence. Father seemed to live in a state of disbelief, unable to comprehend the barbarity. Benny knew him to be a generous man who had regularly shared with street beggars and invited both the poor and the affluent into his home. Father had always pursued a life of dignity. He just did not know how to reason with this situation. It made him feel dishonored. Benny could understand. He, too, despised the invasion into the normal life he once knew.

Sometimes between the bombing assaults, Aaron played his treasured Blutner. The tall man, growing lean, sat hunched over the piano, his fingers moving across the keys searching for notes to relieve his pain, his love of music outweighing his lack of virtuosity. He had only to listen to the melody to bring back beauty and serenity.

When he tired of his own artistry, he moved to his record collection and the old Victrola phonograph, which once belonged to Mirla's mother. A nearby chest held recordings of Chopin, Mozart, and other artists, a collection that would be greatly envied by a music connoisseur. In the past, guests had sat in Aaron's living room and listened to these soundtracks or enjoyed the performance of local musical talents.

Now, Aaron often sat alone, closing his eyes and resting his head against the chair back. The violins and piano of Chopin's "Etude, Op. 3" carried him into the soft ecstasy he so desired. Over and over he played the tunes of Chopin or Mozart while outside the holocaust held sway.

——▸ ※ ◂——

During one of the lulls between twenty-seven days of bombings, Benny took the chance to search for food. He walked through the cluttered streets, often stumbling over rubble and the lifeless, bloated bodies, whose vacuous eyes stared, dictating the boy's response of agony and shock.

Ashes lay where entire blocks once stood. Benny's nostrils stung from the heavy odor of smoldering wood and decaying corpses.

The boy wanted to breathe fresh air -- the rush of air that brushed his nostrils when he rode one of the Arabians on Grandfather Lipman's farm. He longed to feel once again the wind caressing his face as he and the horse moved in rhythm through fields of yellow and pink wildflowers, the horse's long mane touching his cheek as he leaned forward, his arms around the animal's neck.

These moments of terror surpassed those memories. Just as he had been caught up in "the ride," he was now a part of another memory in the making -- one he would not want to remember.

The young boy witnessed the looting of bombed houses and stores, the pilfering of rings and watches torn from lifeless human beings. The haven for peace and well-being, which was Warsaw, no longer existed. Even human life became public property.

Benny's pallid face and drooped shoulders laid bare his exhaustion and grief. Subdued by the disorder in his life, he headed home from the day's never ending search for food. Begging and trashcan searches had become the norm.

Before Benny could reach Ogrodowa Street, daylight crawled into night, the sunset striking a landscape of jagged buildings reaching upward. Gray and black columns of smoke streaked the skies. Occasionally bits of light from fresh flames licked the air. It was a panorama void of hope.

Warsaw lay in devastation, and chaos enveloped its inhabitants. The poor reflected on better times, and the wealthy sought answers to the raging pyre of sudden change.

In his determination to find food for his family, Benny lost his ability to differentiate between right and wrong. He wanted to live. He wanted his family to live. He wanted this more than anything.

Food forage found him dodging rubble and an occasional explosion as he made his way to a pickle processing plant. When he arrived at the factory, he found it in flames. A man, engulfed in fire, ran from the inferno holding a confiscated pickle barrel.

"No! No! Leave me be," the man screamed as he saw the boy approach.

Benny winced.

Baptized by flames the man discharged short, gasping sounds then a hoarse yell -- either a claim to his prize or recognition of death's avowal.

The boy sprung forward, wrenching the treasured pickle barrel from the hands of the dying man.

"I'm sorry! I'm sorry!" he yelled back at the man, now lying on the ground blackened and still burning.

Benny ran as fast as his heavy load and his small frame would allow. He had never stolen anything in his life.

He had just entered Smocza Street when a bomb suddenly exploded the building in front of him. The blast knocked him to the ground, cascading pickles into the street. He looked up to human faces projecting from the fresh rubble. Some were already dead, others pleading for help.

Shuddering, Benny struggled to his feet. He ran, unnerved by the dying noises, leaving behind his treasure. His great hope of salvation from hunger now lay with the dead and the dying -- lost.

Tears stung and bleared Benny's eyes as he limped home. In his rush to escape, he stumbled and fell onto a fallen horse. Dragging himself off the body of the dead animal, he immediately realized he had found food, but the idea of further mutilating the horse disgusted him.

I don't want to do this, he thought. *I don't!*

Benny bit his lip. Clearly he saw Grandfather Lipman's Arabians. His stomach hurt, the huge knot pushing at his whole body. Tears streaming down his cheeks, he reached into his belt for the knife he carried. He wondered if the animal's spirit would forgive him.

When he had finished with the horse he whispered, "Thank you, my friend. Thank you."

He ran away as fast as he could, carrying with him the hunk of meat. He had become primeval in his drive for food.

When Benny came across a bakery open for business he silently thanked the Polish government. Officials gave orders to shopkeepers to sell any available bread to the populace. It was one order that had integrity.

Benny joined the long line for bread in early evening. About midnight a round of German artillery exploded, sending flying debris and shrapnel into the crowd. At the onslaught, Benny shifted his stance in line, pushing his small body against the building and muttering, "Lord, not me. Please, not me."

Even as the wounded fell to the ground near him, the young boy stood bravely waiting for his turn at the bread. Shivering from the cold and refusing to give in to exhaustion, he stood the whole night.

At dawn Benny made it to the front of the line. He laid his precious Zloty on the counter, and the clerk handed him a loaf of bread. He reached for the bread drawing it to him, his eyes devouring it. A thick, brown crust covered the prize. It was too large to put in his pocket and too valuable to hold away from his heart.

The boy headed home clutching his bounty of bread and horsemeat close to his chest much as a mother protects her child. It was the first full meal the family would eat in a week.

THREE

THE MASSIVE GERMAN TANKS, ARMED with mounted guns reaching ominously toward the sky, filled Marszalkowska's broad avenue. Motorcycle escorts, wearing shiny boots and crisp uniforms, preceded the goose-stepping Wermacht, Germany's grand army. A spectacle of flags waved above the neatly uniformed soldiers singing, "s*oldaten soldaten durch die stadt marschieren* (soldier soldier marching through the city)."

Movie cameras recorded the German entry into Warsaw, displaying to the world the virtue of power and strength.

That was how Benny imagined it would be, and he would resist watching the parade, showing no loyalty to the conquerors. They could not make him do that. They could not make him cheer "Heil Hitler" and sing their German songs.

In reality Poland had surrendered on September 28, and within hours, the Wermacht made their appearance in the streets of Warsaw. Movie cameras were there, but it was not what Benny had imagined. The highly disciplined, sleek, and well-fed Germans appeared as benevolent victors, handing out bread to those standing in long lines.

The German Supreme Commander announced that Jews would receive fair treatment and that food would be available for the hungry, but Benny doubted it. How could this enemy army, who left a city in ruins and a population impoverished and starving, suddenly become the charitable conquerors? Who was to make sure the promises were not vacant propaganda? The Polish government officials had fled with the national treasury. They had preached resistance to the nations' people, all the while planning their own escape.

Benny felt contempt for those who left the populace to fend for itself. He loathed those who welcomed the invaders with open hearts. The naive young boy would have preferred to greet them with bravery and resistance.

—◆ ✿ ◆—

Prior to the invasion of Poland, newspapers across Europe had recorded the shape of the Jews' destiny. With each passing day, the future of the Jews seemed more uncertain. The German confiscation of Jewish property by ax and torches in Germany in the 1930s did not deter other European nations from believing they were safe.

Benny remembered the conversation in his father's living room the year before. Aaron had felt safe. The others had not. Yet no one heeded any of the alarms. Even Benny had been doubtful that their worst fears would come true. Things had changed.

Benny's own family and friends refused to consider leaving Warsaw, even after the invasion. They said they preferred to stay and "ride out the storm." The boy tried not to judge their reasoning. It seemed clear to him that the danger existed, and he did not understand why they refused to leave Poland.

With more boyish zeal than facts he initiated a crusade with his family to leave their native country before all doors closed completely. Both his parents rebuffed the suggestion.

"The Lipman family roots are here in Poland," said Aaron. "Why should we give up a birthright that traces back to the sixteenth century?"

"But Father," Benny argued, "look at the signs, the warnings."

"Obstacles have been placed in our path throughout history. We cannot run every time there is a problem." Aaron looked thoughtfully at his son. "I understand you are afraid, and there is something to be said for that, but I believe we should wait it out."

Benny had heard his father's argument before. Aaron and Mirla Lipman did not consider prejudice a part of world attitude. They had lived in an educated, highly cultured, and intellectually curious world. To them their daily lives and their future lay in who they were as humans, not as Jews.

Though they did not consider themselves fully observant, the Lipman family never denied their heritage. They participated in Jewish holidays and traditions. They counted both Gentile and Jews among their friends. Experiencing no wants, Aaron and Mirla readily involved themselves in humanitarian pursuits, giving to all equally regardless of religion or nationality.

The onslaught of degradation both surprised and horrified them. Though there were a few racist remarks when he was a small child, Benny, like his father and mother, had known few enemies. On an errand for his mother he came across an old neighborhood playmate. When Benny's one-time friend saw him, his eyes widened, and he called out to a nearby German Schutzstaffel, pointing his finger in Benny's direction.

"There's a Jude."

Immediately the SS guard rushed to Benny, grabbed him by the shirt and began hitting him in the face. Benny dropped the groceries he carried and put up his arms to cushion the blows.

"You filthy Jew. How do you like that?"

Benny felt the warm blood trickling from his nose onto his lips, but he remained silent. The Nazi stood waiting and watching him.

When the German made no further moves, Benny knelt on the sidewalk, sorting the scattered groceries. As he finished placing them in the canvas tote, he rose to leave.

"What are you doing, Jude?"

Sharp pain shot through Benny's body as the hard boot landed in the middle of his back, sending the boy violently to the ground.

The German bent down, grabbed the bag of groceries, slung it to the pavement once more, and began stomping on its contents.

"Now try to retrieve them, pig!"

Without warning, the SS guard reached down, yanked Benny by the nape of his neck and dragged the young boy toward a truck parked at the curb.

"We will see how you like a little of what we have to offer, Jew Boy." The German smiled as he shoved the youth against the truck. "Get in the back. Now."

A large auditorium on the outskirts of the city was the destination for Benny, along with twenty-five other Jews. Given the assignment of washing and polishing the floors of a large public building, the boy crawled on his knees for ten straight hours. Finally released into the night, he found his own way home.

Not long after the grocery episode Benny and Sala came across several Polish people pressuring a German guard.

"Herr, Mister, give us a cigarette and a piece of bread."

The German snarled, "Why should I give cigarettes and bread to Polish swine?"

"We'll show you a Jew!"

They pointed to a Hassidic Jew across the street. The old man wore a long black coat and a tall hat, the traditional dress of Hassidism. Peyot hung from his ears and a neatly trimmed beard reached to mid-chest.

The German guard quickly crossed the street, approaching the Jew cursing, "Filthy Jew. What are you doing on the street?"

Before the man could answer, the guard grabbed him violently by a curl that hung from his ear, giving it a severe jerk. The German laughed and exhibited strands of hair in his hand. Not content with this display of contempt he began to kick the helpless man, sending him to the ground.

Benny and Sala moved quickly toward the old man.

Startled, the German guard questioned, "Who the hell are you? Are you Jews come to rescue the old bastard?"

"Nein, no. He lives in our neighborhood," lied Benny. "You're right, he is a dirty Jew. We'll get him out of your way."

Satisfied that the two were not Jews, probably because of Sala's blonde hair and fair skin, the German lost interest. Benny and his sister pulled the old man to his feet and took him to the safety of his home.

Hassidism, a Jewish movement to which the old man belonged, was founded in eighteenth century Poland. Members believed despair had no grounds because God was eminent. The Nazi made himself the exalted one. The old Jew would not have defended himself because of his own beliefs.

As he wandered the streets, Benny was to meet with further injustice and betrayal. It became apparent that sometimes the Germans could not distinguish between a Pole and a Jew. On every corner, recruiters enlisted men and boys for the clean up forces. Pushed roughly into trucks, the defensive Poles pointed and cried, "That's a Jew! You've overlooked those Jews!"

While Benny scoured for food one day on Prosta Street two SS guards stopped him.

"Halt, Jude!"

"I am not a Jew," answered Benny.

A group of Polish youths standing nearby yelled in chorus, "Check him out! Check out the runt! He's a Jew."

One of the guards grabbed Benny by the scuff of the neck while another pulled down his pants. Benny's struggle met too strong a resistance, and his pants fell to his ankles.

"See," bellowed one of the crowd, "he is circumcised. He is a filthy Jew." The boys slapped their thighs and jeered.

"Hey, Jew boy," yelled one of the onlookers, "got any yet?" He jabbed his fellow heckler with an elbow. They both laughed.

"Are you kidding?" responded the partner. "Who would want that shriveled up lizard?"

Shrill giggling exploded from the Polish girls among the spectators.

Mortified, Benny reached down to pull up his pants. As he did, one of the SS kicked him. He fell, rolling to his stomach, fearful of where the blows might fall. Benny wrapped his arms over his head and drew his knees to his chest, waiting for more strikes.

A fellow SS, calling to them from the end of the street, distracted the guards from their beating of the boy prey. They ran toward the other guard and a group of workers picking up debris. The Polish spectators ran with them, eager to see the new incident.

Benny quickly pulled up his pants and ran for cover. No longer embarrassed by his own ordeal, he watched the Nazis push the workers beyond their human endurance.

Apparently one of the supervising Nazis believed the men worked too slowly and began striking them with rifle butts.

Suddenly one of the workers broke and ran. A Nazi raised his gun, aimed it at the man's back, and pulled the trigger. The quarry dropped with the first bullet.

Benny thought previous experience had hardened him, but this was the first time he saw a person, running for his life, shot in the back. In the eyes of the young Jew, the daily provocation they faced mocked human dignity. Though tears welled in his eyes, Benny had not yet found the energy to cry.

―――◆ ⚹ ◆―――

By early October, the Germans had almost depleted all the priceless uncut fabrics in Aaron's remaining warehouse. After the bombing ceased, the occasion to conduct business was negligible, yet Aaron walked daily to his office. Soon this opportunity disappeared.

The Germans set up the Transferstelle with sole legal power to import and export goods from the Jewish properties. The Poles received much of the Jewish plunder, intensifying the social conflict between the two cultures, a major part of the German's plan. It would be easier to destroy the Jews with the Poles as partners. The Transferstelle pillaged the remains of Aaron's tailoring and fur business.

Natan Epstein had a similar experience to Aaron's. His Polish partner took over the accounting business they jointly owned. However, Natan had grown weak from constant dysentery and could not resist encroachment on both his personal and business life.

He stopped by the Lipman home to see Sala on the day Aaron received the news about his business. Aaron, Mirla, and Sala huddled around the kitchen table talking, faces drawn and eyes void of hope. Benny sat on a stool by the doorway between the kitchen and dining room, his face furrowed in anger.

Sala looked up as Natan walked in. A rare smile crossed her face as she rose and put her arms around him.

Neither Benny nor Sala had seen him in two weeks. Natan's weight loss shocked him. His shoulder blades protruded, and his clothes hung like those on a scarecrow.

"Natan," said Mirla, "how are you? We have missed seeing you."

He smiled but did not answer. The response was in his eyes, dull and hollow.

"Sit, my son. I wish we could offer you something to eat." Mirla was fond of her daughter's childhood sweetheart.

"Thank you, no," he answered as he sat down.

Natan has lost his appetite, like Father, thought Benny.

"Father's business was confiscated today," Sala said as she moved to stand behind her father's chair.

Aaron stared into space. Mirla sat by his side, her hand resting gently on his arm.

Natan shook his head. "I'm sorry."

The older man turned to him. "What is next?" he asked, his voice full of hurt.

"I don't know." It was a response of dejection, empty of understanding.

Benny still had not spoken. He watched the others.

Sala's eyes flashed anger. "Who knows what's next." She began to pace the floor, waving her arms as she talked. "We're required to wear an armband embossed with the Star of David so they can further abuse us, our businesses are boycotted, and we're kept out of Aryan stores. My God, have you seen the sign in the window of the market on Leszno Street?" She did not wait for an answer. "The poster in the window says *Hunden und Juden verboten*! They are calling us animals and say we're forbidden in the store."

Natan stood and moved to Sala. He took her into his arms, hugging her tightly to his body.

An emaciated woman sells the compulsory Star of David armbands for Jews.
Warsaw ghetto, Poland, September 19, 1941. United States Holocaust Memorial
Museum. (USHMM), courtesy of Guenther Schwarberg

Jews walk past destroyed buildings on Gtzybowska Street in Warsaw. USHMM,
courtesy of Hans-Joachim Gerke, Luftwaffe transportation unit, photographer

Benny could hardly restrain his fury. He wanted his father to have his business back and his sister to look forward to marriage and children. He wanted this monstrosity of a life to go away and allow all of them to recapture the old one.

As he watched Sala and Natan, he was reminded of a conversation that he overheard between his mother and his sister, only a short year ago.

"Tell me, Sala," Mirla had asked, "what did you and Natan decide about the date?"

Benny thought his mother had sounded anxious, and he knew his sister had read her mother's thoughts. He remembered she had smiled, when she answered. "Mother, I will soon be sixteen, and I am advanced in my studies. How old was *buheleh* when she married?"

"Your grandmother was seventeen."

"Not that much difference. I think mothers and accountants are alike. They want everything so precise. Natan's trying to talk me into completing my nursing studies before we marry, and you are saying I am too young."

Benny had smiled as he saw his mother pretending to ignore Sala, busy putting away the dishes.

"Here, I'll take those, Mother," he said. He knew Sala had a head on her young shoulders -- just enough defiance to contrast Natan's sensitive and conservative nature. The boy felt it would be a good match.

Benny knew Mother loved her daughter. Tall, like father, Sala carried her beauty with grace. Mirla often said Sala's golden blonde hair and blue eyes reminded her of her own mother. The boy was proud of his sister.

Finally Mirla had responded, "Well, dear, maybe it is just as well you wait. What are we talking about, two years at the most?"

"No. I want to stay with the first date we talked about, next fall. That will give me time to complete my first round of courses, and that will give you plenty of time to play mother of the bride-to-be. Yes? Yes!"

Sala had moved to her mother, putting her arms around her and leaning over to kiss the shorter woman.

"All right?"

Benny remembered Mirla had nodded her head in affirmation ignoring her daughter's teasing, probably her thoughts already on the wedding preparations.

Now Mirla's eyes filled with tears. Benny was sure his mother was remembering the "next fall" statement. "Next fall" came, but so did the Germans.

"I know your distress, dear," said Mirla softly. "I fear for us all." She looked toward the doorway at Benny. "I worry about your brother on the streets all the time. He is so impulsive and defiant." Benny did not answer. "Poor child. He has had to grow up so fast."

"Are you finding food?" asked Natan, looking toward Benny.

"I went this morning to find a soup kitchen open. So many people are hungry, the lines are long, the food is not available, and our money for ration cards is evaporating."

"Benny tries hard," responded Sala. "When there is food, only small amounts can be obtained. How are we going to survive?" Her voice cracked with the pent-up tears. "Sometimes I go to bed so hungry, my stomach is on fire."

"I know, my dear," said her mother. "I cannot believe my children have given up so much. The worst is not having enough food. Why are these people so terrible to us? What have we done to deserve this cruelty?"

No one answered. No one knew.

During the shelling of the city they lived as others, in a survival mode, refusing to accept this event as anything but a tentative situation.

By mid-November 1939 the Germans demanded the Jewish Judenrat turn over a list of assets of Warsaw's wealthy Jews. Ironically, administering to the needs of the Jewish community was the purpose of that organization. Aaron's long time friend, Adam Czerniakow, served as Judenrat chairman.

The German Schutzstaffel came to the Lipman house early in December. As the family sat at the kitchen table, a sudden pounding sounded at the front door. Startled, they looked at each other, eyes wide with fear.

Before Aaron could answer the door, the pounding intensified, and a gruff voice shouted, "Open up, Jude."

Abruptly the door slammed open with a crash, tearing it from its hinges. Five SS guards rushed through the opening.

"Stupid Jew, don't you answer your door?" barked the Nazi officer. "You never know who may come calling." A mocking smirk spread across his face, changing quickly to disgust.

Before Aaron could respond, the SS guards shoved him aside, causing him to stumble against the stairway. As Mirla and the children rushed to his side, the German SS moved into the living room.

"Ah," exclaimed the officer in charge. "What have we here? A rich Jude, yaw!"

He walked to the fireplace. With his hand, he stroked the ivory and black veins of the magnificent marble. Family pictures in a variety of gold and silver frames, both ornate and plain, adorned the mantle. Mirla had saved them for use as bargaining chips, hoping she would not have to use them. The Nazi picked them up one at a time, setting each neatly back in place.

Suddenly he swept the pictures from the mantle. As they crashed to the floor, Mirla caught her breath. Fine slivers of glass fell on the hand-woven rug covering the white oak floor.

The officer turned to the startled family and smiled as he stomped the frames with his heavy boot heel, grinding the remains of the pictures into the rug. He moved to the sofa, reached down to smooth the Chinese peony damask upholstery and sat down, looking slowly around the room. His eyes rested on the piano.

"Who plays the piano?" he asked.

Hesitantly, Aaron answered, "I . . . I do."

"Play, Jude!" demanded the officer.

Startled, Aaron hesitated, then moved to the piano and began to play Chopin's "Minute Waltz." Mirla stood silently with an arm around each of the children.

Abruptly the German yelled, "Stop!" Looking over at Sala, he smiled and patted the sofa beside him.

Frozen with fear, Sala did not move.

Silence.

The officer smiled once more and patted the sofa.

Sala still did not move. Aaron's fingers froze on the piano keys. He sat very still, fearful of making a noise.

The officer motioned to one of the men standing near the opening to the hall. In response, the SS guard stomped quickly across the room and grabbed Sala by the arm. Mirla gasped, reaching out to her daughter. Sala began to whimper, shaking her head.

"No!" screamed young Benny, moving quickly toward his sister.

A Nazi was upon him immediately, striking him across his face and causing him to fall against the Victrola.

The boy wiped at his nose, looking at the blood on his hand. He looked at his attacker. Furious, he lunged at the Nazi. Instantaneously the other SS guards pulled their pistols.

"Don't, Benny," Sala warned. She turned to the officer. "I will sit with you. Please don't let them hurt my brother."

The officer smiled as he reached over and smoothed her blond hair. "Um, besides being pretty, you are smart. Good girl! How did you end up in a Jude family?" He turned to his men. "Leave the cocky boy alone for now." To Aaron he said, "Play, Jew!"

As Aaron finished the musical piece, the officer began to pound both his feet, the boots making loud clogging sounds against the exposed wooden floor. He motioned for the guards to join him. The boot applause continued for some time. Soon the officer grew tired of the display and ordered it to stop.

Surveying the room, he rose from the sofa. With a flourish of a hand he pointed one by one to the paintings, the gold framed mirror, and other valuables, commanding his men to remove and load them into the truck in which the men arrived. When they had taken the small items from the living area, they checked the dining room.

Soon they had removed as many valuables as they could. They returned to the living area where the Lipman family stood quietly.

The officer eyed Aaron's extensive collection of recordings. Turning to the pianist, he smiled. "Yours?" he asked.

Aaron nodded his head in affirmation.

"Hum," responded the German officer, picking up each record and examining it closely.

Aaron held his breath, not knowing how to respond to the investigation of his treasures.

Abruptly the officer sailed one of Aaron's prizes through the air. As it hit a wall, the record shattered and fell to the floor in pieces. Aaron watched in disbelief, the tears already forming.

Soon the Nazi began to dance in circles, making grunting sounds sailing the records against walls, onto the floor, into the furniture.

Aaron slid from the piano bench to the floor. Kneeling, he looked up at the officer, his hands outreached. "Please, not my music."

The officer, with one sweep, knocked Aaron from his knees to the floor, his heavy boot stomping at his face.

When Mirla cried out, a guard struck her viciously across the face. Startled, she looked in disbelief at the man who had struck her, but she remained silent.

Without warning, Benny jumped on the officer's back. He wrapped his legs around the man's waist and his arms around his neck.

Startled, the Nazi tried to dislodge him, shuffling faster and faster around the room like a bucking horse. Benny stubbornly clung to his back.

Surprised by the boy's renewed resistance, the guards stood watching. They soon regained their composure and entered the fray, pulling and hitting at the young boy.

At last, they knocked Benny to the floor where they began to kick him repeatedly. After a moment, the officer ordered them to step aside. He looked down at the boy and gave him a swift kick in the ribs.

Mirla stood with her hand to her mouth, stifling a scream, tears streaming down her face.

Sala sank back into the sofa, too frightened to move.

The officer turned and smiled at Sala, "You, pretty one. I'll see you again." He pulled his pistol from his holder and aimed it at Benny, lying bloody and quiet on the floor.

Aaron, still on the floor, gasped. "No, please! I beg you!"

The German officer turned to Sala, "You owe me, blond Jude." He looked at Aaron. "You, too, old man."

He slowly raised the pistol from his boy target and aimed it directly at the Blutner. The rapid shots popped loudly, splintering the piano. The first strikes to the instrument's guts made pealing sounds. The last hit caused a guttural drone, which set off reverberations, much like a dying animal.

The officer, followed by his men left the house, laughing.

The tone of the low E piano key, still resonating, drowned out the crying in the Lipman living room.

Aaron Lipman would not discuss the incident, but he began to question ways to leave Poland. Ecstatic, Benny welcomed the chance to try. It would not be as easy now.

The opportunity to escape came when Aaron learned from a Polish friend and a former official of the Polish government that Zloty, equivalent to two thousand American dollars, would buy four passports taken from a dead family named Lapinski.

The Lipman family gave most of their hoarded Zloty to the Polish friend who made the deal with the contact man. They agreed to meet the link to their escape at Dwozec Glowny, the main railroad station in Warsaw. The arranged time was seven fifteen the next evening. Warned to take little luggage, to remove their armbands, and to act as inconspicuous as possible seemed like a reasonable request if it meant possible freedom.

On the evening of departure a light rain fell. Benny welcomed its disguise. Wise to the streets, he guided his family along the least traveled dark streets, alert to movement of German patrols. Luckily they met no obstacles and arrived finally at the station.

They huddled on the bench at one end of the station waiting room. Cold and fear dampened their spirits.

At one point a German guard stopped and asked where they were traveling. Benny quickly answered the man in German. Surprised that the boy spoke the language, the man readily engaged him in conversation. They talked at length before the German bid the family goodnight and wished them a safe trip.

"Benny, what did you say to him?" asked Sala.

"I told him we were Polish with German ancestry and that we were on our way to visit our ill grandparents. He told me about his own grandparents and how much he missed them."

Aaron and Mirla smiled at their son's bravery and good sense.

"I think it helped that you and mother are so fair skinned," Benny remarked to his sister. "You do look Aryan, Sala. I still say you and mother should try to get Catholic papers and make an effort to escape?"

Mirla and Sala argued again that they would never consider leaving the family. Even Sala had resisted this opportunity to escape, but finally she had given into the pleas of both Natan and her mother.

All night the family waited in the cold station, and with each passing hour their hopes diminished. The realization of betrayal came with dawn. There would be no contact person, no passports, and no freedom. They returned home.

Later they learned that the contact person had stolen their money and escaped from Poland to France. Just as quickly as a plan to escape was born it died. Aaron and Mirla Lipman gave up. They would not discuss further flight. To Sala the failure of the plan meant she was to stay with Natan.

It would have been easy for a young boy to give up, but Benny did not. As 1939 ended, he rejected the predicted crescendo of doom. Benny believed he was his family's only resource, and he swore to outlive the madness.

FOUR

A BITTER COLD SPELL, dropping Warsaw temperature to twelve and thirteen degrees below zero, greeted the Gregorian New Year of 1940. The bitter cold continued through February and March, abating only to thirty and forty degrees in April. Coal was in short supply.

Poverty and starvation reeked havoc throughout the Jewish sector of the city. After the Germans severed communications and food supplies from the villages, the Jews found their meager food rations too little for daily sustenance. Soup kitchens could provide food only when it was available. Few people had the strength to find one of the kitchens to make use of the meager helping of soup and bread.

Sometimes the fortunate hoarded food, which left the poor with nothing. Daily, life focused on ways to withstand starving. Czerniakow had predicted that death from starvation would be a common occurrence due to the lack of daily minimum calories needed for life support.

——◆※◆——

Even optimistic young Benny could not have foreseen how his father and mother would react under the pressures of trying to stay alive. The great tower of a man he once believed to be indestructible folded under the strain, overwhelmed.

Staring blankly, Aaron sat for long periods of time not saying anything. The lack of food and dysentery that plagued him left his large frame gaunt. Clothes hung loosely on the once immaculately dressed man.

Mirla, though thin and sometimes very weak, managed the energy needed to gather goods for bartering. Entrusting decisions to her husband for so many years, she continued to follow his lead regarding escape. She lived from day to day.

Sala helped, as she could, either aiding her mother or begging small jobs in the neighborhood. For these she sometimes received a small cloth item or a potato, each considered a prize under the circumstances. The nagging cold assailed her thin frame.

Benny knew that Sala battled the hatred and fear growing inside her. When Natan had insisted they postpone making wedding plans, Sala could not hide her apprehension.

"How did these demons get the power to change my life so drastically," she asked her brother? "Will it ever end?"

"We're going to make it end, Sala." The boy had not lost his edge of defiance. "I've heard that a resistance force is grouping. We should think about joining it."

Sala looked at her brother, longing to find hope in his remarks. "I don't understand where the supplies will come from; where people will get their bravery or even the strength."

"I can't believe you've lost faith."

"Benny, I'm being realistic."

"But we must hang on to hope!" Benny slammed the flat of his hand against the wall. "The *Chutzpa*! The gall of these people! Who do they think they are?"

Sala crossed the room to him, putting her arm around her brother's shoulders. "You have taken on the world, and you're only eleven years old," she said. "Benny, I'm sorry. I wish I had the power to make it all go away."

He looked at her and his lip began to quiver. "Look what's happened to father. Why doesn't he fight back?"

Sala could only shake her head.

The question once more unanswered, the brother and sister went about the business of staying alive. Their immediate goal was to find food for the family. Their small cache of stored staples was running out and the worst of the winter was upon them. The two decided Benny would be the hunter. He had one objective -- the salvation of his family. The single objective soon changed.

By the first week in February, a decree required every male Jew in Warsaw between the ages of twelve and sixty to register for forced labor. The German plans for labor had many facets. They saw it as a means of educating the Jews to "correct physical labor" for the Fatherland and as a way to corral them for security purposes. Idle and disloyal prisoners were expendable.

A group of Jewish forced laborers walk to their worksite. USHMM, courtesy of Hans-Joachim Gerke

No one could predict in 1940 that, by the spring of 1942, the labor force mission would add another dimension. The slave market would provide needed workers for ammunition production.

The Warsaw Jewish Federation issued a February 1940 decree to register the Jews for labor and distributed identification cards to them. Benny received his letter instructing him to present himself at 26 Grzybowska Street. In three months he would be twelve.

Arriving at the headquarters, the boy followed directions to sign up and answer roll call. With no further instructions, he decided to leave. He thought he would not be missed in the crowd, his daily search for food more important. The Germans would answer his bravado.

At two o'clock the next morning, a loud drumming at the door aroused the Lipman family. Mirla moved quickly to open the door and five SS men entered, demanding the whereabouts of Bernard Lipman. Mirla told them her son was asleep. Pushing past her, they stomped up the stairs and threw open the first door on the second floor where they found Aaron. Startled by the intrusion, he asked, "What is it? What do you want?"

Two of the guards roughly pulled him from the bed and began to shake him. "Where are you hiding your son?" They struck him across the face before he could answer.

Benny, clad in his pajamas, appeared in the doorway. "Stop. You don't have to hurt him. I'm here. What do you want?"

"A cocky, bastard young Jude, eh?"

The guards poked a rifle into his back and pushed him toward the stairs.

"Where are you taking me?"

"You will ask no questions," one of the men snarled.

Benny called to his family as he went into the night, "Don't worry. I'll be all right." His insides did not feel as brave as his voice.

Benny arrived barefoot and in his pajamas at an area of the city destroyed by bombs. He worked non-stop throughout the night helping to clean up the trash and bombing debris. Tired and hungry, he was colder than he could remember. He did not know how he could survive the low temperatures. The moment the SS guard turned to other matters, distracted from watching the group, Benny slipped away.

One slave less, he thought. *They won't notice.*

This time he was correct, and his easy escape gave Benny incentive to remain stubborn which amplified his bravado.

Events moved quickly in the days to follow. Benny was on Marszalkowska Street when the incident happened with an old man. People gathered around as German SS patrol members violently tugged at the man's long white beard, traditional among ultra Orthodox Jews. The SS teased and taunted the defenseless man.

Several Polish citizens watching, shouted, "Pull it harder! Rip out the Jew's beard! Send him to Palestine where he belongs!"

Benny watched helplessly. He did not know how to help the man, and he did not want to draw attention to himself. This was a much larger crowd than the other incident with the Hassidic Jew.

In the fray the man's prayer shawl fell to the ground. Immediately one of the SS picked up the *Tallit* and began to tease the old man, holding the shawl within reach then jerking it away. The Jew stumbled as he tried to grab it back.

The crowd jeered and laughed. Egged on by the circus-like atmosphere of the spectators, one of the German guards reached into his pocket and pulled out a can of cigarette lighter fluid. He removed the lid and held it in front of the man's face.

The crowd cheered, "Get a match! Get a lighter!"

Suddenly the German threw the liquid onto the beard. One of his comrades immediately pulled a matchbook from his pocket. Removing a match, he struck it, waving it in front of the man. Then he threw it at the beard.

The startled Jew jumped back but not before his beard caught fire. With his hands, he hit at the flame. When that did not stop the spreading blaze, he ran, flaying his arms and screaming, "Help me! Help me!"

Benny wanted to cry out, "STOP!" but the words locked in his throat. Still he stood watching, his body shivering.

Soon a blaze inundated the man's whole body. Gurgling sounds came from his throat replacing his screams. He fell to the ground. Spectators watched and ridiculed as he burned.

Ironically the Germans suddenly turned on the crowd, rounding up the boys and young men, Polish and Jew alike, herding them into a big truck. Benny could not escape.

The young boy rode in silence. His stomach ached, and the throbbing in his temples threatened to make him nauseous. Instinctively he knew he must control his fear.

I will have the courage to fight the barbarians. I will! He said to himself over and over. I will survive!

Benny tried to fight the terrible thing creeping into his heart. Hatred was not a part of his nature. His Jewish teachings told him he was a worthy and valuable human being. It was up to him to protect his soul. This fervor intuitively gave the boy energy and nerve.

The sounds of city traffic had given way to silence. Benny suspected they had entered the farming area outside the city. A noise at the front of the truck interrupted his thoughts. Near the cab two Polish prisoners protested being selected. One argued that he and his friend should not have stopped on the street to witness the harassment of the old Jew. The friend disagreed. Finally out of frustration, they began to punch each other, swaying with the movement of the truck.

An SS guard, sitting near Benny at the rear of the truck, jumped up when the fight began. In so doing he accidentally got in the way, and the larger of the two Poles smashed him in the face. Unable to keep his balance, the guard sank to his knees.

The second guard leapt from his seat yelling, "Stupid Polish swine! What are you doing?" His rifle butt slammed into the head of the Pole who had struck the German guard.

The fray between the two guards and the two Poles drew the full attention of everyone in the truck. Benny made a decision. Quickly and quietly he lifted the canvas that covered the truck's rear opening and carefully slid down the back and onto the dirt road. He lay still in the middle of the road, hoping not to attract attention in the driver's rear view mirror. It worked. Once again, Benny had taken advantage of the situation.

Benny's chances would decrease with the erection of a wall to imprison the Jews. If the Nazis succeeded, the Warsaw ghetto would become a mausoleum of starvation, disease, brutality, and death, sealing the fate of Benny and his fellow Jews.

Warsaw ghetto wall under construction by Jewish forced
laborers. Warsaw, Poland, October 1940. USHMM, courtesy
of Instytut Pamieci Narodowej

——◆✡◆——

By the middle of November 1940, the wall, eleven and a half feet
high and almost eleven inches thick, had sealed off the Jews from the
rest of Warsaw and any possibility of networking business with the
Poles. Glass splinters embedded in plaster at the top prevented people
from crawling over the barrier. Fourteen heavily guarded entrances
further confined the population in the northern part of the city.

In radio broadcast the Germans referred to the 840-acre area as the
Jüdische Wohnbezirk (Jewish quarter), seventy-three assigned streets.
Imprisoned behind the wall were one half million men, women, and
children, later joined by ninety thousand Jews from across Europe.
Public institutions and schools housed them. This influx of transported
population burdened the already grim shortage of food and fuel. The
European roundup smacked of a holding policy.

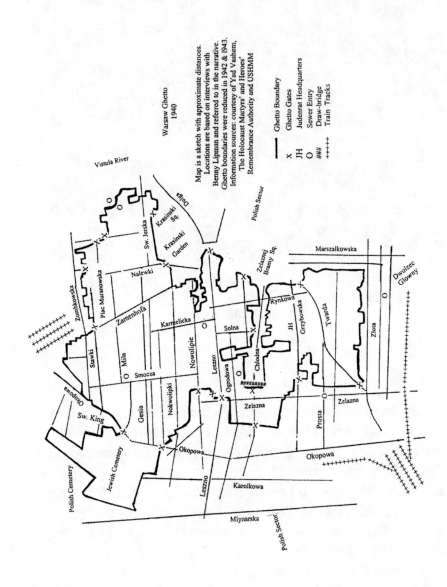

A German soldier stands guard at an entrance to the Warsaw ghetto.
USHMM, courtesy of Hans-Joachim Gerke

Footbridge over Chlodna Street, connecting two parts of the
Warsaw ghetto. Warsaw, Poland, between 1940 and 1942.
USHMM, courtesy of Main Crimes Commission (MCC)

The obligation for the cost of the wall, as well as the construction labor, fell to the Judenrat. The Poles applauded the German mission to incarcerate the Jews.

Severe economic sanctions ravaged the Jews. Compulsory ration cards allotted such meager amounts of food that even the strongest could not survive for any length of time. Segregated train transportation and strict curfews handicapped the ghetto inhabitants. Schools excluded Jewish children. However, the ban on Jews owning radios and other restrictions did not stop the smuggling and black market activities, and strict constraints on cultural events caused the Jews to go "underground" with these activities. But restrictions on the religious leaders hampered official religious life.

Besides the limitation and handicaps, the Jews also lived daily in fear of brutality. Already stories circulated of molestation and rape, if not by the German soldiers then by the Polish gangs.

Ironically, with the sealing of the ghetto wall, the Lipman house on Ogrodowa Street sat only yards away from the gates to freedom.

—➤ ❈ ◄—

Benny had no trouble finding Mr. Czerniakow's office.

"I'm sure he will see me. He's a friend of my father."

"Chairman Czerniakow is very busy this morning, and if you do not have an appointment . . ."

"David, what is the problem?" interrupted Adam, standing at his office door.

"Sir, this young boy says he must see you."

"Benny! Benny, my boy," responded the Chairman, as he walked toward the youth, hand outstretched. "How are you, son? Please come in."

The boy took Czerniakow's hand, pleased to see an old friend of the family but surprised at his surroundings. The chairman's office was not what Benny expected. He had envisioned a more plush and spacious area. After all, he was the chairman in charge of Jewish affairs. Instead Benny found a small drab room, sparsely furnished. Piles of paper covered the small desk.

"Please have a seat," said Czerniakow. "Would you mind waiting a few moments until I've finished the last few lines of this report?"

"Not at all, sir."

The stocky man sat at his desk bending his balding head to the task at hand. Benny knew the man had many worries. Two weeks ago a tall wall sealed off the ghetto, probably creating new deadlines for the chairman's reports. Benny had heard others talk about it. Czerniakow would have to deal with resettlement and inventory preparation for the food and coal supplies in the ghetto. Certainly he must consider the paper work that would be needed for the Judenrat to administer the designation of Jewish buildings in the ghetto. Then there were the problems of rent and possible taxation. When he heard these conversations, they sounded ominous to the young Jew.

Benny wondered if the chairman ever regretted not fleeing with his family when he had the chance. He thought the chairman would not have been able to live with himself had he left his fellow Jews to struggle alone. Benny liked this man very much, as did his father.

During the 1939 siege of Warsaw, Mayor Starzynski appointed Czerniakow Chairman of the Jewish Council, also called the Judenrat. German leadership later confirmed the appointment. The Lipman family was pleased, and it gave them hope. Little did they realize that within a year after the appointment Czerniakow, trying to benefit the cause of the Jews in an impossible situation, struggled in his dedication as a public servant.

Benny believed that most people knew Czerniakow for his compassionate nature and elusion of publicity unless it furthered the cause of the common man. Czerniakow had grown up in Poland among Jews who assimilated into the Polish culture and language. He devoted his adult life to the artisans of Warsaw, numbering one third of the Polish Jewry. That mission and his love for education led him to help develop several vocational schools. His own education was in the fields of chemistry and engineering. No schools could have prepared him for what he would face as Chairman of the Judenrat.

Benny thought the chairman looked tired as though he had had a restless night, and he visualized the office problems starting early in the day. At that moment Benny did not know that the chairman's first chore that day dealt with a family who had hidden their dead members in order to receive the extra food rations. Food was an endless and disturbing problem. Czerniakow had publicly argued that Warsaw Jews would die of starvation within months if they had to live on the prescribed bread ration. Black market and smuggling activities thrived. Jews, mostly children, found ways to crawl in and out of the ghetto, desperately scouring for something to eat. Most families sold or bartered their furniture and belongings in order to have coal for heating and food.

Even as young as he was, Benny believed that their family friend must have felt wedged between the demands of the Germans and those of the needy.

The chairman looked up and smiled. "Now I can put this aside for a while." He moved to sit closer to Benny.

"How is your family?" he asked. "Your father, is he well?"

"As well as can be expected, sir. Thank you."

Benny did not have the heart to tell him the truth. It had been a humiliating experience for his father. His once bright eyes had grown dim and hollow, the look that comes from poverty and hunger as well as disbelief. The Germans stripped Aaron Lipman of everything, like so many other businessmen. In an instant the Lipman business had disappeared. Though they still had their house, frequent trips by the Germans had almost depleted its holdings or left them in shambles. The biggest embarrassment to Aaron Lipman was his lack of ability to care for his family.

Adam Czerniakow was a wise man. Benny knew he understood the stakes all too well and could probably read in his face what his words did not say. The invasion destroyed many lives, not only homes and material items, but also the human spirit.

Before the boy could say another word Adam said, "Benny, would it help if I could give you and your family a few extra ration cards?"

A smile spread spontaneously across Benny's face.

"If your father is up to it, ask if he would like to come and see me."

"I will," Benny said, knowing that his father would be too proud.

Benny took the ration books not realizing the man had shortened his own supply. He reached enthusiastically toward Czerniakow as though to embrace him, but quickly pulled back, embarrassed.

The large man smiled with understanding written on his face. The boy needed to reserve some pride. The chairman held out his hand to him. "Benny, take care of yourself."

"Yes sir," responded Benny, and he turned and went out the door, stopping for a moment, wondering if he should thank him again. He heard the older man sigh and say softly, *"God provide for us all."*

I suppose he wonders, thought Benny, *whether or not a little boy who grew up privileged can survive these monsters.* "I can do it," he said out loud. "My father has told me many times I'm a bright young man and old for my age. I can do it."

As early as the fall of 1939, executions had become commonplace in areas near the city of Warsaw. In 1940 the slaying continued, sometimes secretly in the Palmiry Forest area outside the city, other times blatantly on the city streets.

Death was only one part of the terrorism by the Nazi authorities. The Jews, subject to instant humiliation, often found themselves under brutal attacks. Arrests, recruitment for forced labor, and deportation to newly established concentration camps became commonplace.

Disloyalty by their own peers was one of the most difficult realities that faced the ghetto Jews. Not only was the Judenrat set up to oversee the needs of the Jews but also to implement German policy. In the beginning, the Judenrat supervised the Jewish Police.

Early on, Chairman Czerniakow worried about the bogus police department. He feared its function might endanger the Jews rather than create order. He doubted the credibility of this group, for a large number of them had never taken part in either the political or community life of the Warsaw Jewish sector, the very area they policed.

A group of Jewish policemen stand at the entrance to the offices of the Jewish council at 26 Grzybowska Street in Warsaw. USHMM, courtesy of Hans-Joachim Gerke

Many of them were refugees and unknown to the ghetto Jews. If they were pawns of the Germans, they would not serve the ghetto population in an unselfish manner. Two thousand Jewish Police in Warsaw were identifiable by special caps, the Star of David armband, and the police unit's insignia.

Benny's first encounter with the Jewish Police would not be his last. Selected for a work detail, he and several other Jews traveled with Jewish policemen to Okecie Air Force Base near Mokotów, a suburb of Warsaw. Snow was falling steadily when the truck reached its destination. Immediately the policemen ordered the group to wash the Germans' cars and trucks.

As Benny completed his third truck, a guard approached him, ordering him to take off his shoes. Puzzled, Benny obeyed. He believed he had done his job quickly and efficiently. Obviously the Jewish guards did not think so since he completed only three trucks instead of six in the designated time. Soon others joined Benny in the snow reprimand. They stood barefoot three hours.

The pain of the cold set in immediately; numbness followed. Benny knew about the danger of frostbite. Although Jewish youth training had not taught him how to deal with cruelty, it had trained him to deal with exposure to weather extremes. It would be essential for him to be healthy. If he could not care for his family, what would happen to them?

Anger swept over the boy, warming him. *You will not do this to me, swinia . . . you dirty swine!* he promised silently.

It seemed a lifetime before the group re-entered the building. Once inside, they stood at attention.

Soon a tall, thin German officer, followed by the Jewish guards, strolled into the room and stood in front of them. Arms crossed, he stared, squint-eyed.

"You will learn to comply with orders!"

He began to pace in front of the men, stopping occasionally and glaring at one of them.

"You are stupid! Do you understand? There will be no other chances for such disobedience."

The muscles at Benny's jawbone tightened. *Meshugeneh! You are a crazy man!* He hoped the officer could not read his thoughts.

The Nazi stopped in front of Benny.

My God, thought Benny, but he did not move.

"Your disobedience to orders will not be tolerated."

Benny, as the schoolboy caught throwing a spitball, felt the officer charged him directly.

"The next incident will lead to a firing squad. This kind of behavior is considered sabotage against the Reich. Do you understand?"

The workers stood silently at attention.

Benny understood that if he were to survive, he would have to be smarter than his enemy.

After the lecture, the workers piled into the truck for the ride back to town. When Benny arrived home, he used his youth training to treat his feet, soaking them in cold water. It was three days before he knew he would not lose any parts of his feet.

Not long after this incident, Benny ran into his friend Zygmund Gurdus. Both were looking for food. With a smile and a handshake, the two old friends sized up each other. Each had lost his look of innocence. They were beggars and thieves now, and lack of nourishment had made them lean and drawn.

Rather than appear idle to the Germans, Zygmund invited Benny to his house. "I'm sure my parents would like to say hello. It's been a long time."

Benny hesitated to leave his search for food.

"Besides," said Zygmund, "since I've seen you last, I have a new brother. He's six months old today. Why don't you come help us celebrate his birthday? God knows, we have little to be happy about these days."

"I'd like that," said Benny, welcoming the reprieve.

The two made their way to Zygmund's house, where Max and Rutka Gurdus welcomed their son's friend. Baby Josef, playing in his crib, made a gurgling sound when he saw the guest and reached up to the young boy. Surprised, Benny looked at Rutka.

"It's okay to take him," smiled Rutka as she moved into the kitchen.

"He apparently likes you, son," remarked Max.

Benny did not know much about babies. He felt a little clumsy around them.

"Go ahead, pick him up," encouraged Zygmund. "He won't break."

Benny leaned over and cautiously picked up the baby who immediately pulled at the boy's nose and laughed.

Benny grinned, obviously pleased that the baby liked him. "He's such a happy baby."

Zygmund's father smiled. "It is amazing. He is so happy, even in such stressful times."

Rutka, bringing toast and potato soup, came back into the room.

"We are glad you're joining us, Benny?" she said. "Did Zygmund tell you we are celebrating Josef's birthday -- six months old today. He is a miracle."

"He told me, and I would love to join you." Benny returned the baby to the crib and sat down for his first celebration in over a year.

They had hardly begun the party when a loud knocking sounded at the door.

"Oh, my God," responded Rutka. Nowadays any sound at the door brought fear to the occupants of the house.

Zygmund jumped up quickly, grabbing his jacket from behind the door. "This is the second time they've come for me. I've got to get away!"

As the back door closed behind him, thirteen black-shirt SS barged through the front door demanding the teenager. Told that Zygmund was not at home, the redheaded Nazi in charge ordered his men to search the rooms. He turned toward Benny.

"Who are you?" It was too late for Benny to run.

Benny showed the Nazi his identification card, praying silently that he could avoid being a substitute prey. He was lucky the Nazi, focused more on finding the Jew that got away, only glanced at the ID.

When the SS guards returned to the room without Zygmund, the Nazi supervisor's face turned red, veins in his throat bulging. He screeched, "Pigs, swine, bastard filthy Jews. You better bring your son out of hiding, now!"

He kicked a chair, sending it across the room and crashing it into a wall.

Baby Josef shrieked.

Benny held his breath. Maybe it was a mistake not to have run when his friend did.

Max and Rutka stood silently while the redheaded officer bellowed, gesturing wildly. Rutka moved toward the crib to calm the crying baby. As she did so, the officer raised his palm to her. She stopped. He leaned over the crib.

Max moved quickly toward his baby son. Immediately one of the guards jumped in front of him, his rifle raised above his head. Max pushed past him, and the Nazi hit him with the rifle butt, a resounding thud to the skull. The Jew fell to the floor, lying motionless, blood streaming from the side of his head.

As Rutka Gurdus stood with her hands over her mouth, her cheeks covered in tears, the Nazi supervisor reached into the crib and grabbed the baby by one of his legs. He jerked upward violently, holding the baby upside down and swinging it in mid-air.

The mother reached forward, moaning, "No! No!"

Baby Josef screamed louder, a shrill cry.

A guard jumped toward Rutka, shoving her backwards into the dining table. Recovering her balance, she lunged toward him with a great wailing sound. He knocked her to the floor. She struggled to get up. He kicked her in the head again and again until she lay still, blood oozing from her mouth and nose, her arm extended toward the crib.

A second guard pointed his pistol at Benny, who had risen but was standing motionless. For once the young Jew did not try to match his bravado with that of the Nazis.

The officer, still holding the screaming baby, twisted his mouth into a half smile as he looked at the mother. With great strength, he jerked sideways and slammed the baby into the wall with a resounding thud. As the head jerked sideways from the impact, a cracking noise resonated throughout the room.

Instantaneously red dripped down the wall, spreading over the white and yellow flowers of the wall covering. It diffused slowly, like spring rain, spilling the vital river of life. Evidence of the hit streamed into the crib, where the limp, small body now lay, tangled in the infant's blanket.

No more crying sounded in the room.

As quickly as they came, the guards left, laughing as they closed the door.

Silence. It echoed as a lightening strike catches its victim in a vacuum, sucking. The absence of sound resonated in Benny's ears as pounding. His legs folded under him, and he slid onto the floor, landing legs spread wide, arms dangling at his sides. He sat, staring into space. He could not feel his body. He could feel nothing. Without warning came the heaving, and he vomited.

It would be a year before Benny could cry.

FIVE

WITH HEAD DOWNCAST, SHOULDERS HUNCHED, and hands in his pockets, Benny walked slowly toward his house. He tried to ward off the cold, but he was finding it difficult to deflect the worry. He had not found food today.

As he neared the house he saw a shadow in the window. It would be Sala. She would have crawled onto the window box in the front living area, as she sometimes did, waiting for him. It had been a while since she sat like that, her chores consuming her. The distractions of her daily life kept her from idle reflection. On one of their many visits to the house the SS confiscated the larger pieces of furniture that had blocked the window for the past few weeks.

He knew it was cold in the room. She would have a shawl around her shoulders and her legs covered with her skirt. Wrapping her arms about her knees, she would have them pulled to her chest, resting her chin on them. That's how he visualized her.

They used to sit there as little children, looking out that very window watching the snowfall. Sometimes they played a game guessing the designs of the flakes that gently touched the windowpane. What seemed beautiful then seemed bleak now. He longed for the old days. Sala was fifteen years old when the Germans invaded Warsaw. Benny knew she was a brilliant scholar, graduating into higher studies early and pursuing certification in nursing, her childhood dream. Like their mother and father she had a humanitarian spirit and saw the medical field as a means of satisfying that drive. She had been only slightly distracted from her goal -- by love.

Benny loved the story Natan told about her. The tall, lithe blond could have chosen any number of boy friends. Her sparkling blue eyes and smooth, fair skin caused many to glance her way. She fell in love with him -- Natan Epstein, ten years her senior, the son of long-time family friends.

When Sala was only nine, she looked up at the tall, dark teenager and emphatically stated, "I'm going to marry you when I grow up, Natan."

Natan said he guessed his eyes widened with surprise, but therewith the slow smile crept across his face. He said he could have shrugged off the little girl, but he loved her as a little sister.

"Sala, my beauty," he would say, "I won't have a chance. You'll break their hearts by the time you're sixteen."

He loved telling how, at fourteen, the tenacious beauty had charmed him out of his brotherly affections and toward a more serious attitude. When the two decided to marry after Sala completed her advanced studies, both families approved. A year before the bombing of Warsaw she had persuaded him to marry her when she turned sixteen, promising to continue her studies after the marriage.

He had agreed to her proposition; then the Germans attacked. It drastically changed the wedding plans and their lives. Nightmares replaced their dreams.

As Benny approached the house, he knew his sister would be anxiously waiting for him. She always worried about her little brother. Sometimes he sensed that guilt swept over her because Benny had become the family scavenger. When she had asked to help, he had responded, "No, Sala. It is less dangerous for me."

He knew his assumption of responsibility amazed her. She always told him he was a good boy and a serious student. Now she told him she could not remember anything in their short lives that prepared either of them for this onslaught of danger, hunger, and the necessary begging. They grew up privileged but not spoiled. Taught to share their gifts, they learned not to take them for granted.

His sister told him she worried about his defiance. He told her he called it "courage." She named it "bravado" and told him she feared his attitude could cause him trouble with the Germans or the Jewish and Polish Police. Each time he returned home, she said she thanked God. Sala had assigned herself the task of finding odd jobs close to home and of caring for their father who seemed to be the hardest hit by their situation.

Early on, Benny and Sala had been surprised about their father's reluctance to make an escape. Now, Benny appeared to be the lone member of the family that still persisted. After the one attempt to leave the country met with betrayal, the boy continued to talk about flight for his sister and mother.

"If we could just secure Catholic papers, your Aryan looks could get you out of the country," pleaded Benny.

"It would be impossible to get Catholic papers, son."

"Maybe not, Mother. Mr. Czerniakow may be able to help."

His sister had also changed her viewpoint about escape. "You talked me into trying an escape before," Sala had said. "I won't be talked into it again, not without Natan."

Benny realized his face clearly showed his disappointment at the family's reluctance to talk seriously about escape. He felt his parents knew their early decision might have been a bad one -- now that they faced possible starvation or even death. Though some wealthy Warsaw Jews fared well, the Lipmans did not. Their wealth had once provided a good life for them, but it could not save them now.

The white snow drifted heavily now, leaving valleys on the broken structures that surrounded their house. Once they were homes. Now the buildings stood like white gravestones against the gray skyline.

Many of the houses on Ogrodowa Street received either direct or indirect hits from the bombardment by the Germans. Though spared by the outside assault, the Lipman family fell prey to invasions of privacy in their home. By now, no valuables remained in their house and very little furniture.

Sala was sitting in the window as he thought she would be. He could see her smile as she recognized him. Just as he turned to climb the steps that led from the walk into the house, a man approached him.

"I have news about Natan Epstein," he said. "You should bring your sister to see him quickly."

How much more, thought Benny. How would he tell her?

He glanced up at the window, and her smile faded as she looked into his face. If he could have kept the look from her -- the furrowed brow and the eyes dull with dread, a young boy turning old -- but he was tired, so tired. He looked at the man and shook his head, nodding the affirmation. The stranger walked away slowly.

Benny climbed the front steps like an old man. Both feet resting on one step at a time, he dragged his body forward, reluctant to reach the top of the stairs.

The color had drained from Sala's face. He knew his body language and the look on his face would cause his sister to believe that the news was not good. She opened the door for him.

Benny stood quietly, snowflakes resting on his small shoulders. The two stood in silence looking at each other.

"Sala." Benny's voice was almost inaudible, hoarse.

"Something's wrong, isn't it? Is it Natan?" Her voice was clouded with dread.

"Put on your coat. I'll go with you to his house."

As Sala disappeared into the kitchen, Benny's eyes followed the movement of her fragile body.

What more can she take?

When the two arrived at Natan's home, they found him alone, lying on a pallet in his living room. Natan's only surviving parent had been his father whose feeble hands had accidentally dropped a shovel he was using. An SS guard shot him in the back.

The room, in which Natan lay, was cold, poorly furnished, and dirty. Urine and feces smells permeated the room. The once tall and strong man was almost unrecognizable. Severe malnutrition caused his legs and arms to swell beyond recognition. Skin, now taunt over his cheekbones, had turned gray with splotches of yellow, and his eyes receded into bony sockets.

Sala caught her breath. Benny stood silently, knowing that when his sister last saw Natan he looked ill but she could not have expected this. He watched her kneel and fold Natan into her arms, trying not to show her distress.

"Natan, it will be all right. I will find a way. I promise."

He did not answer.

Sala lay her head on the man's chest. "I love you, Natan."

Natan moved his right arm slightly, raising it upward slowly. It clung to and slid along his body as he pulled it toward his chest with great effort. He touched Sala.

"Don't give up, Natan, please," she pleaded.

His body rose upward against hers then suddenly collapsed downward, the rasping sounds resonating off the chamber walls of his chest, hollow echoes struggling for life. As air left his lungs, wheezing noises escaped through his swollen lips. He had given up.

Sala lay on his body, refusing to move, though she knew that life had gone out of it. No one would have known a year ago that starvation would so quickly affect the lives of so many.

Finally, Benny convinced Sala she could do nothing for Natan, and he assured her he would take care of the arrangements to pick up the body.

Holding hands as they did in childhood, brother and sister walked home. Sala walked in silence while Benny talked of camping trips in the beautiful foothills of the Carpathian Mountains, the horseback riding on Grandfather Lipman's farm, the theatre productions they attended with their father. He talked non-stop, hoping to ease her pain.

Suddenly Sala stopped and put her finger on the boy's lips. She faced him, tears streaming down her cheeks.

"There is nothing you can say, Benny."

"Sala . . ."

"No! I understand what you're trying to do, and I love you for it." Her hand now rested on his cheek. "Don't you see? He was my first love. My only love. I was going to have my babies with him." Sala's voice broke. "He was a gentle and kind man. He didn't deserve this."

As she spoke, her tears turned to sobs. Benny wrapped his arms around her and held her until the crying subsided.

The funeral was brief. Remaining members of the Epstein extended family followed the traditional religious ceremony, as circumstances would allow. Afterward, Sala and Benny followed the open funeral cart on which Natan rode without identity, stacked along with the other bodies like one log in a cord of wood.

At the onset of the German occupation, a horse-drawn hearse with black veiling on its side accommodated the dead. Carts made of wooden planks and wagon wheels with no sides replaced the hearse as poverty and death increased. A single operator pulled the vehicle, usually with five to ten bodies on it. Sometimes, due to the shortage of carts, bodies lay for days before being picked up. Since the bombardment and the overcrowding of the nearest Jewish cemetery, the carts carried the dead to gravesites that accommodated mass burials.

Sala walked alongside the cart -- Benny behind her -- until she could go no further. At the gate of the ghetto wall she said her last good-bye to Natan. The frail girl stood silently watching the cart pass through the gate for an unknown destination, and Benny waited for her.

The rains hammered away, turning the snow into mud. It was mid-afternoon when Benny approached Panska Street. Searching trash and knocking on doors, the boy moved in and out of alleys. For hours he had searched for food with little luck. The woolen cap on his head did not afford protection from the dampness, and his overcoat hung loosely on his small frame. Though he tried to wrap the coat tightly around his body, he could not deflect the bitter mid-November rain. He was cold and very hungry.

Undertakers drive a horse-drawn funeral wagon through the streets of the Warsaw ghetto. USHMM, courtesy of Willy Georg, German soldier and photographer

A German soldier inspects a funeral cart from the Pinkiert funeral home in the Warsaw ghetto. USHMM, courtesy of Hans-Joachim Gerke

Hunger was a constant companion to those in the ghetto. The entrenching of the Jews into a sealed area caused a warping of the economy. While ghetto artisans went unemployed, a labor shortage prevailed outside the wall. Taxing the required ration cards used for bread while the price of bread remained firm further disabled the Jewish community.

Benny never gave up exploring new avenues for food. Still naïve, he believed he could find new sources, regardless of the risk. It was slow death in the ghetto if the forager did not learn to take chances and to survive on little.

Once on Nowolipki Street, he remembered a former schoolmate who lived there. The girl's father had been a material handler for a manufacturing company in Warsaw. He knew the house the moment he saw it. Benny climbed the stairs and knocked on the door. After a few moments, the door opened slightly. Rachel peered through the small opening. "Yes?" she asked.

"It's me, Benny Lipman."

She hesitated.

"You know, from history class."

"What do you want?" she asked.

Benny did not hesitate. He placed his hand on the door and gently pushed it open. The startled girl stood silently, her eyes narrowed. Benny recognized the look. In these times trust was lost in the fray.

"Is your father or mother at home?"

From the next room a male voice called out, "Rachel, who is it?"

Without invitation Benny followed the sound of the voice. The girl trailed behind him as he entered the dining room. Benny's eyes widened with disbelief. The family sat eating at a table spread like a wedding feast. Benny had not seen that much food in almost a year. He could barely restrain himself from grabbing something to eat.

"Can't you see we are busy?" said the girl's father, as he shoved more food into his mouth. "Please go away." The mother and a smaller child sat silently, eyes diverted from their visitor's face.

For once Benny was speechless. He could not believe his reception. Surely hunger showed in his face. Defeated by his own fellows, he turned slowly and walked out the front door. In the midst of their plenty, they had not offered him even a crumb of bread. Hoping he could stop the tears that threatened, he bit his lip.

Even young Benny could guess the source of their treasures. It was obvious Rachel's father was a profiteer, dealing in the Black Market. Organized groups, as well as laborers with passes, both Poles and Jews, involved themselves in smuggling activities. Bribes and inflation of prices were common. Before the Germans began to confiscate packages, some families received food from relatives living outside Warsaw, but the black market food and rationed bread were the buttress of the ghetto.

Benny decided to risk finding food outside the ghetto walls. It was all he could do. Before the wall was completely finished, he was already mapping possible exits. The young Jew walked the streets, watching the building of the barrier, noting areas that might be vulnerable to guarding. Benny checked out bombed buildings near the walls for cellars, holes that could be used as passageways. He needed a master plan if he lived on the streets and foraged for food.

Benny had been successful before with one particular exit. If he were careful, he could slip unnoticed through the empty rooms of Krasinki Palace located northeast of the ghetto and reached from Sw. Jerska Street. It was close to an area where Benny lived as a small boy. He remembered standing at the windows of the fourth floor apartment on Karmelicka Street. From there, he could see the Palace and pretend he lived in the beautiful seventeenth century building that served as the supreme courts since World War I.

At the entrance, two guards usually chatted and smoked, but the youth could get from one deserted room to another if he progressed, sure-footed and cautiously, always alert to any changes of activity. His exit out was Nalewki Street in the Polish quarter. Looking for Polish friends, Benny pocketed his Star of David armband and moved vigilantly through the area. But today Nalewki hosted too many German patrols. He would have to find another way to cross illegally from the Jewish to the Polish sector.

Heading west on Nowolipki, he turned onto Smocza and then onto Gesia, which led him to the Jewish Cemetery opening. Drivers, pulling carts loaded with the dead, paid no attention to the boy as he walked past them and into the cemetery. This was a familiar hiding place to Benny, and it was not always this easy to access. A wall separated the Jewish and the Polish cemeteries. In one of his searches for escape, Benny had found a vine-covered hole in the old wall that separated the two cemeteries.

Zigzagging through the headstones, Benny headed for that secret cavity. Once he was out, he made his way to the Koblinski home in the Polish sector. It was late afternoon, and surprisingly, there were few people on the streets.

The boy knocked at the door. There was no answer. He knocked louder. At his right, a window curtain moved. Benny pulled his right hand from his pocket and motioned to the onlooker. Presently a short, large boned woman in her sixties opened the door. Straining to see, she asked, "Who is it?"

"It's me, Mrs. Koblinski -- Bernard Lipman."

Jews from the Warsaw ghetto congregate at the entrance to the cemetery.
USHMM, courtesy of Simon Adelman

"Benny? Benny Lipman? I did not recognize you, son. Come in." She reached out and quickly pulled the boy into the house. As she did, she glanced into the street, looking both directions. "Daniel," she called. "Come see who is here. It is Mirla's and Aaron's boy." To Benny she said, "Come, son. Come into the kitchen. You look terrible. Take off your wet things. Are you hungry?"

"Of course he's hungry," responded Daniel Koblinski. "You can tell by lookin' at the boy. Sit down, son. Tell us about your family."

Benny brought them up to date while Janka Koblinski warmed some milk and put out bread.

"We are sorry to hear things are so bad," said Daniel. "Sometimes we feel sorry for ourselves, but the Jews have it so much worse. At least I have a job. It is a meager salary, not like I used to make in your father's factory, but it is a job."

"He is correct. Daniel and I do not have much, but we are not confined to an area like you are." She looked at Benny, her brow furrowed. "How did you get into the Polish section? Are you in danger?"

"Yes. I had to sneak out and I'll have to sneak in. It's something I have to do. I need to find food for my family." The boy held the cup of milk with both hands, savoring its smell and warmth, making it last as long as he could.

"*Potepiac*! Damn Germans," responded Daniel. "They may end up starving us all. They give us our food systematically, and the Germans always get first priority. When I see you, I feel guilty that the Poles have priority over the Jews. My God, they have pushed Jewish children into smuggling. Look at you, risking your life for food."

Janka, standing by the stove, moved to her husband's side and rested her hand gently on his shoulder. Her eyes shined, tears threatening. "We have known your family for years. I wish we could do more for you."

"I understand, Mrs. Koblinski. It's dangerous for you to help me, and I will not return."

The couple looked at each other. Janka's eyes welled with tears, and Daniel no longer smiled.

"There will be no more talk of that," said Daniel. "Janka, let us share some of our supplies with Benny and his family and bid him safe travel before it gets too late. It may be more dangerous for him on the street late at night."

The sky cast its night shadows as Benny took his leave with a wondrous treasure -- a burlap bag of food. He thanked the kind couple as he waved good-bye. The Koblinski visit would help sustain Benny when he faced less benevolent experiences.

Shortly after his departure from the Koblinski's home, he noticed the figure of a German guard standing across the street. The light from his cigarette glowed in the early night shadows. The guard glanced his way, and Benny waved to him, calling in German, "Good evening, sir."

The German did not acknowledge his greeting.

Two Polish laborers approached, lunch pails in hand. As they passed under the streetlight, Benny recognized them. Hoping they had not recognized him, the boy ducked his head into his coat collar. Too late. To compensate, he spoke to them in Polish. "Evening. Nice to see you again." Perhaps the calculated friendliness would distract them from identifying him to the German. It did not.

They yelled, "Guard, guard, here is a Jude. Get him! Get him! He doesn't belong here."

Taking no more chances, Benny stumbled forward, burlap bag in tow, and began running.

The startled SS guard paused a moment, threw down his cigarette, and started after the boy.

"Halt!" he yelled. "Halt, or I will shoot!"

Benny's heart pounded in his chest. The bag hindered an easy flight, but he was not going to loosen the grip on his treasure. He swung it over his right shoulder and ran as fast as his legs would carry him. The rough edges of the old brick street pushed through the thin soles of his heavily worn shoes, making the run difficult. When he reached Karolkowa Street, he headed north toward the cemeteries. Hugging the darker shadows from the house fronts, he continued to run. The loud clomping of boots rang out behind him. Another German had joined the chase.

The boy darted behind rubble, moving in and out of alleys. Gasping for breath, he took a chance to rest behind the ruins of an apartment building. If he could make it to the northern end of Mlynarska Street, he would be at the cemeteries. Ahead, he saw their walled outline. Shifting his bag to the other shoulder, he raced for the Polish cemetery. If he could reach it in time, he believed he could re-enter the escape hole. Benny learned to alternate his exits and entries into and out of the ghetto, and he used the hidden hole on more than one occasion.

It was dark by the time Benny entered the graveyard. He could not believe the Germans still chased him. The boy had hoped that nightfall would block their view and the SS would not see him enter. A whizzing noise passed near his ear. The Germans had opened fire.

Benny ran for cover. White, marble gravestones stood out in the darkness, lending an eerie guide for the boy. Using these as shields, he darted in and out. When he approached the vicinity of the break in the wall, he suddenly heard a loud thud. Benny jumped behind a tall monument. Peering around the corner of the stone, he looked toward the noise. Several boys blocked the secret passage as they overturned grave markers and stones. They laughed and joked boisterously.

Polish gangs often ran the streets of both the Jewish and Polish sectors. Little had been done to stop these raids. The gangs had plundered and raped, almost at will. Construction of the ghetto wall had lessened these activities somewhat but had not totally stopped them.

Benny hoped the wall cavity, concealed by foliage, would go unnoticed by the Polish youth. Unexpectedly one of the Poles jumped accidentally into the middle of the vines, causing him to trip on a loose brick.

"What's that?" the Pole asked.

The others walked toward their friend.

Benny held his breath.

Abruptly they stopped as they looked back over their shoulders.

"Listen. Someone's in the cemetery," said one of the youth.

They stood quietly, listening. Soon they heard the voices of the approaching SS.

"It's the Germans," whispered one of the boys. "Let's get out of here!"

The Poles darted through the overgrown graveyard. The commotion from the vandals distracted the guards from their chase. Benny could hear the Germans arguing and ordering the youths to go home. The SS were not angry at the overturning of the stones, but with the boys who had confused their efforts to get their Jewish prey. Finally, the voices grew faint as they moved farther away from Benny's hiding place.

Clutching his precious cargo, he moved prudently toward the hole. Carefully pulling back the foliage, Benny pushed his bag through the small opening and crawled after it. He then reached back through the cavity and pulled the vines toward him. The boy prayed they would continue to hide his precious exit.

Once in the Jewish cemetery, the boy cautiously weaved in and out of the tombstones and toward the entrance. He hoped there were no German or Jewish police lurking. He was lucky. He quickly slipped across Okopowa and into the ruins along Gesia.

Even though it was probably the safest route, Benny decided not to use the Mila and Smocza manhole entry to the sewer system that tunneled under Warsaw. It was the worst possible route to his house but often a necessary one. When he did use it, he had to crouch as he moved through the narrow space. If he were lucky, a recent rain would have washed through the section and saved him from wading deep in excrement. The stench always saturated the damp sewer. Occasionally a rat ran across his foot. Benny had learned to deal with many new situations over the past year, but this was always among the worst. Within the next two years, Warsaw sewers would be used for smuggling arms and food during the ghetto uprising.

Cautiously Benny made his way through the rubble of the streets. As he climbed the steps to the front door of his house, he heard noise from the left. It appeared to come from near the basement window. He leaned over the railing and listened. Benny thought he heard

Sewer manhole cover from Warsaw. Courtesy of Warsaw City Authority
Deportation train. USHMM, courtesy of Instytut Historyczy Instytut
Naukowo-Badawczy

someone sobbing. Moving back down onto the sidewalk and toward
the basement window he stepped on something, crunching it under
his feet. The sobbing stopped. A broken window exposed a single
light bulb hanging from the basement ceiling. Benny peered through
the opening, just large enough for a person to crawl into. Not seeing
or hearing anything, he decided to check the situation from inside
the house.

Benny, hoping not to make a noise, slowly opened the front
door and placed his bag on the floor. The boy could hear someone
in the kitchen, probably his mother or Sala. Not wanting to alarm
them, Benny moved calmly to the basement door under the stairs

and carefully turned the knob. The door squeaked. He waited for a response from the kitchen or from below. None came. He descended the stairs into the basement, one step at a time. From the ceiling, a single light bulb dimly lighted the room, leaving corners only half illuminated.

When he reached the bottom of the stairs, Benny stood for a moment. He heard nothing nor saw anyone.

He supposed Mother or Sala left the light on.

He reached for a board to put over the window.

Suddenly a rustling sounded from the shadowed corner to his left.

"Who's there?" he asked, holding the board, ready for defense.

There was no answer. He moved cautiously toward the sound, carefully stepping over broken glass, overturned boxes, and scattered tools. Someone or several people had been there.

"I know you're here. You'd better answer."

That was when he heard the moan. In the dim light he saw the figure lying on the floor. Sala lay in fetal position, her knees hugging her chest.

"My God, Sala! What happened?" Her torn dress hung loosely from her body. Dried blood smeared her arms and legs as well as her dress.

The girl did not respond.

When Benny moved toward her, Sala turned her head and looked at him. Her eyes were swelled nearly shut, and blood oozed from her split lip. Her blond hair, sweat-soaked, lay in strings, clinging to her neck.

The boy reached out to her, but she jerked away from him.

"Sala, what happened?" His voice was almost a whisper. "When did this happen?"

She looked at him, her eyes vacant, moans beginning from deep within her throat.

Benny could not stand the hurt in his heart. It felt like a heavy stone. How could anyone assault his beautiful sister? He squatted beside her, gently wrapping his arms around her and lifting her.

He whispered, "It's okay, Sala. I'm here."

The boy wondered how no one heard the commotion. Then he remembered Mirla saying she was going to the orphanage during the afternoon to help with something. He did not remember what. It was unusual for her to leave the house. His father would have been in bed on the second floor, the depression blocking out reality.

"We won't tell mother and father," he said.

Sala sagged heavily on his arms. He had read her thoughts.

"I'll get you upstairs to your room. I'll sleep on the floor by your bed tonight. You won't have to be alone. All right?"

Sala nodded.

"I'll think of some way to explain your bruises. Yes? No one will know."

The boy guided his older sister up the stairs and promised to return after she had prepared for bed. As young as he was, Benny knew she felt disgraced. How could they do this to his sister? *Damn it!* She did not harm anyone. If he ever found who did this, they would have to answer to him.

Sala would never again be the same. She would carry her mental wounds to the grave.

Had their mother ventured that night into Sala's room, she would have seen her son sitting beside his sister's bed, holding her hand and singing a Yiddish lullaby.

It was not yet daybreak when Aaron slowly descended the stairs to the front hall. Having grown weak from the constant dysentery that plagued him, he did not often leave his bed. The man was a frail display of protruding bones and skin cast in a gray pallor. Daily Aaron became more confused. He entered the living room where his parlor piano stood, only fragments of what once was a grand instrument of music. Aaron sat at the bench, placing his hands on the remaining keys. He began to play. Obtuse thuds fell upon the silence of the room. Continuing to move his hands over the broken keys, he leaned his head back and shut his eyes as though listening to the swell of Mozart's "Magic Flute."

Startled by the noise from the first floor and missing her husband from their bed, Mirla rushed down stairs, followed by Benny.

"Mother, is he all right?"

"I think so, Benny." Tears welled in Mirla's eyes. "I think he believes he can give the piano life again. It meant so much to him." Her voice trailed off into quiet sobs.

Benny moved to his mother's side and put his arms around her.

"I don't know how much more your father can take. He has changed so much this past year."

"I know, Mother." Benny fought tears. Since the invasion of the Germans, he had not spent much time with his father. Gone forever were the leisure days of camping as well as theatre going. Benny felt almost as if he had lost his father too.

At that moment, the pounding began at the Lipman front door. Startled, Mirla looked at her son. Aaron stopped playing, pushed back from the piano, and walked past the two to the front door. He opened it.

"We want to see Bernard Lipman," demanded one of the two Jewish policemen.

Aaron stood without expression.

Mirla moved to her husband's side.

"I'm Bernard Lipman," said Benny as he moved toward them.

"You are to get dressed and come with us."

Benny knew there would be no use to resist. Their sudden appearance negated thoughts of escape. He started upstairs, followed by one of the policemen. He would not deny he was frightened. He hoped they would not discover Sala asleep.

When the boy and his police escort returned, they found the others standing in silence. Benny did not know what to say to his parents. He did not know why or where the police were taking him. It would have accomplished nothing to ask. He turned to his mother, put his arms around her, and kissed her. Tears ran down her face.

Looking up at his father, Benny said, "Sir, I'll be back soon. I promise."

The boy put his arms around the man's waist and hugged him tightly. Aaron stood stoically, staring into space. As Benny reached the waiting German truck, he looked back toward his home. His father stood at the window, eyes sunken and dull, a look of defeat on his face. Benny would never forget that look.

Mirla rushed to the door and cried out toward the truck, "He is a *yintel*! He is just a little boy! Do not take him, please!"

The truck picked up speed as it moved away from Benny's home. He sat in the rear, staring at his mother standing in the street, stretching her arms toward the moving vehicle.

Giant floodlights drenched Plac Muranowska, the destination for the trucks. As far as one could look, a sea of people, mostly old men and young boys, filled the area. Fathers clung to their sons. Some cried openly while others stood silently with faces etched in heartache and suffering. Sobs, mixed with whispered questions and shouting, created a panorama of confusion.

Sorting people into groups of five to six hundred, the Germans began the selection. Benny was placed with a group of twelve-year-olds and sixty or seventy-year-old men. Loaded into the back of several trucks, they traveled out of the ghetto and through the streets of Warsaw. Eventually, they arrived at the Praza Dwozec Wilenski Railroad Station.

They boarded five boxcars at mid-morning. One hundred human beings stood, packed shoulder to shoulder in each train car. Riding like this offered no choices. They could only wait for whatever was to happen. It was sundown when they arrived at Lublin, some seventy-five miles south of Warsaw.

Young boys, dressed in Nazi uniforms and carrying rifles, herded the prisoners from the boxcars. The boys, no more than thirteen years old, shook their fists and shrieked at the prisoners, assaulting them with rifle butts if they moved too slowly. It was not difficult to displease the youths who yelled again and again, "*Stellt euch an, stellt euch an sechs in der Reihe* (get into line, get into lines of six)." The young guards' contorted faces showed the depth of their hate.

How can they have such maliciousness toward someone they don't know? thought Benny. *Will I be able to outlive this hate?*

Since they were so young and their uniforms different from the SS, he believed they must be *Hitlerjugend* -- German youth trained to be reserve manpower. In 1938, just a year before the Germans invaded Warsaw, a discussion concerning the goals of youth organizations around the world, including the American Boy Scouts and the "Free German Youth," was the focus of several of Benny's Jewish youth meetings.

With the Third Reich playing havoc across Europe, interest in the German youth movement increased, especially in the Jewish youth organization. Michal Strauss, leader of the Warsaw branch, led the discussion at one of these meetings.

"Some of the activities are similar," he told the club members, "such as camping, hiking, patriotism, but since Hitler appointed Schirach leader of the Nazi youth program, the group seems to have a more militant attitude."

"Are they still patriotic to Germany?" asked one of the boys.

"Oh, yes, perhaps more. Hitler is probably brainwashing them toward the Aryan takeover of the world."

One of the young men offered, "I read that they believe that physical health and loyalty are far more important than education."

"Their motto," answered Strauss, "appears to be dedication to the Fatherland, at all costs, even obeying directives that could be questionable. I find it extreme that they participate in para-military training."

Benny remembered the discussion well as he now watched the youth, ready to create an opportunity to show their power.

Startled by someone speaking to him, he turned toward the voice. "I beg your pardon," said Benny.

"I don't think you heard the guard, and I don't want to see you get hurt," said the young man. "By the way, my name is Moses, and this my younger brother, Jacob." He pointed to the person standing next to him.

"My name is Benny." It seemed such an incongruous situation to be exchanging niceties.

The guard yelled instructions, and Benny moved forward. Moses reached out and touched Benny's arm. "I think we would be safer near the front, in the middle."

Quickly Benny followed the two before their movements became too noticeable.

Ultimately the Germans were satisfied with their marshaling of the six hundred prisoners. The march began with both *Hitlerjugend* and SS guards supervising.

Benny looked up at the heavens. No stars were in sight, just a cold, dark night. He wondered if they had withdrawn their gleam to avoid showing the scene below. If he could, he would have.

As soon as the prisoners cleared the railroad area, the Germans prodded them to run, not walk, at a full trot. They rifle butted those who could not keep up the pace. It would have been difficult to describe the eerie night mission and the sounds that exploded into the night. Germans bellowed orders and Jews wept openly. Still the prisoners ran.

As they passed through townships, people watched from their balconies. Streetlights illuminated the harried runners. A few people yelled at the Germans, demanding to know what was going on. Shots fired into the night were their answer.

Benny tried to focus on things other than exhaustion or fear. He bolstered his energy by pretending he was in a soccer match, driving toward the goal. Old men and young dropped in their tracks, exhausted from the running and hunger. The Germans shot stragglers, leaving them by the roadsides. Benny was glad Moses suggested a spot in the center of the line. Psychologically it seemed safer there, away from the madmen driving the group and easier to keep from falling behind.

Benny's heart beat fast, and his mouth and throat burned from inhaling the night air. Would he be one of those that fell behind? *No,* he said to himself. *I'll show them.* Benny had come much too far this past year to die falling behind.

When the group arrived at a compound in the middle of a field, the murky threads of morning streaked the sky. The exhausted prisoners dropped to the cold ground. Electrified barbed wire surrounded their resting-place.

The dirt seemed like a feather mattress to Benny. He did not feel the cold or the dampness, but he did worry about his paralyzed feet and was afraid to remove his shoes to rub them.

Before long an SS officer came out of a barracks-like building and approached the men sitting on the ground. He did not press them to stand. In a harsh and guttural voice he demanded, "Who among you is a rabbi?"

No one spoke.

"I asked, who among you is a rabbi?"

Everyone was afraid to answer, not knowing what lay in store for the man that admitted to being one.

"Unless a rabbi comes forward," yelled the German, "one hundred of you will be executed on the spot. Do you understand me?" Pausing, he surveyed the group of prisoners, and then calmly stated, "It is impossible for any group this large not to have a rabbi."

Finally an old man raised his arm. "I am Rabbi Isaac Abrams."

Benny knew he was not, for he met Isaac, a shoemaker, at Plac Muranowska. Their conversation had been brief.

"Have faith, young man," he had said to Benny. "They cannot destroy tough old shoemakers and courageous young boys."

Benny remembered the man's smile and calm demeanor.

"Come forward, Abrams," beckoned the SS commander.

As he did, the Jews stood up.

The German demanded, "You are to say a prayer for those who died on the march from the train station. What is it you Jews call it, a Kaddish?"

The German's reasoning was systematic. They needed a rabbi to condone the killing.

"A Kaddish -- yes," said Isaac.

"Do not let anyone say that Germans are not humane." The Nazi stood stiffly, shoulders straight and chin tilted, pleased to be a member of the superior race.

The officer selected twenty-five from the group and several guards to go back over the route and pick up the dead bodies.

The rest of the group sat around most of the day. Finally at sundown, the captors distributed to each a small piece of bread and some water, their ration for the day. They had just begun their meager meal when two hay wagons, confiscated from a local farmer, pulled into the compound, loaded with approximately one hundred dead prisoners. The Jewish prisoners took turns pulling the wagons while the guards followed, rifles posed.

Isaac urged the prisoners to gather around the wagons. There, he led them in the recitation of the mourners' Kaddish, the chanting sounding hollow in the middle of a prisoner compound. Afterwards, the Germans chose a detail of men to dig an enormous grave at the edge of the encampment.

Benny watched as the crew unceremoniously dumped the bodies into the hole.

My God, he thought. Out loud, he said, "They're being treated no better than dung, thrown into the ground to fertilize it."

"Shhhh," cautioned the man standing next to him. "You will be punished if they hear you."

"I don't care," he whispered back. "It's not right."

"Right or wrong," responded another prisoner, "Shut up or you will endanger us all."

Benny stood silently. *The Chutzpa! Shame!* he thought. *It isn't fair for them to have this kind of control over the lives of others.*

Benny's lessons regarding fairness and control were just beginning.

SIX

"GERMANY WILL, IN THE END, conquer the world, you know." The brash SS officer had begun another of his lectures.

Light snow began to fall, chilling the prisoners who stood in lines, listening. Bordering on the Polish Uplands and the Central Plains, the makeshift labor camp stood in an open field, vulnerable to blowing winds. Once this farming area grew potatoes and barley. Now it housed prisoners.

Benny, like the others, wore tattered clothing that gave little protection from the spine-rippling chill. Even though the barrack in which Benny quartered had no insulation or heat, it was at least a shelter from the wind.

The boy watched the officer's face. It was not a particularly unique one. His long, thin nose dominated the features, the nostrils flaring as he punctuated the end of sentences with guttural emphasis. The high cheekbones gave a chiseled look to his face. As the officer talked, pacing back and forth along the lines, he stared at his Jew and Pole recruits, his clear blue eyes penetrating, intimidating.

A knaker. Big shot! So this is the super race, thought Benny.

This particular Aryan did not impress the young Jew. Bored by the officer's rambling discourse, Benny cautiously surveyed his surroundings. He was in the middle of a barbed wire pen three times the size of a soccer field. Five barracks sat at one end of the compound, two of which were for the Germans. The ground, once a meadow of lush grass, was now mire created by the weather and the

77

frivolous marching and senseless lineups. Benny felt as though he was a farm animal kept at bay by the electrified fence and a locked gate. A wave of anger swept over him.

"Your effort here is a collective responsibility," droned the SS officer. He had stopped directly in front of Benny. Benny looked him in the eye. "Do you understand?" The boy did not flinch. "If you work hard, the lot of your people will improve. If not. . . ." The officer's voice dwindled into another threat that always accentuated the "talks."

With hands clasped behind him, the SS captain walked the line in front of the prisoners, stopping occasionally to look directly at one of the group as though to emphasize his message.

"Remember, it is polite," he pointed out, "for all Jews to remove their hats in the presence of their captors. This includes privates as well as officers."

The prisoners were already standing bareheaded. Those few who owned a hat held it in their hands.

After each of the hour-long lectures, the group returned to the barracks only to be asked to reassemble outside. It was the conquerors' plan to create chaos and confusion.

"Today," continued the captain, "you will be divided into smaller groups and sent out from Lublin to work."

Benny almost welcomed the opportunity to work. It would be a good way to stay warm, and perhaps the Germans would provide more food for those who did hard labor. He had no way of knowing what lay in store for them. His guess was that he could expect almost anything from the trigger-happy Germans.

On the re-entry into the barracks, Benny crawled onto his bunk and pushed his body against the wall, searching for warmth. Double layers of clothing could not provide much protection. He pulled his knees to his chest and wrapped his arms securely around them.

A gehenem! What a hellhole!

No bedding, not even blankets covered the roughly hewn wooden bunks, stacked three tiers high. The long barracks had wooden plank floors and no heating. A single light bulb hung from the center of the room. The toilet, a short walk from the building, consisted of two long poles suspended about three feet off the ground. The first time Benny experienced this unique facility, he found that he had to hang precariously over the trench in order to relieve himself. He very nearly fell in. Until they learned to maneuver the poles and the trench, many prisoners slipped into the refuse pit.

Once the wind chill left his body, Benny began to move around the room, activity providing some warmth. He stopped by Moses' bunk. "What kind of work do you think we'll be doing?"

Moses stood leaning on the corner pole. He looked at the boy. "I don't know, but you can bet it'll be something the Germans need."

"Your family still in Warsaw?" asked Benny.

Moses looked at the boy, his eyes flat, and the muscles along his jawbone tightening. He glanced toward his brother who sat silently on the bunk above him.

"Dead. My father was taken in one of the first selections. My mother died in the bombing."

Benny did not know what to say. He guessed Moses to be around twenty years old and his brother about seventeen. He felt sorry for them. At least he still had his family.

"My father was a rabbi."

"A rabbi!" Benny could not help but be impressed.

"That's what I wanted to be."

"You still can, Moses." Jacob joined the conversation. "Don't give up your dream. One day this will all be over."

Moses did not answer. The look on his face was chilling. Benny had a strange feeling he could not explain.

An elderly man standing nearby observing the conversation spoke. "I do not know what is ahead of you, my sons, but you are young. Do not make this your graveyard." He reached out a callused hand as though to embrace them. "Keep the spirit, and fight for your life."

The man's words lingered for Benny. Sleep was hard to come by that night. He felt the tears rimming his eyes, but he refused to let them fall, even as he wondered if this was his graveyard. Would he ever again see his parents? He had promised his father he would return. How could he break that promise?

So rapidly did his heart beat, Benny felt that it had distended to fill his entire chest. He tried to calm himself. Lying there on the hard board, he concentrated on one of his favorite melodies. Strains of violin and piano music filled his thoughts. The elegance of Mozart's work gave the young Jew a sense of balance and control. The imaginary melody cushioned his body and his mind, and he fell asleep finally.

—◆ ❊ ◆—

A mass segregation of the captives began, some to be deported to other locations while around two hundred stayed in the Lublin area to build a concentration camp, later named K. L. Majdanek, opened only ten months after Benny's departure. Two to three weeks after Benny left the area, a death march took Jews from Lublin to Biala Podlaska, sixty-two miles away. Shortly afterwards the Germans sealed the Lublin ghetto, and within fourteen months, the nearby Belzec extermination center received thirty thousand deported Jews.

On deportation day Benny found himself in a group of 150 loaded in trucks for transportation to the Lublin train station. Surprisingly they had passenger train accommodations for the short distance to a small town southwest of Lublin. When they arrived in Opole, they transferred into more lines. Benny remembered Moses' directions for marches and inched himself toward the middle. He smiled as he saw Moses and Jacob as well as Isaac. Moses' tipped his hand toward his head and smiled.

"Hello, Benny," whispered Jacob.

"Hello."

Isaac reached out and touched him on the arm. Benny welcomed the friendly touch.

A fresh snow had fallen. Clear now, the sky seemed almost bright as the prisoners marched into the small village that sat in quiet medieval beauty, seemingly untouched by intruders.

To Benny it was a distinct contrast to the bombed shell of Warsaw and the ghetto. Although it was evident that poverty existed, the little stone and brick cottages were neat and clean. As the marchers entered the market place, peddlers, dressed in the traditional attire of the Polish peasant, hawked various items from boots to newspapers. Peasant women sold geese and chickens, sometimes from slatted cages or by holding the bird by its feet and hugging it close under the arm. The cackling and hissing competed with the children playing and the hawkers' shouts. A school bell sounded in the distance, and children with books in hand, scurried toward it. Curiously no one was visibly Jewish if one judged ethnicity by clothing. German soldiers milled about.

Heads turned toward the prisoners, sympathy showing in their faces. Ignoring the German guards, many of the people began calling out words of encouragement and throwing cigarettes, cigars, and hard candies. The SS guards, whose ages ranged from seventeen to twenty, seemed amused.

Over the roofs of the stores Benny could see the spire of an ancient church pointing toward the heavens. The boy wished he could stay here, just for a while, with the smiling faces of people not yet faced with a ghetto. The winter snow covered the rooftops of the ancient structures with a virginal quality. The village existed in Benny's eyes as a fairyland of reprieve from the war.

The group continued their march, sharing the cigarettes, candies, and bread tossed to them by the villagers. Things once commonplace now became priceless.

They left Opole and continued along a paved road, bordered by conifer and hazelnut trees. The rolling terrain and small forest areas blended with farms, creating a collage of a pleasant and diverse countryside. A small road sign indicated that the small village of Józefów na Wisla (City by the River) was nearby.

It was a short walk from the village to their new home, a fenced compound and a drastic contrast to the scenic peace of the village they had just left. They marched six abreast through a large, wire gate. The barbed wire enclosing the three-barrack complex did not appear to be electrified.

Insulated barracks, unlike the Lublin camp, held a big iron stove that sat at the end of each long room. An abundance of wood in the area assured the prisoners they would be able to have this luxury. The toilet facility was similar to the one at Lublin, serving approximately one hundred men at a time, lined up back to back. Shortly after they arrived, Benny was standing in one of these lines when he began to giggle. The others taking their turn frowned, wondering where the boy could find humor in such a situation. The use of poles reminded Benny of movies he had seen that showed American western hitching posts. *There's something ironic about this*, thought Benny. *Work horses, all in a row, collectively taking a pee.*

The living conditions were more luxurious than the last ones, a pleasant surprise for Benny. Sleeping on straw was much better than having to sleep on boards. His bunk was directly over Isaac Abrams.

"Rabbi." Even though Benny knew Isaac was not a rabbi, he called him that because he did not want to give away the man's secret. "Don't you think it seems all right, so far?"

Isaac looked at Benny and smiled. Regardless of the circumstance, Isaac always had a ready smile and optimistic outlook, making life more bearable for those around him. It was obvious Isaac liked the naive young boy who was strong-willed and determined to survive. "Benny, my boy," he answered. "I think it is time to liven up this group. What do you think?"

Benny frowned, puzzled at Isaac's remark.

Abruptly Isaac began to sing a Yiddish folk song. The others had begun to gather around Rabbi. A few ventured to join the singing. Soon Benny sang enthusiastically, drowning out the others. Isaac smiled broadly, motioning the others to be quiet. So caught up in what he loved to do, the boy did not notice that the others had stopped singing. As he reached the end of the song, loud clapping startled him. He looked around, embarrassed.

The prisoners welcomed the reprieve from more fearful thoughts and began to chant, "More, more."

Benny smiled but stood silently.

"I think you should sing some more, Benny," said Isaac. "You have a fine voice. Would you?"

Pleased, Benny chose a raunchy song that caused the prisoners to laugh and slap their thighs. The men, caught up in the moment of merriment, did not hear the barracks door open.

"Halt, *verboten!*"

Benny stopped singing. The prisoners stood paralyzed, unsure of what they should do.

When one of the two guards approached Benny, Isaac stepped forward. "It is my fault. I asked the boy to sing."

The Nazi pushed Isaac, causing him to fall against the bunk and onto the floor.

"Please do not hurt Rabbi. I will not sing further," said Benny in German.

The German stared at him.

Benny stared back.

"Unless . . ." Benny's voice trailed off.

Stunned, several Jews gasped as they looked askance at the other guard.

" . . . unless you would like me to sing it in your language."

Isaac's eyes widened as he waited for the German response, fully expecting the worst.

The startled guard slowly raised his rifle butt toward the boy's head.

Benny waited for the blow. When it did not come, he asked, "What is your favorite song?"

The German lowered his rifle, smiled, and asked Benny if he knew a particular folk song, popular among adolescent German males. Benny knew the number, a universal song sung to the tune of the American Battle Hymn of the Republic.

"*Hel, helu,*" Benny began, motioning for the guards to clap their hands.

Shocked, the prisoners stood quietly.

"*Schön sind die Mädchenvon siebzehn und achtzehn Jahren* (Hallelujah, halloo, halloo, beautiful are the girls of seventeen and eighteen years old from all over the world)."

As Benny pranced around the room, he embellished the familiar tune with impromptu verses. He filled them with sexual suggestions learned from his secret talks with male friends and his out-of-classroom study of the German language.

Soon the two guards were laughing and clapping their feet and hands. The prisoners stood in astonishment, daring not to join in. Benny glanced over at Isaac who was smiling broadly. The older man winked at the young Jew.

All of a sudden a shot exploded at the door. The captain stood with a pistol aimed at the ceiling.

"What is happening here?" he demanded.

The two guards immediately came to attention and moved away from the prisoners.

"I will deal with you two," he said as he looked sternly at the two SS guards. "And you, all of you, we will see how much energy you have left for tomorrow." The officer looked closely at each of the prisoners. All stood silently, heads straightforward. "Perhaps morning should come earlier than usual."

The officer turned sharply and left the barracks, followed by the two guards.

"I'm sorry," said Benny to no one in particular.

"It is okay, boy. Do not give up," Isaac encouraged. "My heart tells me that voice of yours will get you far. Do not be afraid to use it when your gut tells you the timing is right." The older man put his arm around Benny's shoulder. "God has given you a fine gift, my son. Each of us should pleasure from God's gifts. Maybe some day you will be heard in great churches throughout the land."

"Churches," questioned Benny, "not synagogues?"

"Both," answered Isaac with great confidence. "We are all created by the same God."

Benny lay in his bunk thinking about what Isaac had said. Eventually he fell into a deep sleep and dreamed that his melodic voice mesmerized nations of people, and war did not exist.

——◆ ✦ ◆——

Morning came early for the prisoners. It was well before dawn when the German bugler aroused them, followed by several guards who rushed into the barracks yelling, "Outside, outside for instructions."

The prisoners filed out of the building into the dark, cold morning, a smoky haze covering the lighted corner poles surrounding the camp.

The captain began his day's instructions. "First, you will have breakfast."

Breakfast, thought Benny, *a mere drink of weak tea and a piece of bread is hardly breakfast.*

"You will be divided into teams," instructed the captain. "Some of you skilled in the trades will serve as barbers, cooks, carpenters, and such. Those of you with no skills will serve in the labor battalion." Soon it was obvious the younger men and boys would serve as laborers.

The officer continued, "The Wisloka River is near this camp. It is our job to help regulate its flow." He walked back and forth in front of the prisoners as he talked. "The labor group will take sand from the tributaries of the river and pile it up in dunes to act as barriers against flooding."

After explicit instructions, he dismissed them for breakfast, a meal of weak tasting soup and bread. Benny did not take lightly the responsibility of having his own food container. He had punched a hole on the side of his and tied it to his waist. He even slept with his prize possession.

The younger members of the group marched, six abreast, the five kilometers to the river location where they organized for rotation of the duties. While one group stood in the cold water of the river shoveling sand into wheelbarrows, another pushed loaded wheelbarrows along planks, laid single file, extending from the river to the bank. The makeshift bridge, supported with pilings, stretched precariously into the river.

Day after day, twelve to thirteen hours a day, the laborers worked, generally under the supervision of an older SS guard and *Hitlerjugend* assigned to the camp. Rotation of the workers from wheelbarrows to shovels provided the only change of pace.

Marching back to camp at night the SS and *Hitlerjugend* often ordered the tired group to sing songs. The men tried to follow orders, their voices hoarse from cold and exhaustion.

Benny still felt guilty about the display of songs in the barracks, and though tired, he took on the role of the clown for the captors, keeping the others out of trouble. He led the singing, often the only voice heard. For the first time in his life singing was a chore.

—➤❖◀—

Supper was always the same -- a piece of bread and a pint of watered down potato soup without potatoes. The men began to lose weight, the ration of soup inadequate for the hard work. Some learned to manipulate for more food. Isaac and some of the older men gave extra pieces of bread to Benny and the other younger ones. Their jobs, though strenuous, were not as difficult as the boys working on the river project. Isaac found extra food for the young laborers. Because he was the rabbi, the Germans trusted him and allowed him to go under guard to the village on errands. Isaac's money procured bread and a little butter from the Polish citizens.

Newly constructed barracks held more laborers who arrived during the first few weeks of Benny's internment. They brought valuables -- watches, rings, and money. Isaac set up a bartering system with them and used the resources for additional food for all. If the Germans suspected the activities, they did not interfere.

Benny appreciated what the older men did for him. It was Isaac that Benny usually turned to for answers to his questions.

Not long after they began their river duty, Benny asked Isaac, "What do you think the chance is for escape?"

Surprised, Isaac looked up at the boy. Benny was hanging over the side of his bunk, listening anxiously.

"I have to be honest," whispered Isaac. "It does not look good. The routines are too pat. Be careful who you talk to."

The youth nodded his head in affirmation and rolled into the bunk. The thought of escape excited him and boosted his spirits. He believed if anyone could do it, he could.

Benny trudged through the never changing daily routine. Separation from his family plagued his thoughts. While others received mail from home, Benny went without. Perhaps his sudden roundup left the Jewish Federation without enough information to notify his parents of his whereabouts. A nagging uncertainty clouded Benny's mind when he remembered his father standing at the window, forlorn, and his mother sobbing and waving her arms as the truck carrying her son pulled away for its unknown destination.

Even though they were weak and hungry, the laborers were forced to work long hours in the cold. Recruits took the place of those who fell ill. An area in the compound set aside for medical purposes provided only a small space with makeshift assistance. The threat of death hung over any person whose recovery lingered. Determination kept Benny away from the sick area.

In December the heavy rains came, and the Wisloka River reached flood stage. The overflow caused havoc with the prisoners' work.

"Nothing is impossible!" roared the SS officer in charge. "You will find a way to continue to work. Is that understood?"

The Germans never wavered from their systematic control.

The weary and drenched workers, rain plastering their hair to their faces and their inadequate clothing to their body, stood in silence. The rotation of duties allowed the prisoners to take short rests and to claim a brief period of time next to a makeshift stove made by burning logs in a large barrel. The laborers leaned dangerously over the fire not only for warmth but to keep the rain from dissipating the welcomed flames.

What could be worse, thought Benny, *to drown, die of pneumonia, or be shot? At least the first two will be by the elements and not by the hands of a German and his rifle.*

The men, subdued by the cold rain and the power of their captors, forged mechanically ahead, driven by the small chance for survival. Planks and ropes, secured from the camp and carried to the river, added an extension to the makeshift bridge. Several men stood in the muddy current on each side of the bridge, holding it as the wheelbarrows rolled over the wooden planks. Two men stood in the rushing water and shoveled sand. Two more held a rope tied to the waist of those in the water.

It was a tedious and difficult job, controlling the shovel and the sand. Long hours produced little product, but the laborers continued to work collectively under the strict eye of twelve rifle-carrying *Hitlerjugend.*

It was Moses and Jacob's turn to shovel. They had been in the water about thirty minutes when Moses gave in to the rush of ice-cold water and exhaustion.

"Help!" yelled Jacob. "My brother has gone under. He will drown. He cannot swim. Help!"

Suddenly jerked toward the raging river, Moses' holder on the bank yelled, "Help me. He's too heavy. I can't hold on."

Those nearest holding the planks turned loose and reached for Moses' rope, causing the wheelbarrow being loaded to fall into the river. Benny, its handler, teetered dangerously as the planks threatened to overturn him. With outstretched arms, he walked the unruly boards until he reached a point where he could jump to shore. The men holding the rope to Moses struggled to hang on as he bobbed out of the water then submerged again. Digging their heels into the slimy, wet dirt, they pulled, sliding closer and closer to the edge of the water. Finally they dragged Moses onto the bank, followed by Jacob. The rescuers fell to the ground gasping for breath. Others hurried to Moses as he lay coughing and sputtering the muddy water from his nose and mouth. After a while, he rose up on one elbow.

"I praise you, oh Lord," he said out loud, "for you have saved me."

"Heathen," shouted one of the *Hitlerjugend,* moving toward Moses.

Another guard rushed up and demanded, "Why aren't you working, Jude? Who told you to take a rest?" He looked over at Jacob who sat with his head in his hands, trying to catch his breath from the uphill struggle on the muddy bank. "You, too, Jew boy. Get up! Get to work."

Before Moses or Jacob could respond, the German youth, who called Moses a heathen, hit him across the head. Moses fell backward onto the ground. Several of the prisoners jumped toward the guard. The other *Hitlerjugend* cocked their rifles, daring the prisoners to make another move.

The SS guard in charge moved quickly toward the group screaming, "Form your lines! Form into lines, now!"

Benny and another laborer assisted Moses, lifting him to a standing position. They helped him join the lineup.

"We will stop for today," commanded the Nazi. "You see, Germans do have compassion. Now march!"

During the near drowning episode, the *Hitlerjugend* stood watching, making lewd comments, and offering no assistance. Bent on having the last word, they ordered the group to sing. Hitler had done a good job arousing the feral instinct of Germany's young people when he convinced them Germans were "the chosen" rulers of the world.

The rain, defusing daylight, beat heavily on the laborers. Bedraggled men, covered in mud, marched and sang. The croaking pitch of their voices broke through the darkness, ejecting sounds similar to those of inmates in a mental hospital. They tramped through the puddles of mud and water. The farther they marched the louder their sounds. They seemed to give strength to each other. Soon even Moses was walking without help, singing along with the others.

As he marched, Benny remembered why Moses' blessing was familiar. It was from a psalm known by most Jews. He suspected that the Hanukkah holiday had something to do with the rush of memories. The memory of the history lesson and the incident on the riverbank was strange timing. Benny had learned never to take up the sword willingly but to recognize that sometimes no other choice is available. He wondered if the prisoners sang, not to follow German orders, but as a group dedication to thoughts of freedom and survival. It was a small simile, but it was what Benny could hold on to.

—◆ ✧ ◆—

Tired from the struggle against the river and the captives, the laborers filed into chow line with their pint cans. Again, the meager meal consisted of such small amounts of soup it hardly made an impression in the pail. After supper the work battalion lined up outside the mess hall, splashing their bodies with the water provided in buckets. They received a change of clothes, tattered and old. Benny suspected the effort was more to keep them fit for working than for any humanitarian reason.

Benny looked like a scarecrow, jacket sleeves hanging below his hands, the coat to his calves. He rolled oversized pants above his boots that he stuffed with torn pieces of his old clothes. This kept his feet from shifting and causing blisters from the oversized boots. He often wondered where the supply of clothes came from. He later learned the dead from round-ups and death camps sacrificed them.

When they returned to the barracks, Benny approached his friend, who sat on his bunk removing his shoes.

"Moses, I had thoughts of Hanukkah as we marched."

Moses smiled. "So did I."

"I remember the stories of the priest of Modlin and his courage in the face of the Syrian-Greeks. Why do you suppose the story came to me today?"

"I think I understand," answered Moses. He lay down his boots and moved to Benny's side. "In the story the priest was hoping to avoid war, but when he realized he would have to give up his beliefs, he chose death, a survival of sorts. Does that make sense?"

"A survival?"

"Yes, a survival of his beliefs, at all costs. That was courageous, and he won in the end." Moses smiled. "I felt a sense of courage in our fellow workers today. Perhaps that's what you felt."

"Yes, I did, but I have a question. If the priest believed he could not exist as a slave and a free man, what does that tell us? At this moment we are slaves."

"I don't know," responded Moses. "I'm trying hard to remember the lessons of my father and my teachers. It's difficult."

Moses' eyes turned bright, and he looked away from the younger boy. When he had composed himself, he said, "I was taught that life is important, we're to find joy in the world, and we should serve God and our fellow human beings. I have to be honest with you. I'm wrestling with those teachings."

"I believe we should not give in."

Moses looked at his younger brother. "I am not sure how we avoid that." Now, tears ran down his cheeks. With a raspy voice he said, "I love you, Jacob. I want you to know that at this moment. Tomorrow may be too late."

"What are you talking about? We're going to get out of this, one way or another," asserted Jacob, but when he saw the look on Moses' face, his brow furrowed.

Moses turned away from Jacob. He sat quietly, his shoulders slumped and his head bowed.

Touched by the brothers' relationship, Benny thought of his sister. He missed her greatly.

"I think we should celebrate Hanukkah," said Isaac.

All three young men turned toward the rabbi. When they saw what he was doing, they smiled.

Isaac placed a candle on the floor and began lighting it with a piece of kindling from the iron stove that heated the barracks.

"Rabbi, where did you get the candle?" questioned Jacob, his face glowing with pleasure.

"Never you mind," said Isaac, winking, "we are going to celebrate the first night of Hanukkah." Obviously the purchase was clandestine from one of the trips to the village.

The prisoners grouped around the light, eyes intent on its small flame. Perhaps some remembered a real Menorah and special family gatherings.

Isaac, the fake rabbi, stood in the center of the group and began to sing the psalm Moses had earlier prayed.

A loud noise startled the worshipers. They looked quickly toward the door. Several *Hitlerjugend* and SS stood in the opening.

"*Aufstehen schmutzige Juden schnel -- los, los, los*! (Stand up you dirty Jews. Hurry, hurry, hurry! On to it)!"

Those sitting on the floor by the candles jumped up.

"It is my fault," Isaac quickly interjected. "I bought the candles and lighted them."

One of the Nazi youth shoved Isaac, knocking him to the floor. Another rushed up and began kicking the older man. Lying in fetal position, Isaac held his arms over his head for protection.

The others, faces frozen white with horror at the assault of a rabbi, stood trembling.

"Please don't hurt him," cried Moses. "It was my fault. I am the one who started it. We were just discussing a Jewish holiday."

Benny moved to speak. Isaac put his hand up, waving him to keep quiet.

"Stupid, Jude," yelled a *Hitlerjugend* as he grabbed Moses by the collar and pushed him toward the door. The red-faced adolescent bellowed, "All of you, get out of the barracks and assemble outside. Now!"

Suddenly an older man slumped to the floor, his heart weakened by the fright. An SS soldier came forward and ordered the dead man to rise. Receiving no response, the maddened German fumbled with his holster, jerking out his revolver and firing it into the lifeless body. With each shot, the other prisoners flinched, expecting the next bullet to be for them.

The prisoners lined up outside, the night air still damp with light drizzle. The Germans ordered the two brothers, Moses and Jacob, to step forward.

Strolling with his hands locked behind his back and his shoulders erect and rigid, an SS supervisor approached the brothers. "I understand you have been disloyal to the Fatherland by practicing some heathen ceremony."

Benny did not understand the choice of these two for group reprimands. Abruptly he said, "Sir."

"Shut up, boy, I am not speaking to you," answered the officer still staring at Moses and Jacob. "I understand you tried to sabotage the river project today."

Some of the prisoners flinched. Benny could not believe his ears.

The officer's voice droned on. "You are a distraction to the work force. You will immediately give alliance to the Fatherland and deny your obsession with this cult you call a religion."

Both Moses and Jacob stood silently.

"Obviously you do not understand the order," sneered the Nazi, enunciating his words. "Shall I repeat it?"

Bravely Jacob responded, "I cannot speak for my brother. As for myself, I will not deny my heritage. I serve my Lord, not your Fatherland."

Startled by the young man's audacity, the prisoners nervously shifted their stance. Taken by surprise, the Nazi hesitated, then drew his pistol and whipped it across the face of the younger brother. A stream of red ran down his temple and onto his jawbone.

Furious now, the Nazi demanded volunteers from the group. No response was forthcoming. Immediately the officer pointed out four prisoners, ordering them to pick up nearby shovels and lanterns. Benny was one of the four. Then he commanded the two brothers to join the "volunteers."

The other prisoners walked slowly back to the barracks, as an SS guard and a half dozen German youth herded the "chosen" toward the gate. Isaac, among them, looked anxiously back over his shoulder. A wave of sadness threatened to overcome him. As he reached the barrack door, he saw the group march through the gate and into the night.

It was close to midnight when the prisoners reached a field not far from the river project. Strategically placed lanterns glowed through the mist, forming a circle around an area designated by the guards. There was no mistaking the order. A large hole was to be dug.

It was not easy digging the saturated ground. Heavy mud clung to the shovel. The young prisoners, including Moses and Jacob, worked as fast as they could, always prodded unmercifully by the temperamental *Hitlerjugend* shouting and pointing guns at the workers.

Benny thought of Jacob's bravery, and he wondered what ideas crowded his friend's mind.

Upon a satisfactory completion of the job, the SS supervisor ordered the prisoners out. Standing at attention, prisoners waited for his next order.

The supervisor stepped forward. "You." He pointed to Moses and Jacob. "Get back down into the hole."

The brothers hesitated.

Without warning, Jacob vaulted away from the group, racing toward the open field and yelling, "Shoot, you mad dogs! Shoot!"

Benny drew in his breath.

The lantern lights revealed the horror written on Moses' face, aged beyond its years.

The rifle's sharp crack sounded into the night, immediately followed by Jacob's scream. Then silence.

The supervisor pointed to Benny and another prisoner. "Go and retrieve the body."

Benny's heart pounded as he stumbled toward Jacob. When he and the other prisoner reached the boy's side, Benny knelt and raised his friend gently. Jacob gasped for breath, weak moans coming from his mouth.

The two lifted the boy and took him back to the hole. As they lay him on the ground, Jacob tried to speak. Benny kneeled and put his ear to the boy's mouth. He looked up at Moses, struggling to get to his brother but held by one of the Germans.

"Please!" cried Moses as he sank to his knees. "Please let my brother live."

Benny knew it was no use. Jacob was dying even as Moses pleaded for his life. Tears welled in Benny's eyes, but he dared not cry.

"Eventually," said the SS in charge, "you will have to die. It might as well be now, pig." The German pointed to Moses. "Pick up your brother and throw him into the hole."

Moses slowly rose from his kneeling position and walked listlessly to Jacob who lay without movement. He lifted his brother and gently allowed him to slide into the opening. Jacob's limp arms and legs tangled over each other like a rag doll as he fell into the man-made pit.

"Now you," demanded the German, looking at Moses and pointing to the hole.

Moses looked at the guard, his eyes filled with sorrow. Softly he pleaded, "No. Please. No. We have a right to live. We're humans!"

"You're dogs!" responded a *Hitlerjugend*.

He lunged at Moses, shoving him into the pit. The young Jew hit bottom with a thud. When he could regain his breath, he cried out, his pleas cutting through the night.

The SS supervisor stood, stoically, the prisoners, hushed. He then turned to Benny, "You, start filling in the dirt."

Benny looked at the German, his eyes wide with dread. He saw the rifle pointed at his head. Without orders, the other prisoners picked up their shovels and moved quickly to Benny's side. They would not let Benny do this alone.

It took almost an hour to bury Moses and Jacob. Each shovel of dirt muffled Moses' plea for life. Twelve-year-old Benny opposed, stubbornly, the rising surge in his stomach. He shoveled frantically, trying to cover the terrible sound of his friend buried alive. Tears dared to blur his vision. The nausea rose to his throat, burning and threatening eruption. No words could describe the horror the boy felt, as he became an assassin.

Benny believed that, until the day he died, he would vividly remember the agonizing cries and the bestial act that made him an unwilling partner in the death of another.

Benny lay on his bunk, still wearing the mud-splattered clothes. He was pale and quiet, refusing to speak even to Isaac. He wanted to cry. Exhaustion prevented it. Torn between his beliefs and his hate, he could not sleep.

How could God make such unmerciful people?

Benny was still awake when the storm hit. Around three o'clock in the morning, rain slammed onto the tin roof. Thunder rolled in the distance and lighting strikes flashed against the windowpanes. Gusts of wind shook the poorly built barracks.

Benny knew what he had to do. He quietly climbed from his bunk, careful not to awaken Isaac who slept on the lower one. He had made a decision. A stormy night with a strong wind to cover sound was a good time to try an escape. He grabbed his threadbare coat and made his way cautiously to the door, slowly opening it only enough to squeeze his body through.

Once outside he realized it was colder than he thought, and he re-entered the barracks and picked up the first coat he could find. Two would be better than one. The noise of the storm blocked any sounds he made.

Walking hurriedly from the building, he made his way around the toilets to the back of the compound. Benny knew that the barbed wire fencing, though not electrified, would be a task. He bent down and pulled at the bottom of a section. He struggled with the sharp wire, feeling the pointed bards bite into his hands. Pain was of no consequence; the thought of getting away was stronger. Finally after he pulled at the wire and dug into the mud below it, he was able to squeeze into an opening. As he pulled his way under, a barb caught the back of his coat. His body, thick with the two layers of coats, could not move.

In the distance he heard a guard shout to another. He lay quietly, patiently waiting. He saw no movement nor heard further sounds. He placed his hand at his back and tugged at the barb until it loosened. Quickly he slid under the wire. Now outside the compound, he crawled close to ground.

Though the night was black and the rain heavy, he knew he had passed through the open field when he felt the ground cluttered with vines and shrubs. He was in the wooded area. He stood and ran blindly. Twice he fell. Once, he ran headlong into a large tree. He leaned against it, breathless. At length, he quit running.

Benny stood, listening. He heard nothing. Holding out his muddied, bloody hands toward the sky, he let the rain that fell between the branches of a tree wash them. Benny had no idea where he was or where he was going.

SEVEN

BENNY COULD RUN NO FURTHER. His chest heaved, and he wheezed short breaths into the cold night. In the darkness, he saw an outline of what appeared to be a large clump of foliage on his left. Dropping to his knees, he pushed and pulled at the thickness of the underbrush until he could push his body underneath. It was a narrow place but surprisingly dry and a place to be still. He was cold. Hunger gnawed at his stomach. Benny would rest here, just for a time.

From inside the belly of the shrub he could see nothing. The boy shuddered at the horrors that could lurk in the woods. If he were to rest, he would have to fight his sense of panic. Questions raced through his mind. Had the camp officials discovered his escape and looked for him? Would the others be punished? What if he had accidentally lost his sense of direction and circled back to the detestable camp? The boy fought an intense war with his imagination before he curled into a ball and fell into an uneasy sleep.

"Please don't do this to me," cried the voice.

"He's alive, alive, alive," echoed voices from the dark.

"I'll save you, Moses. Hold on. I'll save you!"

"I can't breathe. My God, I can't breathe."

Is that my own voice? thought Benny. *Am I sane or not?*

His pounding heart made him think his ears would explode, and he struggled to open his eyes. The lids would not budge.

"*It's a dream. It's a dream,*" he told himself. "*Wake up.*"

Benny's body jerked. He struggled to move, but the bush hemmed him in. Startled, he opened his eyes. It was no longer dark. Through the trees, the thin, gray lines of dawn brushed the sky. The rain had stopped.

He lay quietly, alert to possible sounds. Hearing nothing, he crawled cautiously from his hiding place, pulling his stiff body erect and stretching his arms and legs. He must decide which direction to pursue. More than likely, he had moved almost directly north since escaping from camp. If that were true, the river project and the village of Józefów would be south and behind him. With luck, if he continued on this course, he should reach the town of Opole soon.

Benny picked his way through the underbrush and trees, intent on watching and listening for signs of movement. He had walked a short distance when he stumbled onto a road. The squeaking sounds of a wagon bed, as its springs moved to the rhythm of its wheels, sounded a short distance away. The boy quickly jumped back into the woods. He waited quietly as a farmer rumbled past him in a horse-drawn carriage, transporting his cargo of milk and butter for market.

Using the woods for cover, Benny followed the wagon. Soon house rooftops appeared on the morning horizon. A cock's shrill cry sounded in the distance, and dogs barked at the early morning noise.

When he reached the village of Opole, the houses sat shuttered against the night. Benny sighed with relief that few people stirred. The mud-crusted boy would cause questions. If he could find a Jewish home marked by a Mezuzah, he could find refuge. He looked up and down the streets for a door that would have the familiar box attached next to the entrance. Benny had fond memories of placing his family Mezuzah next to their door. It was a Jewish tradition to have the container holding a parchment listing the beginning verses of the Shema, a basic Jewish prayer.

As he turned into a street that branched from the market plaza, his heart skipped a beat. Two German military policemen approached from the cross street two blocks away. They wore combat helmets, and each carried a rifle with drawn bayonet, the blades pointing ominously toward the heavens. The two casually strolled and chatted.

Benny could not rely on their continued preoccupation. He turned and walked back around the corner from which he had come. The boy had almost reached the end of the street when he saw it, the two-story stone house with the Mezuzah at its doorway.

As he crossed the street, he looked both directions for a patrol or a curious neighbor. There was none. He knocked on the door. No answer. He knocked again. When no answer was forthcoming, Benny's hopes began to fail him. He knew it was imperative to get off the streets before the morning activity began. His renewed knocking gained no response. Dejected, he had turned to leave when a sound came from inside the door.

"Who is there?" asked a hoarse voice.

"My name is Benny," the boy answered softly, for fear of disturbing the neighbors whose houses butted next to this one. "I am a Jew, and I need help. Please, help me!"

Silence.

Benny saw the German patrol only a block away. They walked slowly toward him.

"Please," he whispered loudly. "In the name of God open the door before the Germans catch me."

The door opened a small crack, from which a stooped old man peered. "Quickly, come in young man," he said, gesturing nervously with his hands.

As soon as Benny entered, the man bolted the door. Benny thought it was ironic that someone would think a double lock and crossbar could stop the devils he knew.

He said to the man, "My name is Bernard Lipman -- Benny."

The old man looked closely at the boy. "I am Kuba Borenstein. You must call me Kuba. You said your name is Benny?"

"Yes sir," answered Benny. "Benny Lipman, from Warsaw. I've escaped from the labor camp."

Kuba's eyes widened, smile lines creasing the corners. He put his hand on the boy's shoulder and guided him gently toward the kitchen where the family stood around a table waiting to begin morning prayers. Patting Benny on the back, Kuba introduced him as "this courageous young man." Kuba's daughter, Rika, and her six children smiled broadly. Her husband, Stephen, neither smiled nor spoke.

"You must get out of those muddy clothes," said Rika. "We will wait breakfast for you." She turned to one of the children. "Josef, please prepare a washbowl of warm water for our guest." The boy, several years younger than Benny, obeyed quickly.

"I will take him to my room," said Kuba.

Benny followed the old man to the back of the house. The room they entered was small and sparsely furnished. Josef followed, placing the basin of hot water and a washcloth on the nightstand. He smiled at Benny as he left the room.

Kuba walked to a large oak armoire that stood in the corner of the room and opened it. Reaching in, he removed several items of clothing -- a suit, a shirt, a brown felt hat, socks, and a pair of high-cut, lace up boots. With his arms full, he turned to Benny.

"I have no need for these. I do not believe I will survive these monsters," said Kuba. "Since you are young, perhaps you can. I pray you can." Kuba laid the clothes on the bed and walked out of the room.

In the privacy of the man's quarters, Benny cleansed himself. When he finished his toilet, he put on the trousers, one of the shirts, and the fresh socks and boots. Surprisingly the clothes fit well. As he returned to the kitchen, he felt a sense of order, the first time in many weeks.

"That is better," remarked Kuba, smiling as the boy entered the room. "Now, come stand here by me, and we shall say a blessing."

Following the *hamotzi*, the meal began. Scrambled eggs, dark bread spread with chicken fat, and tea delighted the insatiable hunger of the young boy. Benny could not remember the last time he had eaten eggs.

When they had finished the meal, Kuba said, "You need rest for your journey." Benny had told them he wished to return to Warsaw and his parents as soon as possible. "May I suggest you rest awhile in my room," said Kuba. "We have business to be about. You will be safe."

Sleep came effortlessly. For once the nightmares did not intrude. It was mid-afternoon when Benny awoke feeling refreshed.

Kuba, seated by the stove, was reading a book when the boy entered the sitting room. He looked up, smiling. "Ah, my boy. I hope you are rested."

"Thank you, sir," replied Benny. "I will remember your kindness."

Kuba patted the stool beside him. The boy sat down. Kuba reminded him of his grandfather Lipman. Physically the two men were very different, except for the long white beard. Grandfather Lipman was very tall and thin and had reached the age of 105. Kuba was a small frame man and short, like Benny. The boy found similarities in the way they gestured with their hands and in the soft, reassuring tone of their voices. This man made him feel comfortable as his Grandfather Lipman did.

"Sir, may I ask you a question?"

"Certainly," answered the old man, closing his book and placing it on the table beside him.

"I couldn't help but notice that Stephen is nervous about something. Is it my being here? I would not want to put you in danger."

"You have to understand," said Kuba, hearing the concern in Benny's voice, "he is frightened, especially for the children. The German butchers shot his father in the market place only last week because he was unable to keep up the work pace."

"But the village seems so peaceful, even with the patrol I saw. When we marched through here some weeks ago, everything seemed so normal."

"Perhaps it appears that way to you. You have not been here long enough to see what is happening. The Germans came in '39, set up a Judenrat, formed a Jewish police force, and organized forced labor."

"What kind of labor?" questioned Benny.

102 Song of a Sparrow

"We work on the road repairs, on local farms, and in the sugar factory. Stephen works at the factory. Rika and the children work on a dairy farm, and even though the milk and butter mostly go to feed the Germans, the Polish family that owns the farm shares potatoes and other food stuff with us. I have been spared, so I do the chores here at home."

"You're lucky you have no ghetto like we do in Warsaw."

"You are wrong," answered Kuba. "The Germans have been working since summer to create one in the older section of town. They have already brought in around twenty-five hundred Jews from Putawy."

"Oh, I'm sorry."

Kuba sighed and looked at Benny. He said, "Enough of my stories. What about you, my boy? I have a feeling you have seen much for your young years. It must weigh heavy on you. Would you like to talk about it? Even at the age of seventy-five, I am not sure I have answers, but I listen well."

Benny did not know where to begin -- it was such a gruesome story. Finally he told of horrors of the bombing, of his family's plight, his fight to stave off starvation, and the evil he witnessed.

As Benny talked, tears soon streamed down Kuba's wrinkled cheeks. Occasionally the old man interjected, "May God bless you."

Benny told him of the labor camp and of Moses and Jacob. His voice cracked as he struggled with his story. Finally spent, the boy sat silently, his eyes welling with tears. The only sound in the room came from the crackling wood in the iron stove and the clacking of the mahogany clock on a table near by; the pendulum swinging back and forth echoed the silence in the room.

Kuba lighted his pipe. The sulfur of the match strike caused Benny's eyes to smart and his nostrils to flare. The poignant smell of the tobacco brought back early memories of his father. The boy struggled against the threatening tears.

Kuba's head rested on the back of his chair. His voice was soft, reflective. "You are so young to have experienced such atrocities. I believe God measures our actions. A child murdered, though his life may have been short, means more than the long life of the murderer."

Benny thought of baby Josef, his friend's six-month-old brother. "It is difficult to understand," said the boy. "I was taught that God is the creator of the universe and that all human beings are made in his image. I have seen people -- Germans, Poles, and Jews -- who don't fit that image."

"I understand your confusion. It is difficult to understand the actions of those who portray evil."

"Yes."

"I am old," said Kuba. "I am supposed to gain wisdom with my years. I, too, must ponder this confusion."

The man rose, reached for the poker, and opening the lid to the old stove, stoked the fire. The wood snapped and the sparks flicked in several directions. The iron lid clanked as Kuba replaced it and returned to his seat. He sighed. "I may be wrong, but somehow I believe our faith will prevail because we are bound to God's covenant."

He looked closely at the boy who leaned toward him, waiting. "It is our strength the Nazis do not understand -- no one has. Our faith is our strength, our measure, even if we die in the hands of our captors." He looked earnestly into Benny's eyes. "If we hang onto that certitude, we overcome."

Benny looked puzzled. "Our captors are people, and if people are made in the image of God . . ."

"I believe," responded the old man, "that those who have done the evil deeds against us will have less measure in the eyes of God, and ultimately that is all that really matters." Kuba paused. "Do you understand?"

"I think so." The boy looked closely at the old man. "Sir, if some of us survive, do you think our memories will teach the world about dignity of the human being and brotherhood of humankind or the lack of it?"

"Very profound," smiled Kuba. "You are a *mentsch*." He placed his hands together and applauded quietly. "However, there will be some Jews," prophesied the old man, "who will lose their faith while others prevail in theirs."

Benny felt comfort in Kuba's words. The boy wondered if he would meet others, like this man, who could guide him in the impossible and perilous journey he faced.

—➤ ✦ ◀—

Early the next morning Benny said his farewells to the family. Sharing the traditional Friday meal had brought him memories of his own home and childhood. He would treasure his visit with this family, but he longed to see his own.

Rika packed Benny a burlap bag with food and the extra clothes Kuba had given him. The boy said his good-byes at the door where Kuba leaned forward and kissed him on the forehead, quietly slipping fifty Zloty (ten dollars) into the hand that held the old man's brown hat.

Kuba, eyes rimmed with tears, said, "You have already lived beyond your years. A boy like you will never get lost in the fire. You remember that."

Benny laid down the bag and put both arms around Kuba. He tried hard not to cry. "I don't have words to thank you, all of you. I'll always remember your kindness." Benny looked at Stephen. "I'm sorry about your father, sir."

Stephen nodded and put his hand on the boy's shoulder.

"Go with God," said Kuba. "He is with you always."

Benny put the money in his pocket, set the old brown hat on his head, and picked up the bag. Turning to the family, he smiled and tipped the hat. Already a sense of loneliness and sadness crept over him, as he entered the streets of Opole.

Benny, skirting the busy streets, walked though the village. Surprisingly he saw few Germans or Jewish police. He soon came to a road that led out of the city. The boy paused and looked back at what seemed to be a peaceful village. He shuddered at what might become of it.

In February 1941, only two months after Benny's departure from Kuba's house, two thousand Viennese Jews entered the Opole ghetto, followed in a month with eight thousand more Jews crowded into the confines of the village. The severe overcrowding and dire conditions resulted in an outbreak of typhus and typhoid, killing fifteen hundred people.

By late May 1942, the Germans deported most of the Jews in Opole to Sobibór extermination center. The Nazis murdered nearly five hundred others before they could leave.

A light snow had begun to fall, blanketing the countryside in white. For the first time in several weeks, Benny felt happy as he walked down the country road. Farmers, with teams of horses pulling carts loaded with eggs, milk, and other dairy products, passed him on the road. Life seemed normal.

By noon Benny's feet were tired. When he saw a small farming community, he decided to find a place to rest. At the first house the wooden door swung open to his knock. A stout, middle-aged woman stood staring at the boy.

"Good morning, my name is Benny Lapinsky," said the boy, using his fake name and his knowledge of the Polish language. "May I rest? I have walked from Opole."

"Lapinsky?" She smiled "Are you related to Anna and Jake?"

Startled, Benny stammered, "I, I don't think so. Are they from Kazimierz?"

"No," she said, "Wilków, just up the road."

"I'm from Kazimierz," lied Benny.

"Come in young man. I'll bet you're hungry. We are just about to have lunch."

Benny followed the woman into the kitchen where her husband sat at a small round table. He frowned as Benny walked into the room. The smell of fresh baked bread permeated the air. Confidently the boy moved quickly to the farmer and stuck out his hand. "Hello, sir. My name is Benny Lapinski."

"He is from Kazimierz," remarked the wife.

The man reluctantly shook hands with Benny. "The name is Urbanosky. Have a seat."

Benny laid down his burlap bag and sat down opposite the Polish farmer. When the woman put a plate of homemade bread and fresh cheese and butter in front of him, he smiled broadly. "It smells like my grandmother's fresh bread, Mrs. Urbanosky."

A smile spread quickly across her face.

"So you are from Kazimierz?" asked the farmer between bites.

"Yes. I'm traveling there. I've been visiting in Opole."

The man appeared reserved, almost suspicious of Benny.

"What do you think about the Germans?"

The farmer's question startled Benny. He paused for a length of time, pretending to chew his food. He answered, "What do you think, sir?"

The man answered directly, "I do not know what the outcome will be, but it is not such a bad idea the way the Germans are handling the big Jewish businessmen."

"Um," Benny muttered, concentrating on his food.

"I think it is high time the Jews get what they deserve. Don't you?"

"Yes sir," answered Benny, shifting uncomfortably in his chair.

The farmer talked at length about the economy, the German take-over, the Jews, and the weather. Benny thought he would never take a breath. At last he paused. With this opportunity, Benny stood up. "Thank you for the food. I really have to get home. I have work to do."

"Well, I could take you the distance, I suppose," offered Mr. Urbanosky.

Surprised and not wanting the man to suspect that anything was unusual, Benny answered, "I could pay you a little." Benny was thankful for the money Kuba gave him. He thought he might have more than enough for a boat ticket to Warsaw out of Kazimierz.

"How about ten Zloty?" asked the farmer.

"Sure," said Benny. "I would appreciate the ride." That would leave him enough money for the boat ticket and maybe a little more.

Benny turned to the farmer's wife and thanked her for her generosity.

"You are welcome, young man. May Jesus Christ and Mary be with you always."

Benny smiled at the Catholic blessing invoked on him. "Thank you ma'am. I'll light a candle for you and Mr. Urbanosky at mass on Sunday."

"Oh, what a wonderful Polish boy and a good Catholic, too," gushed the woman.

Benny smiled and thanked her graciously. He wondered what she'd say if she knew that he was a Jew?

A square box with high sides and a board that provided a makeshift seat was not the most comfortable mode of transportation. The horse-drawn cartwheels seemed to fall into every mud hole in the road. The boy concentrated on the winter scenery. Trees, mostly conifer, lined the country road. Small hills rose behind them. Enough morning snow had fallen to layer the tree branches in a virginal coating of white and to partially cover the rolling terrain.

He remembered, as a boy of eight or nine years of age, traveling near here with his Jewish youth group. They camped in the hills between here and Kazimierz, some fifty or sixty boys and girls. Benny smiled as he remembered the ceremony at the end of the four-week outing. He had received three stars for his merit badge as a good watchman, performing his duties well. What fun it was to play the watchman game! Competitors from other Jewish youth organizations tried to sneak into their camp and steal the flag. The group whose flag was best protected won honors. Benny had saved his group's flag from capture.

In reflection, those days were golden for Benny. He would never have guessed his life could change so drastically in such a short period of time. Now looking at the hills, he saw the same beauty in the landscape, but the splendor in his life had dimmed. He wondered if he could ever recapture it.

The sputtering of a motor jolted Benny from his thoughts. A German motorcycle patrol came toward them from around the bend in the road. Benny's stomach muscles tightened. As the cycle with the two SS patrols sped past, the farmer raised his hand in greeting. Benny mimicked his gesture. Several more patrols passed them over the length of the trip, but none stopped.

Flat farmland, interlaced with woods, stretched for miles. Farming consisted primarily of raising wheat, potatoes, beets, and onions. In the spring this farmland would look like a giant carpet of green with rolling waves of grain stalks. Stacks of hay would dot the landscape at harvest time. Now they looked bleak under the gray winter sky.

Benny held to the thought that every mile brought him closer to his family. He pictured his father with a rare smile, pleased that his son had survived his first labor camp and had returned home. Perhaps the boy's escape would encourage Aaron to find a way to leave Poland.

Suddenly a German jeep with four SS guards came into view. The jeep, parked close to a hay barn, was only several yards away. Distracted no longer by daydreaming, Benny focused on the occupants of the vehicle.

His mind raced. *Will they stop us? What can I do?*

As the wagon in which they rode approached the barn, one of the SS climbed out of the vehicle and strolled toward the road. He gestured, and the farmer brought the horse to a halt. As he watched the German come toward the cart, a lump in Benny's throat threatened to choke him.

"Where are you going?" asked the German.

"To Kazimierz," answered the Polish farmer.

The German held out his black-gloved palm. "Let me see your identification papers."

Benny's heart stopped.

The farmer pulled papers from his pocket and handed them to the officer. After closely examining them, the German handed them back and reached for Benny's.

"I . . . I don't have them with me," he stuttered in response to the outstretched hand.

"Did you forget your papers at home again?" asked the farmer.

Startled, Benny shook his head up and down.

"Is this boy related to you?" asked the German.

"He is my nephew."

The German looked closely at Benny then at the farmer. "You should tell your nephew to be more careful."

"Yes sir," answered the farmer.

Without wavering from his fabrication, Benny met the German's eyes. He thought the Nazi would stare at him forever.

Ultimately satisfied, the German gestured them to move on.

Nodding to the German, Benny and the farmer continued their journey. When they had gotten out of sight of the patrol, Benny stood up in the wagon and stretched his arms and legs. He looked at his host. "I have a lot to learn."

The farmer smiled and reassured him, "Do not fret. Nothing is going happen to a good Polack. Keep your faith and the sun will shine on you forever."

I guess I can be a good Polack when I need to, thought Benny.

They reached the outskirts of Kazimierz late in the afternoon. Benny paid the man and shook his hand. As the man rode away, Benny sighed, relieved he not been found out.

The boy, hoping to buy a ticket on the passenger boat that traveled between Kazimierz and Warsaw, made his way to the Wisla River harbor. Surveying the docks, he saw little activity. Benny decided a straightforward approach would cause less suspicion. He walked straight to the ticket window, determination outweighing doubts of succeeding. The woman at the ticket window watched him approach.

In Polish, Benny said, "I would like a one-way ticket to Warsaw."

She stared. "I need to see your identification papers."

Benny searched through his coat pockets. He looked into the burlap bag he carried. Continuing his pretense search, he said finally, "I must have forgotten them at home."

"Where is home?" she asked, raising an eyebrow.

"Opole."

"Opole, hum?" She leaned toward the window and whispered, "Do not worry young man, I will sell a ticket to a Jew." In a normal voice she said, "That will be fifteen Zloty." She pulled a ticket and handed it to him.

Benny tried not to show his surprise. He slid the money to her without saying a word. Their eyes met for just a moment. She looked past him. "Next," she said.

Clutching the precious ticket in his hand, Benny picked up his burlap bag and moved nonchalantly toward the pier and the boat. When he boarded, there were ten or fifteen people already on deck. He did not know how many were below. Benny took a seat next to the cabin, one adjacent to the ramp, just in case he had to make a quick exit. Besides, the cabin wall would help block the cold wind. He had made up his mind that he would not sit below where he would feel closed in.

The boy surveyed the station area for any signs of a German patrol. As he watched, the woman from the ticket booth came out of the building with a German SS, talking and pointing at the boat. Benny caught his breath. An exit out of view was not available, unless he wanted to go overboard. The SS moved quickly toward the boat. As he climbed the ramp, he looked in Benny's direction.

Oh, my God! thought Benny. *He's going to come over here.*

It was too late.

"The ticket lady told me something about you," said the German in Polish.

Benny tried to keep an expressionless face. He did not answer.

"She said you like strudel. Is that so?"

"Strudel?" Benny's eyes widened. *Strudel?* he thought. He answered, "Uh, yes. Sure."

"Well, she has given me this sack to give you. She says it will be a long trip and that you might enjoy the snack and some company." The German handed the brown bag to Benny. He smiled, "Maybe, for my effort in bringing it to you, I can have a taste. It's been a long time since I had strudel." The soldier winked.

Benny took the sack. He hoped his hand did not shake.

"The lady says you are traveling to Warsaw. Is that right?" Before the boy could answer, the German said, "So am I." He sat down beside Benny.

Startled by this turn in events, Benny concluded he would make the best of it. He handed the officer one of the strudels. "I will be happy to share with you," he said in German.

"You speak German?" The spontaneous smile revealed dimples.

Obviously homesick, the young officer talked continuously. He spoke fondly of Germany and his family, especially of a brother near Benny's age.

The shadows of night had already begun to fall across the water when the boat whistle blasted three times, and the boat began to churn the water and pull away from the pier. Slowly the harbor grew smaller, vanishing finally from sight.

Soon the swaying boat caused the conversation to dwindle as the German became drowsy and napped at last.

Relieved by the respite, Benny savored the familiarity of the countryside, even through the dusk. As they motored along the great Wisla River, they moved past small villages where lights twinkled from the shore. Benny watched the shore lights and imagined families gathered behind them. The idea of home spurred Benny, and he longed for the trip to end even though he faced danger at the end of his destination. He could not sleep.

After a while, the boat docked for passengers at Denblin. Benny remembered the business trips with his father in the pre-war days. A large population of Jews owned businesses and shops in the area.

As the boat moved through the night, Benny began to question his decision to return to the ghetto. How would he get back into the city without being spotted and arrested? Polish policemen guarded the docks, perhaps Germans, too.

The need to see his family overcame his worry. At length, he drifted into a restless sleep.

When they docked at Góra Kalwaria to let passengers off and on, Benny woke up. Childhood memories of visits to the historical area and the home of Rabbi Kozienico, a great Polish religious leader, pleased the boy. Benny loved the story of the rabbi's forefather who predicted Napoleon and his army, camped there, would suffer defeat and end up in exile. For a moment he considered departing and seeking advice of the rabbi.

How foolish, he thought. *What chance do I have of finding him? I need to return to my family.*

Well into the morning hours, the boat passed an old fortress where Benny, as a young boy, camped and explored. Benny remembered rumors that told of a German massacre of the populace in 1939, retaliation for resistance to the Third Reich. Suddenly gloom once more filled the youth's heart.

When the shore lights became more clustered, Benny knew they were moving closer to Warsaw. Snow had given way to a drizzly and damp gray dawn when they neared the suburb of Praga Warsaw. As they pulled into the dock, two Polish policemen at the end of the gangplank were checking identification papers. Was he to come this far and be caught?

The boy turned quickly to the SS officer with whom he had been traveling. He touched him on his arm. "Sir," he said. "We have arrived in Warsaw."

The German stretched his long arms and stood, stomping his legs to start the circulation.

"I'll walk down with you, sir," Benny said. "I enjoyed our earlier conversation."

The German smiled and accompanied the boy down the ramp. He passed in front of Benny as he walked past the policemen and onto the dock. Benny followed closely.

"Halt," said one of Polish policemen. "I need to see your papers."

Benny paused. The German looked back over his shoulder. "It is all right," he said to the policeman who stopped Benny. "He is with me."

The boy followed the German from the docking area. When they reached the street, Benny confidently slung the burlap bag over his shoulder, said his farewell, and headed for the Polish section. He wished he could thank the ticket lady for her brilliant plan to get him safely to Warsaw.

Early morning traffic influenced Benny's decision to skirt the busiest spots. By foot, the trip to the ghetto would take a good hour, and Benny must avoid drawing attention.

He wove his way through the Polish sector. Some things had not changed; others had altered drastically. He paused for a moment at the bombed remains of Zamek Krulevski Palace. As a child he visited the once beautiful national shrine, home of Polish rulers for many years.

Saddened by its destruction, he turned his thoughts again to entry into the ghetto. He ruled out re-entry this time of day by the cemetery or through the old palace on Nalewki Street. When he came to the Polish section of Leszno Street, he looked for the area he tunneled out several weeks before his roundup for labor camp. He used it in one incident to avoid capture by the Jewish Police and the SS. After the Germans blocked access and exit to the palace, he had looked for new methods of escape.

When Benny found the hole, it was littered with debris. He knew it was a risk to enter it during the daylight, but he had no choice.

He stood for a while observing the few passing by. When he felt it was not too obvious, he sat down by the hole, and as inconspicuous as possible, inched his way behind the boards. He pushed his body through the narrow opening and came out on the ghetto side. No one was in sight. A smile spread across Benny's face as he stood up and ran toward home.

No sound came from within the house. Benny moved directly to the kitchen and unloaded the food from the burlap bag. Calling to his mother and sister, he moved back through the first floor rooms. Trash and the remains of broken glass and shattered pieces of furniture cluttered the area. Benny ran up the stairs toward his father's room.

He reached it just as he saw Sala coming out of the toilet. She stood looking at him, her face pale, eyes wide with surprise. She tried to speak.

"It's me, Sala," said Benny. "I'm home."

The girl ran to her brother, embracing him tightly. Benny asked, "Where is father? And Mother?"

Her eyes focused on the floor, and she answered hesitantly, "Mother is out."

"And father?"

Sala stood staring at Benny, her lip quivering.

"Sala, where is he?" demanded Benny.

Sala did not answer. Fear griped Benny. He ran into the other rooms on the second floor. They were empty of furnishings. He ran back downstairs calling out for his father. As he reached the kitchen, Mirla came through the kitchen door from the basement.

"Benick," she cried. "My son, my son." Tears streaming down her cheeks, she ran to Benny and took him into her arms.

Benny pulled away from her. "Mother, where is Father?"

Mirla looked past Benny at Sala who had entered the room.

"Benny, sit down. I will tell you," she said.

"No! I want to know where Father is!" demanded the boy.

After a long pause, Mirla looked directly into her son's eyes. "Benick, we could not save him."

The boy's worst fear had come true. He slumped into the chair beside his mother.

"Dr. Solowejczyk came. You know what a dear friend he was." Mirla dabbed at her eyes. "He was one of the best doctors at Csysta Hospital, but he could not save him."

Benny could not breathe.

"He did everything humanly possible," continued Mirla. "Your father's entire body swelled from malnutrition and the constant dysentery as well as high fever." Struggling with her story, she reached out and placed her hand on her son's arm. "His heart gave out, Benick."

Benny sat for a while in silence. Sala and Mirla wept quietly. At length, Benny rose from the chair, put his arms around his mother and kissed her on the cheek. He moved to Sala and did the same.

"I'm going to my room now," he said, his voice almost inaudible. Benny felt like a mere dot in a world crumbling around him.

The young Jew climbed the stairs with great effort, his thoughts on the man he had worshipped. Now he was dead. Total frustration and hopelessness tormented the boy. His father was one of the kindest men who ever lived, and the Germans had murdered him as surely as if they had pulled a trigger.

Benny's room, even with some of the furniture missing, was a contrast compared to the clutter he saw in the other rooms. A mattress and bedding lay on the floor where his sturdy childhood bed once stood. The covers lay folded back waiting for his return. Next to the bedding, set his oak desk and chair given to him by his grandfather Lainveinber, his mother's father.

His beloved astronomy books and a picture of his father still sat on the desk, his telescope and tripod standing next to it. Benny walked over to the instrument, gently touched the scope and leaned over to look into it. He ran his fingers along the books he loved to read. Turning to his father's picture, he stood for a moment looking at it, his fingers caressing the surface. He picked it up and held it against his heart.

The trembling of his body startled him. Soon the shaking overpowered him, drowning his ability to control his own passion. He held the picture in his hands and shook it violently. His voice cracked with pent-up emotion as he wailed, "Why? Why? Why didn't you listen to me? I begged you over and over to leave." The unwelcome thoughts flooded out of him. "*Potepiac*! Damn it to hell! Why didn't you try, father? Where was your courage? You were my hero."

The boy gave in to the emotions that consumed him, and with great force slung his father's picture to the floor and stomped on it, again and again. With his arm, he swept the books from his desk to the floor. He reached for his beloved telescope, picked it up and threw it against the wall. As the loud cracking sound of falling objects came, so did more anger. All the months of hurt, the horrors, and the fears came out of him like a deluge. He whirled around and around, flinging himself into the walls, pushing his fist into the air. He was like a wild animal throwing off any attempt to be tamed.

"I kept my promise," he sobbed. "I came home. I survived. You weren't here, Father. Why? Why?" His voice cracked with emotion and the tears streamed down his face.

Gradually the feral explosion eased, and Benny, shaking his head, began to pace the length of the room, his fists clenched. As suddenly as it began, it stopped. Exhausted, the boy slumped to the floor. He lay there whispering, "I love you, Father. I love you, Father."

He reached toward the broken frame that held his father's picture and pulled the print from the broken glass. With the picture in hand, he crawled to the mattress where he curled into a fetal position. Holding the picture next to his heart, Benny gave in to the quiet sobs. He had not cried in a year. Eventually the tears became silent drops on his face, and the tired and disillusioned young boy fell asleep.

EIGHT

BENNY CAME DOWN THE STAIRS reluctantly, deliberately delaying seeing his mother and sister. How could he face them? How could he face another day?

He had slept fitfully, horrible nightmares assaulting him. Would he ever again have a peaceful night's sleep? Would the hurt live with him forever? Last night's tears had drained all his strength. He had held them within for so long.

As he reached the bottom of the stairs, he heard his mother's voice in the kitchen. What would he say to her? Unsteady, he gripped the banister and looked around the room they used to call the living room. Now it was only a shell, just like him. In the corner sat the once beautiful piano, a shambles. How many times had he stood at that piano and sang as his father played their favorite tunes? That seemed so long ago.

The anguish swept through his body, and he felt he could not breathe. How could he go on with his life? He would never again see his beloved father.

I just want my life back, Benny reasoned silently. *I just want to be a regular boy again. I want to go camping with my father and to play soccer with my friends. How can life ever, ever be the same? How can the horrible memories be eradicated, the hurts put away forever?*

Benny raised his arm, and with the sleeve of his shirt he brushed the tears from his eyes. *I will be brave*, he thought, standing straight and squaring his shoulders. *I must be brave. I have to for Mother and Sala. I am the only one they have left.*

The boy moved to the kitchen doorway. In the kitchen his sister sat with her head bowed, tears dropping onto her lap. Mirla stood at the stove as she stirred groats. They did not realize he stood watching them.

"Benick's reaction to his father's death was so unsettling," said Mirla without turning to Sala. "Did you see the hurt in his eyes when I tried to explain that Aaron had the best possible care?"

Sala did not answer. She smoothed her dress where the tears fell. The hand that wiped the teardrops was red and callused, and Sala's once lustrous hair hung limply around her face, the youthful, fair beauty faded.

"Oh, Sala, there was so much hurt in his eyes, and a dreadful silence crept over him."

Sala did not respond. "He just stood there looking steadfastly at me as though he had just heard a news report." Mirla's voice choked, the tears welling in her throat. She stood silently now, reaching for her apron corner. She brought it to her eyes and smoothed the teardrops.

"Mother," said Benny quietly.

Mirla turned quickly toward the door, and Sala raised her head.

"Oh, Benick, Benick," cried Mirla as she rushed to embrace her son.

"It's all right, Mother. Please sit down." Benny took his mother's arm and guided her to the nearest kitchen chair.

"My God! What have I done to my children? Why did I not fight to escape?"

Benny put his arms around Mirla, but she would not be calmed.

"Oh, Lord, forgive me," prayed Mirla out loud. "Forgive both Aaron and me." She began to sob.

When she and her husband had chosen to stay in Warsaw rather than escape, they had made an irreversible mistake. The sorrow had left them helpless. The grown-ups had become children, and the children adults, especially young Benny who shouldered most of the responsibility for the family's food supply.

Finally Mirla's tears abated.

"It was you, Mother, wasn't it who covered me as I slept?"

She nodded her head.

Mirla did not have to answer. Benny knew his mother well. To him she was an angel. When she heard his rage two floors above, the storm that engulfed him would have drowned her too. He suspected she had reacted by wrapping her arms across her chest and holding her body, rocking back and forth, silent tears streaming down her cheeks. He had seen her do that since the Nazis came.

Then as the upstairs' noise abated, Mirla would have stopped rocking, stood, and walked out of the kitchen, both her body and mind numbed by the sadness that enveloped her home. Slowly she would have climbed the stairs to the attic room and paused outside his door, listening until his sobs became muffled. When no further sounds came from the room, she would have entered, knelt beside his bed and gently pulled the covers over him, tucking them around his shoulders as she kissed him on the forehead. Soon afterward his mother would have risen from her kneeling position and slipped quietly out of the room.

Benny would never forget the scenes from the bygone days of his childhood. Whether he skinned a knee or quarreled with a friend, he could still hear his mother's remarks, "Still so young and vulnerable, my little Benick"; now she would add, "yet so old."

Last night she had probably found him cuddling his pillow as he had as a small child. She used to tell him that he slept like a little kitten, curled into a ball. But last night his sleep would have been uneven -- his body jerking, his emotions formidable. He knew her heart ached for his lost childhood. He had heard her say that.

Benny knew, too, that Mirla would have been stubborn about selling Benny's bedding, his boyhood desk, and the telescope, stoically keeping the room intact for the day she knew her son would return home. She would have sold what was left of the other household linens and furniture to supplement the food rations and to pay the tax on the ration cards. It was surprising to Benny that the Nazis had taken only his bed frame and chest of drawers. After all, they had already robbed him of his father.

The tears threatened once more, but Benny reached deep within his soul to be courageous for Mirla and Sala. He would not cry.

I will not give the Nazi beasts the satisfaction.

The boy knew his mother lived with false hope, believing the nightmare would end, and one day she would renovate the once splendid apartment. The possibility of renovating the human spirit was a part of both her denial and her hope.

Over the next week Benny went solemnly about the business of preparing the repast services for his father. Finding the minyan, ten people for the traditional ceremony, was difficult. It was Benny's job to round up the men and provide food for them. Stoically he carried out his duties. His mother had not seen him cry since the day he heard of Aaron's death.

The minyan stayed only for the Kaddish and the food. Benny, barefooted and sitting on a small stool, prayed for seven days and completed the rest of Shivah by himself. Determined to follow the tradition of the eldest son in a Jewish family, Benny ate only bread and potato soup during that time. By this ritual, he was giving his father a formal and final good-bye.

Normally family members and guests took part in the ceremony. These were not normal times. No matzevah would be placed on Aaron's grave. An unknown grave has no stone.

Mirla swore to do her part to help her courageous son. She told Benny she recognized that this was the most important thing he could do for his father, and even with the threat of death, she would protect him from any German obstruction. Benny knew she meant it. He smiled at her bravery.

"Benick, my son, we must make plans to get out of this terrible mess. I have decided that worrying will get us nowhere."

Surprised, Benny looked up from his meager bowl of soup. His mother's drawn, colorless face showed signs of malnutrition. Her hair had grayed, and her short, once robust, frame had become delicate.

My mother is an angel, he thought. *She always was and always will be.*

After having hardship and privation for a constant companion, Mirla had somehow become inured to it. The loss of her beloved husband, rather than crushing her vitality, seemed to revive it.

Benny was sure his mother felt Aaron's spirit guiding her, just as he felt it leading him. "What do you suggest, Mother?"

"Remember when all of this started, you thought we could get Catholic papers for Sala and me?"

"Yes," replied the boy.

"Do you think that is still possible?"

Mirla's suggestion both uplifted and took Benny off guard. "I don't know," he answered. "I don't want to say it's too late, but I don't know."

He looked at Sala, who sat silently, her eyes pleading.

"It's worth a try," he responded. "I'll go to see Chairman Czerniakow."

The smile on Mirla's face stretched wide. A hint of a grin crossed his sister's face.

"It's peculiar you should bring this up this morning," said Benny. "I've been thinking about trying to get into the Russian sector, but I was worried about leaving you."

Mirla looked puzzled. "The Russian sector?"

"Yes. People tell me if one can make it across the border, there's more chance to earn greater sums of money and less harsh treatment by the Russians. If we can get you and Sala to Wodzislaw to stay with our family there, I can work, get money, and return for you."

Both women listened intently.

"Our chances are increased to get out of Poland if we have money to bribe for false passports."

"But, Benny, is it not dangerous for you?" Mirla questioned.

"It's dangerous to stay here. Why wait for the butchers?"

"I think it's worth a try." The voice was soft, almost a whisper.

The two looked at Sala. Mirla reached out and squeezed her daughter's hand.

"Then it's settled," said Benny. "I will go to see Czerniakow tomorrow."

—➤※◄—

The Judenrat Headquarters on Grzybowska Street swarmed with activity. Eyes of the milling mass reflected a broken populace -- bodies shriveled and hope too distant to discern. The cold was fierce and the hunger, worse. Mothers held children, sickly and weeping. People bundled in rags drifted aimlessly, moaning. While refugees continued pouring into the city, vendors, hawking their goods, lined the street. Hundreds of thousands crowded the "Jewish sector." The Nazi propaganda machine preferred this terminology to the word "ghetto."

The New Year arrived promising more shattered lives in 1941. Early in January the Judenrat gave notice there would be no St. Sylvester feast in the ghetto. The ban on the Polish activity, often attended by Jews, was a further attempt to withhold ceremonies from them. The synagogues, now boarded, offered no activities. It would soon become obvious that many of the Nazis' worst deeds occurred on Jewish holidays.

Wearing his oversized river project coat, Benny made his way through the crowd. The Jewish Police guarded the entrance and dispassionately shoved those who sought food or shelter. Benny pushed his way toward Czerniakow's door. Suddenly a sharp pain crossed his shoulders. A Jewish policeman stood, holding a nightstick above his head and daring the young boy to move further. Benny fell to the floor on his hands and knees moving swiftly between the legs of the crowd.

People shoved forward as the policeman tried to find the perpetrator. The crowd soon closed in on the Jewish Police guard, blocking them from Benny who had reached Czerniakow's outer office door. He reached up and turned the knob. The door gave way just enough for him to squeeze through to the other side. A guard standing just outside the chairman's office moved quickly toward him.

Jewish council chairman Adam Czerniakow, meets with a
German Air Force officer in his office in the Warsaw ghetto.
USHMM, courtesy of Hans-Joachim Gerke

The ruins of the former Warsaw ghetto Jewish Council building
after its destruction by the SS during the ghetto uprising.
USHMM, courtesy of National Archives

Benny shouted loudly, "Mr. Czerniakow, it's me Benny Lipman!"

The boy strained against the policeman as he tried to hold him. The president's door opened, and Adam Czerniakow stood a moment viewing the scene.

"Come in," he said sharply, motioning for the policeman to return to his post. "What is it?"

Czerniakow's less than friendly greeting puzzled Benny. Lines creased the man's face, and dark circles shadowed the skin under his eyes.

"I'm sorry. I know you're busy, but I'm desperate."

"You and thousands of others." The chairman moved toward his desk, cluttered with stacks of papers.

"I must turn to someone. My father is gone and . . ."

Czerniakow's face softened. He moved toward the boy, placing a hand on his shoulder. "I am sorry. Your father was a good friend."

"Sir," pleaded Benny, "I must get my mother and sister out of Warsaw."

Czerniakow's eyes widened. "You ask the impossible, Benny. It is too late now."

"Sir, nothing is impossible. I have escaped from a labor camp and back into the ghetto. I believe we can find a plan. I need your help. My father trusted you, and so do I."

Czerniakow shook his head and slumped into a chair. Finally he answered, "Let us not speak of this now." He picked up a pen and began writing on a piece of notepaper. "Come to my apartment in a couple of days. I will try to give you advice as to what to do, but I cannot promise anything." He handed the slip of paper to Benny. "Come at night and be careful."

Benny reached for the note. "Thank you, sir. Thank you."

He looked back at the man, already attacking the mound of paperwork. Czerniakow did not look up as the boy left the room.

The next two days Benny sorted the possibilities of meeting with Czerniakow. The fearful moments sometimes consumed the hopeful ones. Would he place his mother and sister in greater danger? Could the chairman do anything at this late date? Would they ever escape from their tormentors?

Two days after the visit to Czerniakow's office, Benny knocked at his apartment door.

"Come in, Benny. Please sit down." Czerniakow pointed to a sofa where the boy joined him.

The apartment was small and sparsely furnished. A desk stacked with papers, much like the one in the chairman's office, stood in the corner. A desk light revealed reports on which he was working.

"Can I get you some tea?" asked Czerniakow.

"No thank you, sir," responded the boy. "I'm afraid the foremost thing in my mind is escape for my mother and sister."

"I understand," responded Czerniakow. "Have you any idea where to go?"

"I've noticed less German activity in some of the small towns. I hope they will be safe with my mother's parents in Wodzislaw. And my father's parents don't live far from there."

Benny saw the look in Chairman Czerniakow's eyes. There was no mistaking its meaning. Czerniakow felt Benny was disillusioned about the safety of small towns. Probably even as they spoke, roundups had begun. But Czerniakow said instead, "And you? Will you not go with them?"

Looking squarely at Czerniakow and without hesitation, Benny answered, "My ultimate mission is to find a way for us out of Poland. I will need a great deal of money and luck to accomplish that. I can go to the Russian sector, earn the money, and return to get my family."

"Perhaps," said Czerniakow, his voice lacking confidence. But he smiled. "You are brave to seek ways to escape. You have a good head on your shoulders -- intelligent and persistent. But always be wary."

"I will, sir."

"Your father was a good friend, a man of sterling quality. I urge you to fight hard to carry on his name."

Tears filled Benny's eyes when Czerniakow spoke of Aaron. "You have found a way to help me?"

"I am not sure. It is dangerous but worth a try. Once before, I suggested to your father that arrangements be made through a Polish judge I know. Because Mirla and Sala look Aryan, we may be able to get them to Wodzislaw." Czerniakow hesitated. "I can't remember, does your mother speak Polish?"

"Yes, but she does not often speak it."

Czerniakow looked thoughtfully at the young boy. "I repeat -- it will be dangerous." Benny nodded. "I have secured the identification papers of two Polish sisters who perished near the end of the siege in '39. The pictures do not look like your mother and sister, but the papers are worn. Perhaps the lack of resemblance will not be noticed."

"Is it that simple?"

"It is not simple at all. Tell your mother and Sala to practice their Polish, and they will need to learn to write the signature, in case they are asked to verify. I also believe they will need supplemental information to support their claim."

"What kind?"

"Knowledge of the Catholic church. Some are asked to quote prayers known to Catholics or other information relating to the religion."

"And things that can prove they're Polish?"

"Yes. There is one church in the ghetto still open, a Catholic church near Leszno and Solna, open to Jews converted to Christianity. The Polish parishioners, as you know, not only had to find another home outside the ghetto but also another church."

"You're suggesting we may be able to get information there?"

"Yes."

Czerniakow stood up, walked toward his desk, and began to sort through papers. "Before I received the dead sisters' papers and after I talked with you, I spoke briefly with the priest, Father Edelman. He is willing to help."

Benny sat forward on the sofa, listening intently, hope filling his heart.

"Be careful. Father Edelman is closely watched."

"Yes sir."

"Good. Let's talk about getting you to the Russian sector. I cannot guarantee your safety or that you will make it to your destination."

"I understand."

"The borders are tightened daily. I can supply you with the name of a man who knows someone skilled in ferrying refugees across the border. My contact's name is Singer, and he lives between the Bug and the Narew Rivers -- but a short distance from the Russian occupied section of Bialystok. You will have to find a way to get to him." Czerniakow looked earnestly at the boy. "It will be dangerous."

"I face that every day," said Benny.

Czerniakow looked at him and smiled. "You are a courageous boy. Now let us see about your papers."

"I've been using the Lapinsky name. I have no actual papers."

Czerniakow took from the corner of his desk another paper and handed it to Benny. "Here is new identification. It belonged to a Polish boy only two years older than you -- Adam Borski. There is no picture. That may help you. It may hurt you."

"I understand," said Benny as he took the treasure and stood silently looking at it.

"Is there something else?"

Benny found it difficult to ask this kind man to do more. It was possible he had dealt with the underground to acquire the identification papers or even the Polish judge whose loyalty could be questioned in the face of German threats.

"Sir, I have only a small amount of money. Probably not enough to get me to Drohiezyn, and I'm not sure about the train trip for mother and Sala."

The man looked thoughtfully at Benny and quietly excused himself. Benny could hear voices in the other room. After several moments, Czerniakow returned and handed Benny five hundred Zloty plus twelve extra ration cards.

Pocketing the treasure, he asked hesitantly, "May I ask a personal question, sir?"

"Certainly," said Czerniakow.

"You're in a position to save yourself and your family. Why haven't you?"

Czerniakow's brow furrowed. He said, "It is true; I had the opportunity. General Frank and I attended university together. Twice, early on, he told me he would see that we left Poland safely."

"I don't understand why you didn't leave."

"I suppose it is difficult to comprehend, and I do not wish to sound like a martyr. In the beginning I did consider it -- but decided I would stay with the Jews. My wife supported me in that decision. I will tell you there are many times I feel I cannot do enough for the Jewish populace. I do the best I can, but my hands are tied."

Benny saw the tears welling in Czerniakow's eyes and sensed the guilt the man carried. His own son had disappeared without a trace.

"Sir," he said, "please thank your wife for the money and ration cards, and I thank you from the bottom of my heart. My father was truly fortunate to have you for a friend."

A hint of a smile crossed Czerniakow's tormented face. This time he moved toward the boy and took him into his arms. Little did they know it would be the last time they saw each other.

The small lamp on the kitchen table revealed a large scrap of paper, showing a crudely drawn map. The three people, who sat around the table, focused on the map's contents like strategic commanders planning an attack. The map governed their plan -- the design for escape out of the ghetto.

The two women listened earnestly as Benny pointed and clarified. "I've re-examined every exit that I've used out of the ghetto -- the ruins near Mila Street, the courts on Nalewki, the Jewish cemetery, and the sewers. Because there are three of us, I'm not satisfied with any of the choices." Benny explained that it was too far to the Mila and cemetery exits, and the court's outlet was heavily guarded.

"At all cost, we will avoid the sewers," he said. "It's not a choice I would make for my mother and sister." The boy explained that the pipe-like tunnels, besides being filthy, were narrow, and a person must stoop the entire distance, sometimes thrashing through deep excrement.

The women looked at each other, surprised that Benny knew of such things. Caught up in their own survival, they had never questioned his resources for supplies.

"The sewers coil under the city like a gigantic snake, making it easy to get lost in one of the many branches. We can't risk that. If I were alone, it would be different. There's no way out at the exit where it widens. It empties into the Vistula River." Pointing at the makeshift map he said, "Look here." His finger rested on a spot marked with an "x." "The ghetto wall extends through the ruins of a building right about here. I've been through there a couple of times."

The two women looked closely at the spot Benny indicated.

"What street is that?" asked Sala, a spark of interest appearing in her voice.

"The building sits at the intersection of Grzybowska and Rynkowa."

"Son!" Mirla's eyes widened with anxiety. "That is near the Judenrat Headquarters!"

"Just down the street," answered Benny.

"That is a crowded area with many people and police!"

"That's the point, Mother. We can be more easily lost in the crowd."

Mirla sat back in her chair, her shoulders slumped, arms folded across her chest.

"Mother, we talked about the danger," said Sala.

When she realized the real possibility of escape, the girl's demeanor had changed. Daily she walked more erect and smiled more often. She studied the information on the documents Chairman Czerniakow had given Benny and spoke Polish daily, as they had decided to do. Slipping accidentally into Yiddish would make their secret known. From the false identification, she and Mirla had become Ana and Beth Chevzinski and Benny, their nephew.

At Benny's advice, the women practiced using the new names, writing the signatures, and speaking only Polish to each other. They gleaned every piece of information they could about the Catholic church. He was not sure they were completely ready for the escape.

The exit instruction continued. "We will leave the house in our daily clothes with the usual Star of David armband. I will carry a large duffel bag holding our change of clothes, some food, and a small flashlight. If they stop us, we're to say that our destination is the Judenrat Building." Benny looked at his mother who watched him, smiling. He questioned her look. "Yes?"

"Benick -- Adam," she said sheepishly, shaking her head and trying to remember his new name. "Have I told you how much I love you?" Tearfully she said, "I am so very proud of you. I only hope my own courage can match yours."

Distracted momentarily from the role as leader of the escape plot, Benny became the young boy, Mirla's son. He reached across the small table for his mother's hand and glanced at Sala. The three, holding hands, sat quietly for a few moments.

Benny dabbed at a tear on his cheek, and with renewed energy he explained, "We'll need to be out of the ghetto before six in the evening. Daylight actually helps us in this case. We should arrive around four thirty at the Judenrat while it is busy. We will casually walk east toward the intersection. You will need to follow my directions. At the last moment I will determine the best way to enter the rubble without being seen. Do you understand?"

The two women nodded affirmatively.

"We'll change into our better clothes once we're in the cellar."

"Where will we exit from the cellar?" asked Mirla.

"On the Aryan side at Plac Zelaznej Bramy while it's congested with people returning home from work. From there we take a trolley and transfer to the railway at Praga. In fact, it might be wise to take the first trolley we see."

When Benny chose January 31 for escape, he did not know the Germans would collaborate his efforts. The Nazis planned to march three thousand uprooted Jews from Pruszkow and other cities in Poland to the Warsaw ghetto. Exiling them into an already overcrowded indigent area would be a further attempt by the Germans to starve the Jews and expose them to life threatening diseases. The date for the arrival of the Pruszkow Jews was January 31.

The last day of January arrived finally. Upon rising that morning, Mirla made tea and buckwheat groats. During the German siege, she had hidden some of their good clothes, waiting for the liberation for which she had dreamed.

Benny knew that Mirla had given up preserving the material things she so loved in the house. What the Nazis had not taken or destroyed, she had sold.

After Aaron died and the coal supply worsened, she and Sala moved their bedding to the kitchen. The kitchen and the attached toilet were the only two rooms in which they lived. The sparse furnishing in the attic room awaited Benny's return, for Mirla had never given up hope.

When three thirty came, Benny saw that his mother struggled with memories and leaving her home. Finally she closed the door. Benny wondered if she thought she would one day return.

The three joined the surge of people on the sidewalk. With full-throated voices, the growing numbers of vendors hawked their various goods in the jammed streets. They sold sugar, rags, post cards, and Star of David armbands -- anything they could get their hands on.

Some people sat idly on the sidewalks bundled in rags. Children and adults alike begged. Both the dead and the dying crowded the sidewalks. Having no strength for anything more and lost in deep thoughts for survival, their comrades passed them by.

When the three prospective escapees reached the Judenrat, long lines of people stood outside awaiting entrance to the building. The walk from Ogrodowa Street to the Judenrat Building had taken forty minutes. Poorly clothed and sometimes without shoes, people swarmed the street.

Recruits for the butchers no doubt, thought Benny.

Strutting Nazis herded, sometimes cruelly, the sea of people with dissolute stares. Besides the SS guards, many Jewish police roamed the area. They wore the billed cap of policemen, and on their right coat sleeve an amber strip of cloth warranted their public service.

Since the completion of the ghetto wall, the Polish police patrolled the Aryan sector. It was a relief to Benny to no longer worry about the large, red-faced, often drunk and cruel Polish policemen. It was more than enough to deal with the Nazis and the Jewish betrayers.

As Czerniakow had predicted, many of the Jewish police were not sympathetic to their peers but harbored a single mission of survival for themselves. Although they could not carry arms, only rubber clubs, they were sometimes vicious in their attacks.

At the corner of Grzybowska and Rynkowa, the three stopped next to the ruins of a once tall building. The ghetto wall edged the east side of the ruins. As the three stood talking casually, Benny's sharp eye surveyed the area. The nearest policeman stood across from them on Rynkowa Street.

A cart carrying a load of skeletal bodies approached from the south. Day and night the carts moved the carcasses to a gigantic common burial ground. Still the carriers could not keep up with the dying. Often the dead lay on the streets for days before being picked up for burial.

Benny whispered, "A burial cart is coming close. When I tell you to move quickly into the rubble and get on your knees, please keep quiet."

The women nodded.

Two Jewish policemen stood across the street. An intense conversation ensued, and one pointed toward an on-coming wagon. Benny watched them carefully. As the cart of bodies came beside Benny and provided cover from the policemen, he pushed his mother and sister into the rubble of the building. "Hurry!" he whispered.

As soon as they entered the ruins, he jumped into the pile of bricks. Inside, he motioned them to follow him, and the three crawled through the rubble as they zigzagged behind and between parts of walls. At last they came to a hole that, upon entering, revealed the remains of a room.

Mirla caught her breath. Benny stopped her with his outstretched hand. Two corpses leaned against a wall. As the threesome crawled past, the stench of rotting flesh invaded their nostrils. Cold air only slightly decreased the odor's intensity. Sala began gagging and heaving. Benny quickly turned, cautioning her with a finger to his mouth. His face darkened as he glanced toward the opening from which they had just crawled. Distinct voices sounded on the other side of the wall.

Benny pointed toward a crevice in the corner, motioning them to crawl inside. He followed, pulling a larger piece of concrete as a partial cover. The boy prayed for secrecy as he sheltered them with outstretched arms, pulling their bodies close to the ground.

Sala, holding one hand on her throat, struggled with the nausea. Her eyes were wide and her face pale. Her brother gave her a threatening look.

A Jewish policeman, followed closely by the cart driver, walked into the remains of the room "There are the bodies to be removed," the policeman said, pointing at the carcasses. "Do your job quickly."

Holding his nose, the policeman exited in haste. The undertaker grabbed one of the bodies by a foot, dragging it across the uneven surface, the rag-doll-body flopping over the stones. He removed the second body as unceremoniously.

Once the area was clear, Benny and his family crawled from their hiding place. The boy guided them to a narrow hole in the wall that led to another room.

In the second room, Benny moved to the center, laid down the bag, and began to push at a large piece of concrete. It barely moved as he struggled with it. Finally he was able to shove it aside, revealing a hole in the ground. Benny retrieved the flashlight from the bag, flipped it on, and pointed it in the direction of the hole. He dropped the bag into the opening and urged the two women to descend. Unable to see the bottom, both hesitated. The meager light revealed only an old wooden ladder resting inside.

Unsure, Mirla ventured down the wobbly ladder, followed by Sala, holding the flashlight.

With a last glance behind him, Benny climbed into the hole, reaching upward to try to pull the piece of concrete over the hole.

As he worked with it, the ladder squeaked and shifted. Precious moments passed as he struggled with the piece of concrete. Satisfied they would not be easily discovered, he climbed downward. Without warning, the ladder gave a quick jolt and broke. Benny fell into the hole.

"Benick, are you all right?" whispered Sala.

"Shhh," he answered. "The noise may have been detected. I'm not hurt."

They waited silently. When all seemed clear, Benny stood up and placed the bag straps around his neck so that the bag rested on his back. Taking the flashlight from Sala, he walked across the cellar. The women followed.

He turned to them whispering, "We must crawl through this tunnel to get to the other cellar. Keep as quiet as you can."

The boy dropped to his hands and knees and entered the tunnel. Mirla came directly behind, Sala following. Small, hard clods of dirt, harsh to their hands and knees, layered the narrow burrow. A strong scent of urine penetrated the area. Moving slowly, Benny stopped occasionally, listening for sounds.

All at once, the tunnel became black.

Gehenem! Damn, thought Benny. *The flashlight burned out!*

The darkness was like a tomb. He heard the women breathing heavily, too frightened to speak.

"It's okay," murmured Benny. "Stay close."

Suddenly something ran across his hand.

Oh, God, he thought. *They will find their voices now. Please don't let them scream.*

Before he could caution them, the rat ran back toward the women, passing Mirla without incident. Benny prayed Sala would not scream. He knew how she felt about mice. He held his breath. Then he heard her.

"Ohhh," she moaned softly.

Benny smiled. His sister was trying hard to be brave and ignore the furry creature crawling beside her. She knew she must not yell but could not resist a groan. The rat, as scared as she, scurried past her.

Minutes later, Benny crawled into the next cellar. He stood, laid down the duffel bag, and helped the women from the tunnel. As Sala came through the opening, Benny smiled and took her into his arms.

"You were very brave," he said quietly.

She grinned and ducked her head, whispering in his ear as she had done in their childhood days, "I hope I didn't mess my clothes."

The two had difficulty controlling their giggles. Mirla, still shaky from her first tunnel crawl, frowned.

Benny patted his mother on the shoulder. "You did well, Mother."

She smiled in spite of herself.

Retrieving the clothes from the bag, Benny whispered, "Change over there." He pointed to a dim corner of the cellar. "I'll change here."

A smile crossed his face, and a sense of sadness overtook him when he saw the clothes his mother had saved for him. She had altered one of his father's suits as well as a raincoat. *That took a lot of altering*, thought Benny. *Father was a large man.* Often Aaron had remarked that Mirla was one of the best seamstresses he knew. The bag also held Kuba's clothes. Benny felt lucky in them and would need the additional clothing in Bialystok's colder climate.

After they changed, Benny pushed the clothes, along with the hated armbands, between two loose bricks in the wall. Picking up the bag, now filled only with food and the extra clothing for himself, he whispered, "There, beyond that second wall, is the opening to the outdoors. We must be very careful. Follow closely and don't speak."

Benny heard the sound of heavy traffic and the clanking of a trolley. Peering over a broken wall, he watched for the right moment. The sidewalk teemed with people on their way home. He gestured for his family to move up behind him. In a few minutes a trolley screeched to a stop near by. Sidewalk occupants ran for it. At this moment he whispered, "Move quickly with me to the sidewalk and run with the crowd."

The three jumped onto the walk and joined the crowd moving at a fast pace toward the trolley. They were the last passengers to get on. Benny pulled the correct change for the three and handed it to the conductor. He looked closely at the other passengers, intent on returning home.

Benny smiled to himself. *We blend right in. Isn't it amazing! When we were on the other side of the wall, we were different than these people, but on the Aryan side we are the same.*

The trolley ride and further transfers proved to be uneventful. At the train station, Benny bought tickets for his "aunts" and walked them to the gate.

The German guarding the entrance looked closely at the sisters' papers and remarked, "You may want to update your papers. They are worn."

To which Mirla quickly responded in excellent Polish, "Yes, young man. You are quite right. Thank you."

Even Sala ventured a smile at Mirla's audacity in trying to impress the German.

Good-byes were difficult.

As he hugged them, Benny whispered, "Don't worry. I will return from Bialystok to get you. I love you."

They waved from their window until the train was out of sight.

Please dear Lord, prayed Benny silently, *let me see them again.*

Six months after Benny's family left the ghetto, Hermann Göring signed an order giving authority for the "solution" of Europe's "Jewish question." The Warsaw ghetto, a holding pen for the *Aktion* activities, continued to receive refugees, victims for extermination.

NINE

"WHO THE HELL ARE YOU?"

The unshaven man stood at the door in his long underwear. He yawned and ran his hand across his head, tousling the sparse hair.

"Singer sent me."

"Yeah? Well, don't let the cold air in."

"You can take me across the border?"

Motioning the boy into the room, he answered, "Maybe. We'll talk about it in the morning." He was Benny's height and thick set, his neck big and muscular, his shoulders broad. The boy guessed him to be about sixty.

"You can sleep over there." The man pointed to a fireplace where a fire crackled and red sparks fell onto the stone hearth. A large iron pot sat to the side.

The man reached for a blanket from the coat hook beside the door. "Here," he said, handing the cover to the boy.

Benny set his bag in front of the fireplace and turned to his host. The man, already walking toward another room at the rear of the house, growled over his shoulder, "Put out the light."

Benny, taking in his surroundings, stood for a moment. It was a small rustic room with stucco walls and pine flooring as well as pine beams across the ceiling. The worn, roughly hewn floorboards were smooth with age. The sparsely furnished room held a kitchen table and two chairs. A kerosene lantern occupied the table.

137

Benny walked to the table and extinguished the lantern wick. The room glowed from the light of the fireplace. He lay down on the floor, punched his duffel bag into a pillow, and pulled the blanket over him. The boy stared for a long time at the flickering flames as they caught the remaining logs.

How feasible was his plan? Benny was not sure. He was in a strange house with a strange man. Though the train trip had been relatively uneventful, and the man Czerniakow told him to see had treated him well, he was still unsure. Singer had fed him and given him good directions to this house. Had it not been for a clear night with a bright moon and those instructions, he could have easily passed up the house. It sat several yards off the path in the thick woods.

Benny fell asleep finally. The smell of coffee awakened him at dawn. He sat up, disoriented.

"Want something to eat, boy?" asked the man sitting at the kitchen table drinking coffee and eating bread and cheese.

"Sure."

They ate in silence. Abruptly the man asked, "How did you get to Drohiezyn?"

"Train."

"Right through the Germans?"

"Yes sir."

"Well, you got some spunk or you're a lucky son-of-a-bitch. How much money you got?"

Surprised by the man's directness, Benny answered, "Fifty Zloty."

The host slapped his thigh, laughing loudly.

Benny figured in his head. He needed money once he got into Bialystok.

"A hundred fifty Zloty," he offered.

Squinting his eyes, the man stared at Benny.

"A hundred fifty," Benny said.

The man did not answer.

"Two hundred Zloty," said the boy slowly.

"That's more like it. I'm not in the business to baby-sit, you know. This is a dangerous game. You understand, boy?"

Benny, nodding his head, wondered if he should have stuck with his lower offer.

Too late now, he thought.

"You'll have to burrow in for a while. Can't leave till the weather turns bad. Gotta have cover," said the man.

The weather stayed fair and cold. Benny spent the time helping the man with chores, mostly cutting wood. They talked little. The man did not seem interested in the boy nor in sharing information about himself. Benny imagined it was less dangerous in case the enemy caught either of them. When he considered what might be in store, he felt a tightening in his stomach.

Four days after Benny's arrival, it began raining. He lay in the dark, listening to the spat, spat sound as it hit the roof. Soon the light rain gave way to pounding.

The man came into the room and lighted the lantern.

"Get up, boy. Time to go. Gotta make use of the dark and the rain."

"What time is it?" asked Benny.

"Almost dawn," said the man, heading for the door. "Stay close boy."

Benny barely had time to get his extra coat and his father's raincoat from the duffel bag. He pulled them both over the thickness of his clothes, picked up the bag and followed the man.

Benny stayed close to the man as he navigated not only the darkness and heavy rain but also the dense underbrush that hemmed them in. They had walked a kilometer from the house when the man stopped short. He stood, listening, then he led the boy to a small dinghy tied to the riverbank. He touched the boy on the arm and motioned him into the craft. The boat made a small sloshing sound as Benny stepped into it. Motionless, the man took note of every sound. At length he untied the boat and climbed in. Stealthily he reached for a long pole lying in the bottom of the skiff. Again he waited, listening and peering into the murky morning darkness. The rain spattering on the river surface and the water sloshing against the sides of the small boat that churned in the storm were the only sounds.

After awhile, the man stuck the pole into the water and propelled them along the riverbank. He was very careful to put the pole into the water with as little sound as possible. Benny hunkered low in the boat, warding off the thick, cold rain.

As they changed directions to move into the river proper, the man suddenly stopped pushing at the water and thrust the long pole slowly toward the river bottom to idle the boat. Something moved in the water ahead of them. The man reached out and hit Benny's leg, indicating he should remain silent. Benny could barely make out the outline of what appeared to be a large raft. Ghost-like apparitions, obviously on the same mission as the boy, poled the vessel across the river.

Benny and his host sat in silence, watching. The raft was about three-quarters across the river when the sound of machine-guns rent the air. As gunfire sprayed the raft and its passengers, screams and splashing pierced the dawn. Benny scarcely breathed, the realization of death only a short distance away. When the chaos ended, a malignant silence surrounded them, the only sound -- rain striking the water.

The boatman and Benny, frozen in place, waited as long as they dared, then the man poled the skiff out into the river, piloting them away from the massacre site. He motioned for Benny to lie low and make no sound. As the experienced boatman manipulated the pole, they propelled forward. Each time they braked to a stop, Benny's heart skipped a beat.

After what seemed an eternity to Benny, they reached the other side. The old man gestured him out of the boat and pointed in the direction of the Russian outpost.

Benny crawled quickly onto the bank. When he turned back toward the boatman, the man had already eased into the river current, disappearing into the dark and rain.

Hoping not to cross German guards, the boy made his way cautiously through the woods. Only drizzle remained, and daylight emerged when he came to a clearing. Two uniformed Russian soldiers stood several yards away. He hoped a jeep parked near the guard shack would take him the last distance to Bialystok

———❄———

"Who is next?" the man growled in Russian.

He was a large-boned man with a striking handlebar mustache. He wore the baggy uniform of a Russian officer.

Benny took a deep breath and answered him in Russian.

Surprised, the man smiled and offered him a seat. Benny reached across the desk and handed him the identification papers.

"Adam Borski?" asked the Russian officer, looking closely at the papers then at Benny.

"Yes sir. I'm Polish."

"How is it that you speak Russian or try to speak Russian?"

"I learned it in school, sir, but I'm a little faulty in my memory." Benny wondered how much to embellish his story.

"Where is your picture?"

Benny was unsure how to answer. "They didn't give me one, sir."

The Russian peered over the rim of his glasses. "I assume you have come here to work?"

"Yes sir, and to bring my mother and sister here."

"Well, perhaps we can assist you."

Benny could hardly believe his good fortune. The officer was almost too friendly and helpful. The Russians allowed refugees from the German occupied zone into the area, if they could reach the border. Benny believed this was why it was a comparatively easy entrance for him.

Perhaps I am too familiar in dealing with Germans to recognize friendliness?

The Russian officer for NKVD (People's Commissariat of Internal Affairs) nonchalantly handed him a paper and casually said, "However, before your family can join you, you must sign this paper."

The officer handed it to Benny as though he were passing him a cigarette.

Puzzled, Benny took the paper.

"You will be allowed your choice of cities -- Moscow, Stalingrad, Leningrad."

The officer leaned back in his chair, smiling broadly, tapping his fingers together.

"There are many places to work. For this privilege all you must do is sign this contract for a period of five years."

There it was -- the thing Benny's knotted stomach was trying to tell him. He did not want to sign the contract, yet he did not wish to infuriate the officer.

"Thank you, sir. I really appreciate the opportunity, but since I've just arrived, I'd like to see the city. It will give me some time to think over your offer."

The officer leaned forward and slammed the palm of his hand on the desk. "Sign the contract, you son-of-a-bitch, unless you want to eat shit rather than Farina."

Benny was smart enough to realize that he would gain nothing by answering. He kept his tongue in check while the Russian lashed out. The cursing tirade subsided finally.

Benny stood politely for a few moments and then asked, "Sir, if I could have a pass so that I may enter the city proper?"

The officer, taken aback by the boy's brashness, stared at him. Pulling a pad from his desk drawer, he signed one of the forms, ripped it from the pad, and handed it to Benny.

"Here is your pass. I will hold on to your identification papers for you." He smiled a crooked smile.

As Benny entered the city, he noted the cloudy skies giving way to the presence of a winter sun.

A good omen, he wished secretly.

Bialystok, an old city established in 1807, was one of the few cities in Poland he had not visited as a child. He knew from his father's business that its major industry was textiles. World War I destroyed many of the factories. After the war, the rebuilding began. Prior to the German and Russian occupation, Jews owned seventy-five percent of the factories. The Germans invaded in September 1939, and shortly afterward handed over the administration to the Soviet Union.

Looking for a shelter or signs of Jewish families, Benny strolled the streets. He thought he could find out how to make a living and avoid signing the Russian paper.

Narrow streets held neatly arranged houses that clustered close together. Benny passed a Christian church that stabled horses. Other churches housed pigs and cows. Cribs and mangers replaced pews, and swill troughs fed swine. The Russians had heeded the Communist hard line and closed all churches to the public. Benny noticed an absence of people on the streets, even though the population was estimated at forty to fifty thousand, the largest segment being Jewish.

Soon he came to a synagogue where a Star of David hung above the door. If the Russian officer suspected that Benny was Jewish, he had not said. This was the shelter to which the Russian directed him.

The people milling around reminded Benny of the Warsaw ghetto, but here they seemed less desolate. Some ate crusts of bread and herring while others sat talking with their fellows. A few gambled while others sang familiar songs.

Although a Russian checked his pass, no one asked for his identification. Some of the shelter occupants welcomed Benny and gave him a dinner of potato soup with real potatoes in it, some dark Russian bread, and pieces of dried salmon.

After he had eaten, he noticed a young Jew leaning against a pole, and he walked over and introduced himself as Benny Lipman. The Jew offered the boy a cigarette, which Benny took. He had begun the habit in the ghetto but had little chance to obtain cigarettes.

"How should I go about finding work?" Benny asked.

"Some people travel," the man answered. "They peddle merchandise from city to city."

"That would require city passes. Correct?"

"Yes."

Benny did not think this was a feasible plan because it required more passes, difficult to obtain.

"There's something you must be cautious about," advised the man.

"Something to be cautious about?"

"Yes. It's easy to be accused of dealing in black-market here. The Russians believe it's a crime against the government." He pulled long on the cigarette, blew the smoke to the ceiling and looked hard at Benny. "Punishments are not minor. Some stupid man sold the Russians floor wax for edible spread. When it was discovered, they placed placards throughout the city. Someone turned him in. They called his actions treason. No one ever saw him again."

"No idea what happened?"

"None."

"It doesn't sound like the Russians are too different from the Germans," volunteered Benny.

"Well, let's put it this way, I wouldn't indulge in any political matters if I were you. Don't act too smart or too dumb. And don't say to anybody what you just said to me about the Germans."

Benny was glad to get this advice. After a couple of day's observing normal commercial activities, he decided to open a shoeshine business.

With the remaining Zloty transferred to rubles, he bought boards, brushes, and shoe polish as well as rags for polishing. He set out to find customers, Russian officers and soldiers.

Within one week, Benny earned two hundred rubles, and by the end of the month he had earned five hundred. It pleased him that his idea was original and it was making money. Some of the soldiers were repeat customers and tipped well. At this rate, he would be able to help his mother and sister in a short period of time.

Then the unthinkable happened. Early one morning two Russian soldiers barged into Benny's shelter and pulled him from his third tier bunk. They ordered him to follow them to the NKVD office. Grabbing his duffel bag and coat, he obeyed.

"Where are you taking me?" he asked.

They did not answer.

"Have I done something wrong?"

The soldiers stopped. One turned to him, slapped him hard, and told him to stay quiet. He yielded.

It was not yet dawn when they reached the commandant's office. Benny sat and waited for what seemed to be hours. At length the officer he met during interrogation entered the room. The Russian looked at Benny and smiled.

"So we meet again."

"Sir, I don't understand what I've done wrong."

"Let's see," answered the man, leaning on the front of the desk, resting his elbows. "Shall we start with operating an illegal business?"

Benny started to interrupt, but when he saw the look on the man's face, he remained silent.

"All Russians, from privates to generals, clean their own boots. You have interfered with the discipline of the Russian army. That, my boy, is sabotage."

"Sabotage? But, sir . . . "

"Shut up, Borski or whoever you are! You have no privileges at this point! Do you understand?"

Benny did not answer. The man turned from him and walked out of the room while barking orders to the guards outside the door. Benny picked up on a few Russian words -- "transport" and "train." His heart stopped.

It was mid-morning when Benny and the guards approached the cattle car. Several hundred men and boys assembled at the tracks. Unlike German deportations, this one lacked organization. Eventually he joined forty people and one Russian guard in a pine slatted boxcar. No one knew the destination. The boy thought only the Germans did such things. Dismayed at his misfortune, Benny found a corner and sat down.

The old coal burner train finally sprang forward with a jerk, its wheels squealing loudly. It soon gained momentum. Peering through the pine slats, Benny could see the countryside, sterile farmland lying fallow, covered with snow. Once in a while, the train passed small cities.

Twice daily the passengers received soup and a large hunk of bread. Toilet facilities did not exist, except when the train stopped. That was not often. When an older man among the prisoners developed a case of diarrhea, the Russian guard ignored his request to stop the train. Before long an awful odor permeated the air. The others moved to one side, leaving the sick man alone. After several days the man died, and the Russians eventually removed the body. Even in the cold, the terrible stench lingered.

Benny could not guess how many days or weeks they traveled. It seemed an endless journey. He had kept his duffel bag and money as well as his papers. While in Bialystok, he bought a notebook and pencils for his business notes. Now he used them for a journal.

It helped to focus on his childhood. He wrote:

> Life is like a great thunderstorm. As the clouds darken and approach, they foreshadow what is to come. When I was seven, I didn't care what was to come. Today is so important; tomorrow seems an eon away. I remember 16 Karmelicka Street, my early childhood home and the hub of my universe, as though it were yesterday. My father was a tower of strength, a fountain of kindness and a never-ending river of understanding. My mother lacked his giant stature but matched his heart in her kindly deeds. Her acts of generosity were well known, especially with the orphans of Warsaw.

Benny paused as the movement of the train caused an unsteady hand. Remembering the way Mirla used to be brought tears to his eyes. He steadied his hand and continued.

I vividly remember my mother's soothing voice.
She was incapable of raising her voice in anger. She
gave so much meaning to life. And now, what does
she face -- nothing but unkindness.

Villages appeared less frequently now; only woods and fields
were seen through the slats. It snowed heavily. The air became bitter
cold, forcing the group to huddle together for warmth. Even the
Russian looked miserable. He sat in a corner sulking.

After what seemed an eternity, the journey was finally over. The
travelers disembarked and followed their captors to a local office of
the NKVD where each man acquired a second-hand Russian winter
coat and a number that was later sewn on the trousers.

"Do a good job for Russia and you will be able to eat well, sleep
well, and eventually make good Russian citizens."

This was the advice given to the group upon arrival. Benny's
dream was far different from this.

In groups of fifteen, they marched to their new quarters, huts
made of limestone walls and thatched roofs. Each hut had two
rooms, a small kitchen with a stone stove, and plenty of firewood.
The fifteen men slept in a communal bunk extending from one end
of the room to the other. Straw covered the giant bed, and each man
had his own blanket.

The Russians marched the laborers to a wooded area and gave
them the task of felling giant trees. Four men at each saw and four
with axes made up the work crew. It took three hours to hew each
broad-base tree. Once down, the laborers trimmed and cut them into
varying lengths. Sometimes the clump was three feet long -- other
times eight to twelve.

The men worked eight-and-a-half hours a day. Within a short
time, Benny's arm muscles grew as well as his appetite. Plentiful
food and the hard work enabled the men to sleep well at night. They
were too busy and exhausted for conversation.

Two days after arriving at camp, the laborers received orders
to attend Lenin-Marxist classes twice a week. Although he obeyed,

young Benny already detested the doctrine of communism and considered these classes useless.

The bitter cold made Benny nervous, and he prayed each night for survival until he could reach warmer climes. Thoughts of escape were only fleeting moments for him because the Frigid Zone was not conducive to escape. One could easily freeze to death or starve provided a bullet did not get him first.

In the second week, Benny began running a high temperature accompanied by chills. A Russian guard urged him to work harder in order to feel better. When a saw slipped from his hand several times, the guard sent him to a hut located across from the NKVD office. The sick room held two cots and a stone fireplace.

On the second evening in the sick room, one of the workers who bunked next to Benny came to visit.

"Strange things are happening," revealed the man.

"What strange things?" asked Benny.

"Our work group is reduced from fifteen to ten."

"Why is that?"

"I was offered an opportunity to go home if I signed a paper. When I read it, I found I would be signing up for a job in an ammunition factory in Leningrad for five to ten years."

"My God, that's what they tried to get me to sign in Bialystok. What did you do?"

"I lied. I told them I would consider it. I learned that one of the men refused to sign, saying his family expected him back. The Russians berated him and called him stupid. They said he would get out only as a dead man. Since then, he and several others have disappeared."

"What are you going to do?"

"I don't know, but I thought you should know this."

Conversation ended quickly with the entrance of Dr. Ivan Miernoff, the camp doctor. The co-worker made his excuses and left, leaving Benny alone with the doctor.

The boy wondered if he should use this opportunity to confide in the man. "We're in Siberia?" asked Benny.

The doctor looked up from his stethoscope examination. "That's right," he said. "Sverdlovsk."

"And the mountains we came through on the train?"

"Southern Urals."

"It was a long ride. What is the date?"

"It's mid-April."

Surprised at the time lapse, Benny scrutinized the tall, dark-skinned doctor as he counted out medicine tablets. The man's cheeks were deep red, and the lines in his face gave him a craggy appearance. He wore a thick beard, and his handlebar mustache reminded the boy of pictures he had seen of Stalin.

Benny decided to take a chance.

"Doctor, I'm not Polish. I'm Jewish," he blurted out.

The doctor looked at him, his eyes narrowing. He offered no comment.

"I went to Bialystok to earn money in order to get my mother and sister out of Poland. My father died of starvation in the Warsaw ghetto. If you could help me, I would be most grateful."

The doctor did not respond. Handing his prescribed tablets to Benny, he picked up his bag and left.

Can I trust you? thought Benny.

After the Warsaw invasion, he remembered feeling like a fly caught in a spider's web. He still did. He would never forget the suffering he felt when friends turned informers. It took the very soul from him, causing him to mistrust everyone.

Forty-eight hours passed before Benny saw the doctor again. While standing at the window, Benny saw the man disembark from a horse-drawn sled and walk into the NKVD office. The boy, wanting to appear ill, returned to his bed.

About twenty minutes, later Dr. Miernoff entered the hut, bringing with him a rush of cold air.

"I still do not feel well," volunteered Benny.

The doctor looked closely at him. He flashed a hasty smile, which left as quickly as it appeared.

"Remove your shirt," commanded the doctor.

Benny obeyed. Dr. Miernoff listened to Benny's lungs and heart.

Abruptly the doctor said, "I am the son of a rabbi."

Startled, Benny turned to the doctor. "A rabbi?"

"Yes, my father taught Hebrew and was a shochet, one who slaughters kosher meat."

"In Communist Russia?"

"Yes," answered the doctor. Changing the subject, he said, "I can tell you are not really ill. Unless you wish to sign these papers, you must return to the work force." He pulled them from his bag, handing them to Benny.

The boy stared at the papers in the doctor's hand. How could he have misread him? Disappointed, Benny refused them. The doctor pushed them towards him.

"Here, read them."

Benny shook his head. He looked directly at the doctor. "I will not give up five to ten years of my life to Russia when my mother and sister need my help now."

"And how do you propose to help them from Siberia?" asked Dr. Miernoff.

"I'll find a way."

"Read the papers, my boy."

Puzzled by the tone of the doctor's voice, Benny took the papers and read them. His head jerked up in surprise.

"These don't look like the work papers I was asked to sign before. Help me with these words. Does this say. . .?"

The Dr. leaned toward him and said quietly, "How would you like to go home? You and I both know that you are no longer sick, but they do not. I am going to make arrangements for your return home. I will say you are unable to work."

The paper was a passport to freedom. The doctor had indeed arranged his escape.

"How is this possible?" asked Benny, his eyes wide with delight.

"I will drive you to the train station. Your duffel is in the sled. First, we must go to the NKVD office and secure the train ticket and your identification papers. It might be wise for you to appear ill."

Benny dressed and followed the doctor into the cold. A sense of renewal swept over him.

Burning larch scented the air, and fresh snow covered the thatched roofs where smoke floated skyward from chimneys. All this gave the compound a fairyland look.

Benny was going to see his mother and sister.

The boy's passenger car accommodations were better than the cattle car in which he had traveled to Siberia, even if the seats were wooden benches. During less crowded conditions, he could use the seat for a bed. He also had the freedom to walk around and to receive meals twice daily. Benny had long since removed his heavy clothing and packed it in his duffel -- along with his journal. Wearing Kuba's clothes brought back fond memories of the old man.

The train rumbled toward its destination, and Benny pondered the twists and turns of his life as he wrote in his journal.

> My father was not immune to the events that were transpiring. I remember the SS guards taking him in a roundup of forty-three hostages to be executed by a firing squad for the murder of a German actor, born and raised in Poland. Of course, none of them were guilty. This didn't matter to the Germans. At random, the Germans chose twenty-five of the group for execution. My father returned home, bruised but alive. I will never forget the look on his face, the disbelief that his life had made such a dramatic change.

Benny, unable to see through the tears, stopped writing. Aaron Lipman had once prided himself on his ability to care for his family.

Benny had watched his father's eyes grow dull as humiliation overwhelmed him, and his circumstances ravaged his soul.

It would have been better for him to die by execution, thought Benny, *rather than to suffer the agonizing death of starvation. I will try to remember him in his glory.*

As the train left Siberia and crossed the southernmost point of the Ural Mountains, the land tapered into lowland, becoming a part of the Great European Plain.

They had long since left the severe climate and barren land of Siberia. Now fields lay green and fertile, and forests were thick with spring growth.

The train passed through groves of conifer and deciduous trees interspersed with stretches of rich farmland, where barley, cabbages, and potatoes grew. Other timberland held proud maple and oak trees. Occasionally deer and small animals bolted from clumps of standing timber. The days turned to weeks, and Benny continued his journey across the Russian plain.

The click, click, thud of the metal wheels on the track, and the rocking movement of the car lulled the boy to sleep once more. His head, bobbing to the shifting rhythm of the train, rested against the windowpane.

Benny dreamed that he and Sala were running across Grandfather Lipman's fields. Stopping occasionally, they picked wildflowers or watched a rabbit scurry from their path, their peals of laughter filling the summer air. Huge, fluffy clouds decorated the heavens, and the sky between them shone a brilliant sapphire.

Brother and sister had bet on who could reach the stream in the north pasture first. Sala's long legs already outdistanced the boy. As she ran, she looked back over her shoulder. A broad smile stretched across her flawless skin, and her eyes sparkled with happiness.

"Come on, Benick. Come on!" she cheered. "I'm going to beat you!"

Suddenly he saw his mother running out of a clump of trees. Fear clouded her face. She ran, reaching out toward Sala. Piercing screams filled the air, "No! No, Sala. Come back."

Benny felt his heart racing. He did not understand his mother's fright. He and Sala were only playing -- just racing for the stream. It was all right to play.

The boy ran faster. When he reached the banks of the brook, his mother and Sala had disappeared.

Water trickling over the smooth stones drew his attention. Swirling white rushes of clear fluid created miniature waterfalls, captivating his imagination. Mesmerized by the gyration of the moving water, he did not notice the change in its color until the entire stream ran burnished red.

Panic set in. He felt the on-coming hysteria, and he heard himself cry, "No! No!"

"It's all right," said a voice.

Startled, Benny jerked straight up. For a moment he did not know where he was. A man stood in the aisle next to his seat. Benny remembered seeing the tall, robust Russian come aboard at the last station stop.

"May I join you," asked the man in Polish, "now that I have awakened you from your sleep?"

Benny nodded his head and the burly man took the bench facing him.

"My name is Roman Nikovitz," the Russian said, offering his hand to Benny.

"Mine is Adam Borski," said Benny, shaking his hand.

"What is your destination?"

"Bialystok and after that southern Poland. And yours?"

"I'm going home to Minsk to see my three wives."

Benny tried to remain expressionless. It was obvious he failed, for the Russian laughed boisterously, showing his tobacco-stained teeth. He looked like a huge bear, his large stature covered by a thick fur coat.

"Going right back into the Germans, huh?" remarked Nikovitz.

"I must. My mother and sister are there."

"Well, at least you're not a Jew, huh?"

Benny nodded.

"Things are a little unsettled right now in Bialystok," said the Russian. "If I were you, I would not linger there long. How will you leave Bialystok?"

"I don't know yet."

"You know the ferry that runs back and forth between Bialystok and Drohiezyn?"

Benny nodded in the affirmative even though he did not know.

"Take the ferry which has a boatman named John. Tell him Roman sent you, and he will help you."

Benny's good fortune continued, both pleasing and surprising him. He learned that Roman Nikovitz was a Belorussian Slav on a brief furlough before being sent on a new assignment. Nevertheless, he could not answer Benny's questions about the obvious military activities in the villages where the train stopped.

When the two parted, the Russian offered Benny the contents of a bag he wore strapped to his groin. It held sugar, bread, salt, pork, saccharine, five pounds of Machorka tobacco, and cigarette papers. Benny was sad to see the jolly man depart the train.

The sun burned off the early morning haze as the ferry moved across the river away from Bialystok. It was June 1941, one month after Benny's forgotten thirteenth birthday.

He was disappointed that his plan to make escape money fell through, but he eagerly anticipated seeing his mother and Sala. They would make a new blueprint for escape. The dream he had on the train still haunted him. Looking back at the skyline of Bialystok, he tried to be calm and positive.

I will make a better plan, thought Benny.

On June 27, 1941, only days after Benny's departure from Bialystok, the Germans conquered the city. War had broken out between Russia and Germany.

At the hands of the Germans, two thousand Bialystok Jews were burned to death on a day recorded in history as "Red Friday." Within the first two weeks of German occupation, they murdered four thousand Jews in an open field near Pietraszek.

The Germans occupied Minsk, Roman's hometown on June 28 and established a ghetto on July 20. By August 1 they had secured the Bialystok ghetto.

TEN

FROM HIS POSITION at the window, Benny could see the singular organization of the Germans. It reminded him of an epic played out on a movie screen.

The train station at Warsaw Praga was a din of humanity. The teeming crowd surged at the captors' will. With drawn rifles, uniformed SS herded the sea of people, their facial muscles twisted with confusion and fear. Even through the window glass, the roar of the human battlefield was unmistakable.

Train engines belched smoke, blending gray with the early morning haze. Occasionally, the waves of people herded onto the trains receded only to have the gap closed by another wave -- men, women, and children -- all together an eerie backdrop.

Benny felt his heart racing, threatening to engulf his chest in a great spasm, and his throat was so dry he could not swallow. He wondered if anyone ever suffocated from fear. How could he come so far and be caught? The boy made an instant decision -- he must change trains for Wodzislaw as he planned originally.

He rose, pulling his duffel from the overhead compartment and heading for the front of the car. As he opened the door to the divider between his car and the next, he heard a gruff voice.

"Halt! Where are you going?"

Benny stopped and turned toward the source of the order. A tall SS guard stood on the lower platform, only a few feet away.

Jews from the Warsaw ghetto are boarded onto a deportation train. USHMM, courtesy of Zydowski Instytut Historyczny Instytut Naukowo-Badawczy

"I am exiting in order to catch another train," said Benny in Polish.

"Get off the train!" barked the German.

"Why?"

"Do not argue!" He reached his black-gloved hand toward Benny. "Let me see your papers."

Duffel in hand, Benny stepped down onto the platform and into the surge of people. As he reached into his pocket and pulled out the papers, the crowd pushed into him, causing him to drop them. Benny stooped quickly to retrieve them, and in so doing blocked the path of an old man.

The elder Jew fell against Benny, knocking him to the platform and unbalancing the SS guard. The guard immediately responded, drawing his pistol and cuffing the old man across the face. Bleeding profusely the man covered his face with his hands and moved forward hastily to lose himself in the crowd.

Benny, on hands and knees, searched frantically for the papers while the German hovered above him.

"Please, I dropped them. Let me find them," pleaded Benny, looking up at him.

As he spied the papers just ahead, the boy pointed, "There! There they are!"

Simultaneously the surging crowd, concerned only with their fate and not the papers at their feet, kicked them forward.

"Get up, Jude, and move on," scoffed the German, grabbing Benny by the arm and shoving him into the teeming mass.

Overcome with desperation Benny cried, "Let me get them, please! I am Adam Borski. I am Polish."

A fire exploded in his groin the moment the SS responded. The agony between his legs forced Benny to double over. Writhing with pain, the youth rolled onto his stomach. Again, the SS kicked him hard. The lost papers, lying on the ground just beyond his reach, were the last things Benny remembered before he lost consciousness.

---※---

When the train jerked to a start, Benny came to, instantly consumed with excruciating pain that threatened to make him nauseous. Contorting his body into a variety of positions did not give him relief.

Eventually Benny rolled to a sitting position and surveyed his surroundings. A small, slated window provided the only light, revealing bags and boxes stacked at one end of the car. He was alone at the other end. Only the sound of clacking wheels and the popping car -- swaying down the track -- kept him company and hinted at what was happening.

A perfunctory glance proved enough to convince him that escape from the steel car was hopeless. It struck him as strange that the SS put him in a baggage car rather than the usual cattle car and left him a loaf of bread and a canteen of water. By now, nothing his captors did seemed logical. The mind of the SS proved so erratic it would be impossible to keep up with their pattern of behavior.

Always curious, Benny made a painful move to examine one of the bags at the other end of the car. It contained shoes, evidently taken from unfortunate victims of the German purge. Benny dug into the bag and fit himself with a beautiful pair of eight-inch laced shoes.

Next he investigated the boxes where he found a great array of fur coats of varying degrees of value. He extracted several of the heavier coats, turning them to their satin lining to make a soft bed. This would surely ease his continuing pain. He sometimes wondered if he would ever be able to run or walk naturally again.

As the train gained momentum, the exhausted boy finally closed his eyes. The click-clack of the wheels striking the metal tracks hypnotized Benny into deep slumber. He slept through the remainder of the day and night.

When he awoke, the sun shone through the slats. Benny painfully pulled himself up to the little window and peered out. He had no idea where he was.

Vast meadows lay adjacent to rich farmland. Small, whitewashed houses, some with dark gabled roofs, sat in clusters near freshly mowed plains covered with yellow and green haystacks.

Benny thought of his mother and sister. What was their fate at this moment? For that matter, what was his? Time seemed both enemy and friend. He was alive, but how soon would he know his destiny?

Kuba's words came back to him. "I believe our faith will prevail because God is with us. It is our strength the Nazis do not understand. Our faith is our strength, our measure."

He wanted the words to fill him with fresh courage, but the reality of his father's death and the atrocities he witnessed had weakened his confidence. It was difficult to hang on to hope day after day.

Finally the boy drifted once more into sleep. In his dreams he saw Sala running ahead, her dress and blond hair swirling as she ran. Her infectious laughter gave him great joy, causing him to run faster and to call out, "Flowers, sky, I love you!"

Then he did not hear her anymore. And the river's water ran red.

Abruptly Benny sat straight up, perspiring profusely. It was the same dream as before.

Is it an omen? Will I find Sala dead, as well as Mother?

Benny refused to believe this. He made his mind think of happier times, memories that would sustain him.

The boy lost track of time. It was night when the train pulled into a station. Lights illuminated a sign with German words. Hope suddenly seemed to hang by a thread. The sign might as well have read "Hades," if he were in Germany, for he felt sure the words were synonymous.

The door rolled open and Benny became part of an identical scene recently witnessed in Warsaw. He emerged from his private car and joined the hundreds of people disembarking from the train. Prodding SS guards herded the pathetic human beings like animals. The captors were the only ones who knew the destination. Benny felt they all rode on a perpetual merry-go-round in Hell.

The twentieth-century supermen barked their orders, forcing Benny into a group of young children and women. Mothers -- faces distorted in fear -- tried to soothe confused children, who tearfully and sheepishly followed the Nazis.

"*Stellt euch an! Stellt euch an!*" yelled the "supermen." Over and over they shouted to the people to get in line.

Old stuff, thought Benny. *I'm still amazed these cold villains revert to traits of caveman and maddened baboons.*

Benny found himself in the center of the group surrounded by young children. He smiled encouragingly at them, but the terrified souls could only put up their hands to ward off danger. His compulsion was to be strong in front of these children. He wiped away the beginning of tears with his sleeve.

How had he been able to resist without bending or breaking?

Confused by his good luck, he knew how fleeting it might be. He felt deep in his soul that determination for survival would empower him.

Soon a swaggering SS officer marched the people away from the train station. The feeble army of captives moved forward to his command, marching under the summer moonlight down village streets of a peaceful German village. Tidy cottages and beautiful flower gardens in full bloom staged a dream-like backdrop, a stark contrast to the herd of people dressed in drab, loose clothing, heads hung in confusion and fright. Yard dogs barked freely, while human prisoners marched, stripped of their dignity, and wide-eyed children quietly surveyed their surroundings.

After three or four kilometers, Benny noticed a high concrete block fence. Six tall structures with peaked roofs, placed at intervals along the fence, held guards surveying the area.

The group stopped at the entrance to a large gate. Above it a sign read -- "*Arbeit mact frei.*"

"*Work makes you free.*" *Are you kidding?* thought Benny. *Under Nazi rule, it enslaves and degrades both the physical body and the human spirit. That is the reality.*

The big gate swung wide to accommodate the marchers. A second fenced area surrounded the inner compound. Barbed wire, rolled at the top and strung with spools, indicated electrification. The new "guests" of Dachau Camp were unaware they had just arrived at the first concentration camp opened by the Germans in 1933.

Promising that all was well with nothing to fear, the Germans pushed their group along.

Drek! Sanctimonious bullshit!

It seemed to the youth that thousands of vacant eyes stared as the group stood in the roll call area. Several hours passed while others marched through the gates to join them.

It began -- the inevitable selection system. Benny had learned from experience that to be put in the left line usually meant extermination, the right line -- labor. As the Germans sorted men, women, and children into right and left lines, they separated families. A five-year-old child ran from his designated line to rejoin his parents.

A large Nazi, face contorted in a frown, screamed and pointed, "*Stellt euch an!*"

When the child did not respond to the orders, the German pulled his pistol and aimed it at the little boy.

"No, please!" screamed the mother.

"*Stellt euch an!*"

The child ran toward his mother. A shot punctured the night air and the little boy's back arched sharply as he fell forward onto his face. Screams from both children and parents pierced the air while the young boy, only an arm's length from his mother, lay on the ground bleeding.

By the time the selection was over, several children, ranging in age from five to ten, lay inertly on the bloody ground. The others awaited silently their fate, faces frozen in wide-eyed disbelief.

Throughout the inhuman spectacle, Benny stood with clenched fists. The muscles of his neck and shoulders knotted until they ached. He struggled not to cry. How he loathed these barbarians!

Suddenly it was Benny's turn for selection.

"You, boy, move to the left," ordered the large brute.

Left? thought Benny. *It can't be!*

Benny knew he was in imminent danger, and he followed the order. Struggling for composure, he watched carefully every move of the Nazis.

A brisk breeze had begun minutes before, shadows playing across the moon. The smell of summer rain penetrated the air, and thunder rolled in the distance as raindrops began to fall. Soon the wind blew in uneven gusts. With the rain intensifying, the beams from the huge spotlights cast down eerie light on the sordid affair. Nazis raced about, and the confused and drenched prisoners stirred restlessly.

While thunder rolled and popped all around them, the Germans, screaming through the rain at the prisoners, increased their tempo of segregation.

Suddenly a clap of thunder -- the lightning not far behind -- heightened the bad dream. Instinctively Benny made his move and jumped to the right lineup. He anticipated an angry shout or worse -- a shot. It did not come. The preoccupied Germans had not noticed his own selection.

As the separation continued, the youth stood patiently. Rain streaming over his body plastered his hair to his face. New groups marched through the gate and stood waiting. Finally, the Nazis herded Benny and his group back to the train station and on to the dreaded cattle cars.

The nightmare at Dachau would not be his. Another waited. Dachau would eventually intern more than 200,000 prisoners from thirty-seven different countries. Compulsory labor, executions, and sinister human experiments marked the camp.

It was in July 1941 that Benny experienced his brief introduction to Dachau. A mass execution in the fall of 1941 took the lives of six thousand prisoners. Certified deaths at the Dachau concentration camp numbered nearly forty thousand between 1933 and 1945.

Upon entering the car, Benny had maneuvered to the only window that was barred with several wooden planks. He estimated that at least seventy-five others shared the cattle car with him. The Germans left no food or water. If they wanted this crew for labor, they would have provided sustenance. Realizing this, Benny's mind filled with ideas of escape. At the same time, he considered a labor camp might be safer than the attempt to escape. What if there was no labor camp but something even more sinister? The thoughts seduced him.

The wooden walls and flooring of the old car reeked of animal manure. That stench, coupled with the heat and body odor of his companions and the corner toilet, seared his nostrils.

They had traveled two days. Sitting under the window and leaning against the wall of the car, Benny dozed most of the time. He knew from experience that sleep helped him retain energy and to think more clearly.

He had awakened thirsty and hungry. Intuitively he knew he could wait no longer to find a way to escape. The window was the only way out.

He pulled himself to a standing position, difficult to do with the press of people. If he could find a way to loosen the boards that slatted the small opening, he might be able to push through. Pulling at the boards was useless. He needed something with which to pry them free. A smile crossed his face, and he slid down the wall to a squatting position. He began unlacing one of his shoes. Removing it, he stood up, placing the toe of the shoe under a slat. Forcefully he pried the board. As it loosened, he hammered it away from the frame.

"Stop!" warned one man. "You will be heard!"

Benny only looked at him and began to work harder at the slats.

"Stop, boy!" said another in an angry tone. "If they catch you, they will kill us all."

Benny stopped and looked at those staring at him. "Look," he said, "we're all slated for death, so what difference does it make when we are killed?"

The others stood silently as Benny spoke. "I would rather die trying to escape than be killed like some helpless animal at their will!"

Benny turned from the group and continued hammering away at the possible escape route. Instinctively he knew he must not miss this opportunity.

As he worked industriously at the wooden slats with his newfound crowbar, the first shadowy streaks of daylight showed in the eastern sky. He had already broken two of the boards. He knew he must intensify his efforts as daylight would not be conducive to escape. Perspiration beaded his forehead, and his heart beat rhythmically with the ramming.

The others watched, fascinated at the boy's persistence. Finally Benny broke several of the boards. First, he thrust his head and shoulders through to make sure he fit. Satisfied, he hunkered again and put on his shoe, patiently lacing it. Reaching for the fracture above the window, he tried to thrust his feet out, but his hands were in an awkward position. Altering his hold by reaching outside and grasping the window top, he lunged forward as he catapulted outward.

He felt the harsh jolt to his body when he fell into the culvert and rolled several feet, some distance from the track. The pain was faint compared to the joy he felt. Simultaneously rifle fire sounded from the train car dividers. He realized others were jumping from his escape hole, one landing a short distance from him.

Benny lay quietly, detection an imminent threat. When the train had safely passed and the firing ceased, he took immediate stock of his surroundings. Through the gray dawn he saw the shape of a large bridge. He had unknowingly chosen for his escape a spot only a short distance away from the structure.

After catching his breath and getting his bearings, Benny crawled along the culvert. He came across the body of a man who lay distorted in his unorthodox grave. Another body lay on the bridge. "*If I had waited to jump,*" thought Benny, "*it could have been me in the ditch or on the bridge.*"

Saddened by their failed attempt at escape, Benny felt extremely grateful for his own good fortune. He was a seasoned veteran of escape at thirteen years old.

At the river, with the train out of sight, he stood up and walked into the woods.

——◆※◆——

The door stood ajar as Benny entered, and he walked toward the sound of voices. At the kitchen door, he stood watching his mother and Grandmother Mirke Lainveinber working. Suddenly his mother stopped her activity and turned toward the door. When she saw him, her eyes widened.

"Benick, Benick, my son! You have come back!"

She ran to her son and gathered him into her arms, smothering him with kisses and hugging him tightly.

At length Mirla turned to her mother, who stood in disbelief, both hands over her mouth. Behind her, Mirla's father rose slowly from a chair, eyes wide, a smile beginning at the corners of his mouth.

"Mama, Papa, it is Benick! He has come home." Tears streamed down her cheeks.

Grandmother Mirke held out her arms, "Benick, Benick," she sobbed. She grabbed him and kissed him repeatedly. Finally she released him but could not resist brushing his hair from his forehead, much as she had done when he was a small child. Grandfather Lajbis, laughing and crying at the same time, patted his grandson's cheeks and slapped him on the shoulder.

Benny felt safe for the first time in a long while.

Immediately the women plied him with questions.

"Let the boy rest," said Grandfather Lajbis. "He must be hungry. He will answer your questions in due time."

Reluctantly leaving his side, the two women puttered about the kitchen preparing food. Soon they laid a spread before him, and as they sat at the table watching him devour the food, the questions began.

He shared with them his miraculous escape from the train and downplayed their inquiries about his bruises. Between bites Benny recanted his trip.

"I met a man who lived near the river. He told me we were near Przytów. I couldn't believe my luck! I had lost track of time in the cattle car, but to be so near Wodzislaw when I escaped . . ."

"Truly the hand of God!" exclaimed Lajbis. "Did the man know you were a Jew?"

"I told him I was Benny Lapinsky."

"And he did not suspect?" asked his grandmother in amazement.

"He said I did not look like a Pole. I teased and told him I knew that. I told him it was too bad I did not take my looks from my beautiful blond sister." Benny had seen Sala enter the kitchen.

Smiling broadly in response, his sister pulled up a chair beside her brother and put her arms around his shoulders.

"The man laughed, obviously satisfied," said Benny. "He told me he meant no offense, but the Germans would wreck his home if he was caught harboring a Jew." The boy paused for a moment. "Should I continue?"

"Yes, yes!" cried his audience.

"I walked for a while. Around midnight I heard motorcycles approaching."

The boy stopped to drink his milk and take another bite of Grandmother Mirke's coffeecake. Everyone waited for Benny to continue.

"I hoped to avoid detection so I lay flat on the ground. When three motorcycles passed, their headlights swept from side to side almost catching me in their glare. They were so close I could hear the Germans talking and laughing, even over the roar of the cycles."

"How frightening, Benick!" Mirla cried.

If she only knew the things I've seen, thought Benny.

He smiled at his mother and said, "Well, I have learned to play the cat and mouse game with the Germans. Anyway, in the middle of the night I found a house where a man in his twenties took pity and let me stay. The next morning he took me to the train station, got me a ticket, and here I am."

Sala's eyes were wide. "It was dangerous to travel by train. Yes?"

"Sure," answered her brother, "but it's dangerous anywhere. I had to be as inconspicuous as possible. When I got on the train, I immediately saw the conductor, accompanied by two SS officers. There was no avoiding them."

The others gasped.

"I decided to meet them head on, nonchalantly. I walked toward them."

"Toward them, my son?" questioned his grandfather.

"Yes, and guess what? They ignored me and continued on! It was evident they were searching for something because they were examining packages in the overhead rack. For once I was not the prey."

When Benny finished this story, his family wanted to know about Bialystok. Benny's good fortune to escape so much disaster amazed his family. He was careful not to frighten them with unnecessary details.

Sala squeezed his shoulder. She understood. She, too, knew things she had not revealed.

"And what about your being here in Wodzislaw?" inquired Benny.

His grandparents looked at each other, a shadow of fear crossing their faces. Sala and Mirla sat quietly.

Grandfather Lajbis was the first to speak. "We have not yet been molested by the Germans, though surrounding towns have felt their brutality. Waiting for what you know will come is very hard. We wait for the Germans to create a ghetto, like in Warsaw."

Mirke reached over and placed her hand on her husband's arm.

Grandfather's pallid look concerned Benny more than the building of a ghetto. He did not agree with him. He could not imagine a wall built in such a small town.

"A Federation has been set up to supply names of laborers from Wodzislaw Jews," stated Lajbis. "Right now the jobs include cleaning the streets or working in factories. I understand if you do not appear for work, the Germans come and are quite unpleasant. Area Jewish police treat locals well but not strangers."

Mirla glanced at her son.

"I will sign up," said Benny. At the moment bravery seemed appropriate. He smiled at his mother. "It will be all right, Mother."

Mirla showed only a hint of a smile, the worry crowding her eyes. Sala sat, her head bowed.

"I think that is wise," remarked his grandfather. "You are young and have a better than fifty percent chance to come through all right."

Grandmother Mirke quickly changed the subject. Soon the family discussed the impending Friday Jewish holiday and preparation for a lavish meal. Once more Benny felt at home. It was easy to feel that everything would be all right when he was in the arms of family and traditional routine. He promised himself he would go to see his father's parents soon.

———※———

Nowhere in the world was there a fragrance like Grandmother Lipman's kitchen. Six-year old Benny sat on a stool watching the aged woman make fresh bread. He smiled as he inhaled deeply. Her hands, caressing the dough, moved like magic as she rolled and pounded it into loaves. Momentarily the first batch would emerge from the oven, and the boy would spread it with fresh butter and devour it.

"Grandmother, something happened recently that I do not understand."

"What is that, my boy?"

"I was walking home from school and someone hit me with a rock."

"Perhaps it was an accident," she had answered, not missing a beat with the kneading of the bread.

"No," he answered, "he meant me harm. He called me a filthy Jew. I don't know why someone would want to harm me for nothing."

"Benick, come here." Cerke held out her arms, and the six-year-old Benny moved into them. "Sometimes these things happen. Who knows? Remember, you are a good boy." They had stood for a long time embracing, the boy welcoming the safe feeling.

Startled from these memories, Benny, now a veteran of abuse, turned to see Grandmother Lipman standing in the kitchen door. The boy did not know how long he had sat in the kitchen remembering his visits to his father's childhood home. He longed for those days.

"Benick, what are you thinking? Daydreaming?"

"Oh, I was just remembering a time when I was little and I was here in the kitchen while you were making bread."

Cerke smiled. "To me you are still little, Benick."

Benny wished it were that simple. He smiled at his grandmother and rose to accept her huge hug.

"That's a good boy," she said welcoming the opportunity to embrace him again. "Your grandfather has awakened from his nap. Why don't you join him on the front porch?"

Benny moved toward the door.

"Benick?"

Benny turned back to his grandmother.

"We are so glad you came to see us. We are very old. It is nice when our grandchildren think of us."

"I love you, Grandmother."

"I know," she answered. "I love you always. You remember that."

A sense of farewell sounded in her voice. Benny moved away from her reluctantly.

His grandfather sat in a high-backed, oak rocker. Benny had seen it in the very same place on this porch for as long as he could remember.

The large porch wrapped around the old house, and from there one could see the fields stretch to what seemed "forever" to young eyes. It was a very pleasant place to be. Benny and Sala had played here as children, sometimes leaving the porch to climb the large oak tree nearby or to scamper freely through the meadow.

To Benny, Duvet Lipman was ageless. He could not remember how his grandfather looked without the silver hair and the long beard worn by many Jews his age. His tall frame still filled the rocker. The wrinkled face and ready smile had not changed. Duvet's eyes brightened the moment he saw his grandson.

Benny moved quickly to the rocker and kneeled down beside the old man, allowing his grandfather's long arms to encircle him.

"Benick, I am glad to see you."

"Me, too, Grandfather."

"Sit. We will talk."

Benny slid his grandmother's rocker next to Grandfather Lipman.

"How long can you stay, my boy?"

"Until morning."

"Good! Good!"

"I must return and sign up for the Federation."

"I see."

A silence stretched between them. Each hesitated to speak of Aaron.

Finally, Duvet said, "Benick, I know the circumstances of your father's death. Sala came to visit."

Benny did not answer. He had not talked about his father since his death. A throbbing began in his throat.

"You are strong, my boy. You will go through many valleys. Do not dwell in the chasm and wonder what is on the other side of the mountain. Climb the mountain and stand on top! Fear of the unknown will only deplete your energy." Duvet reached over and placed his knurled hand on the boy's knee. "What happened to your father, happened."

Benny looked thoughtfully at his grandfather, unashamed of the tears that rolled down his cheeks. Duvet raised his hand to his grandson's face and wiped away a tear.

"Your father was a good man, and now there is you. Ask God to speak to you, Benick, at your moment of need."

The boy took his grandfather's hand into his.

"When you are feeling the absence of God," continued the old man, "remember that love sometimes comes in disguised ways, sometimes through the heart of a friend. Do you understand?"

"Yes sir." Benny thought of Kuba.

"Everyone needs hope -- goals. It is up to you to create your own future. The mark of youth is driving compassion." Duvek Lipman smiled and whispered, "Thank goodness."

Benny would remember the feelings of security and love and the smell of fresh bread when he visited the Lipman farm. The memories would often sustain him through the hard times.

Before dinner, Benny saddled one of his grandfather's beautiful Arabians. As he rode into the late afternoon, a gentle breeze brushed the boy's face, and he breathed fresh air for the first time in two years. The horse seemed to understand his rider's ecstasy, and he moved in pace to the rapture of the moment. At the river they paused; a golden ray of sunlight touched the water, creating streaks of shimmering sparkle.

It seemed to Benny he had been asleep for years, dreaming the nightmare, and now he relished these moments of peace. He jumped from the horse and lay on the meadow grass beside the bubbling stream. Yellow flowers and soft, swaying grass beat a rhythm of summer grace. A soothing tranquility spread over him. It would have to last a long time. If one could measure serenity, its magnitude reached the far corners of the meadow.

Benny reported to work detail the day after he registered. After distributing shovels to the laborers, German SS and Jewish policemen marched the group to a highway where they worked in ten-man crews, five on each side of the road. The prisoners shoveled gravel with only a half-hour break for lunch. At sunset the guards dismissed the workers from the detail and marched them back to the Federation building.

It all seemed so simple. Under these working conditions, Benny could live with his family and do day work.

The next assignment was at Sedieszów, a small town between Kielce and Wodzislaw. There, he joined a detail crew loading and unloading high explosives and putting bombs onto carts brought in by trains or onto the rail cars for distribution. Stored bombs, covered with tarpaulin to protect them from the rain and snow, remained at the train station.

Each day, German trucks transported two hundred men and boys to the work site. Five hundred Jews from all over Poland comprised the workforce. Beatings left many crippled for life when they refused to work on the Sabbath.

After three weeks of labor, the Germans assigned Benny to Schultz Construction, a private German company located on the outskirts of Sedieszów. There, also, were the impatient and cruel foremen who dealt severely with the laborers.

The days were long, and for the next few weeks the boy helped lay new train tracks and dig trenches for electric conduits. After awhile, the German construction supervisor released Benny to go home for further sign up.

—◆ ✳ ◆—

"Benny, I'm glad you're home at last. Come inside quickly. We must talk." Sala's relaxed demeanor had vanished. Dark circles under her eyes showed she had slept little.

"What has happened?" he questioned.

She took her brother's hand and led him into the house. The once neat living room lay in shambles, furniture in pieces. Pale and speaking breathlessly, she continued, "They came last night, kicking in the door before we could reach it."

Benny put his hand on his sister's shoulder. "It's all right, Sala. Calm down. What else happened?"

"The SS, demanding the whereabouts of someone named Horowitz, shoved their way into the room. No one knew who he was, but the Germans ranted and raved."

Choked by tears, Sala's voice trailed off. Benny put his arms around her, holding her until the sobs stopped.

"They threatened all of us with extermination if the man was not found," she cried. "I pleaded. I told them the man was not in the house nor had we seen him, but they wouldn't listen. They shoved me aside and began overturning anything that could hide someone."

"You were very brave, Sala. What happened then?"

"Finally at two thirty this morning, the maniacs called off their search. They probably went off to molest some other family."

"Where is everyone now?"

"In the kitchen, talking with Cousin Stephen. He's trying to get our grandparents to leave."

As the two entered the room, Stephen pleaded with Lajbis to consider leaving immediately.

"Under no circumstances, Stephen, will I run."

"But don't you understand, Grandpa," Stephen persisted, "the Jewish Federation is being forced to supply names of various families for work details. It's not the usual work detail. Everyone believes it's just pretense. These families are being sent to Sandomiez, who knows what for!"

"Here is Benny," said Lajbis, looking up. "He will say we do not need to leave our home."

All eyes turned to the young boy. Mirla patted the chair beside her, and Benny sat down.

Benny wondered how he could make Grandfather see the inevitable danger and not frighten mother. It was the same story with his other grandparents.

Stephen turned to Benny for assistance. "By this morning twelve persons were killed as a result of last night's search. The SS won't stop there. You know, and I know this, Benny. We've talked. You understand."

"I know nothing about Sandomiez, but I will tell you this -- if it is as I suspect, there is cause for worry."

His grandfather sputtered in disbelief.

"Grandfather," Benny looked thoughtfully at the old man. "I don't wish to bring bad news, but I suspect the public has no knowledge of Sandomiez. If they did, they would panic."

"Oh, my God!" cried Mirla. "I thought we were safe in Wodzislaw!"

Sala moved close to her mother.

"I am aware of incidents where families are already being segregated," said Stephen. "I heard this morning that the Gestapo, Polish police, and Ukrainians surrounded a village called Dzialoszyce yesterday. It is only a short distance from here. Some of the younger people have escaped and come to Wodzislaw."

"Are you certain, Stephen?" asked Benny.

"Yes," he answered emphatically. "I learned that people tried to hide in attics and other places but to no avail. One Jewish family paid a Polish farmer to hide them in his farmhouse, only fifteen kilometers from here. The Nazis axed the Jewish family to death in their beds and severely punished the Poles."

"My God, Stephen, must you be so graphic?" reprimanded Lajbis.

"Grandfather, listen!" said Benny. "It's necessary for you and Grandmother to leave now!"

"We will not leave," answered Mirke, taking her husband's hand in hers. "We will stay in our home."

Mirla looked at her parents, tears streaming down her cheeks. She glanced at Benny. He knew her question and answered it.

"Yes, Mother, we must leave -- you, Sala, and I."

"You should," said Mirke to her daughter. "You and your children run to safety. Understand, we must stay here."

"A warning . . ." said Stephen to Benny, "do not speak of your plans to anyone. Do not ask questions. Germans are plying both Poles and Jews with gifts and money to get information. Of course, in the end it only delays what they will do to them."

"Any ideas where we should go, cousin?"

"You might try Sedieszów. You know Sedieszów and the construction opportunities. Perhaps you can find work as a Pole, then make your decision."

"I know the area," said Benny, looking at his mother and sister. "We'll leave this evening."

A cloak of despair fell over the household. At dusk, sounds of gunfire echoed from the Village Square. As it grew dark, Benny waited for the right moment. Mirla and Sala stood by with a duffel bag containing extra clothing and food.

The lights of the German vehicles on their way to the marketplace flashed into the shuttered rooms and illuminated the walls with ominous stripes of light. Once a group had passed, Benny motioned for his mother and sister to follow closely. Benny used the less traveled streets for their escape. His eyes, trained to the darkness, observed every shadow, and he listened carefully for unusual activity.

Soon they were on the outskirts of town. It was close to midnight when they came to a cluster of farmhouses.

From behind them, they heard the sound of a truck approaching. Benny pointed to a barn about fifty yards from the road.

"Sala," whispered Benny. "Run for the barn and stay low to the ground. I'll bring Mother."

Benny shifted the duffel to his left shoulder and grabbed his mother's arm. Just as the headlights showed on the road, the three reached the barn, Mirla breathing heavily. Benny motioned for Mirla and Sala to move to the side of the barn away from the road and to crouch on the ground. After peering around the corner to observe the truck, Benny followed.

It passed, followed closely by another. The wailing human occupants broke the night silence as the trucks sped to their destination.

After resting for a while, they walked most of the night. At dawn they passed a group of people headed in the direction of Wodzislaw. Benny cautioned them as to what might await them, but they ignored him and continued walking toward their destiny.

Two days later, the roundup of Wodzislaw Jews for deportation to Sandomiez began. Lajbis Lainveinber died of a heart attack shortly before the roundup. Though the Wodzislaw library records show the history of both the Lipman and Lainveinber families, there is no trace of Duvet and Cerke Lipman, or Mirke Lainveinber and the many relatives of that area.

Early in 1945 Wodzislaw became the distribution center for sixty-six thousand evacuees, mainly Jews from overcrowded Auschwitz and its satellite camps. The prisoners boarded freight trains for extermination camps. It was a desperate attempt by the Germans to speed the demise of the Jewish populace before their liberation.

Europe
Major Nazi Camps
1943-1944

Map is a sketch with approximate distances.
Information: Courtesy of
United States Holocaust Memorial Museum
(USHMM)

E designates extermination camp
C designates concentration camp

Germany
1 Buchenwald	C	9 Columbia Haus	C
2 Dachau	C	10 Dora-München	C
3 Bergen-Belsen	C	11 Sachsenburg	C
4 Ravensbruck	C	12 Gross-Rosen	C
5 Flossenburg	C	13 Lichtenburg	C
6 Esterwegen	C	14 Niederhagen	C
7 Neuengamme	C	15 Oranienburg	C
8 Sachsenhausen	C	16 Wewelsburg	C

Poland
1 Auschwitz-Birkenau	CE
2 Lublin-Majdanel	CE
3 Belzec	E
4 Treblinka	E
5 Chelmno	E
6 Plaszow	C
7 Sobibor	E

Estonia
1 Klooga	C
2 Valvara	C

Yugoslavia
1 Jasenovac	C
2 Sajmiste	C

Latvia
1 Kaiserwald	C

Lithuania
1 Provieiski	C

Prussia
1 Stuthof	C

Austria
1 Mauthausen	C

Netherlands
1 Vught	C

France
1 Natzweiler-Struthof	C

ELEVEN

"ARE YOU MR. MARONSKI?" asked the scrawny boy, standing with his cap in hand.

It was mid-afternoon, and the Polish engineer was standing at his office window when the voice sounded behind him.

"Yes. Who are you?"

"My name is Benny Lapinski. I'm looking for work."

Maronski looked at him a moment then returned to his desk and sat down. He began to shuffle papers. "Have you construction experience?"

"Yes," lied Benny.

The Pole looked up from his papers. "Mortar? Carpentry? What?"

Benny hesitated. "To the tell truth, sir, I've done mostly road work and cutting trees, but I'm a hard worker. I have very strong hands, and I learn quickly. Also I can speak several languages."

"How old are you?"

"Fifteen."

Maronski raised his eyebrows. "Fifteen!" he said, looking as though he did not believe the boy. "Twelve or thirteen, maybe?"

"I am strong. I can do the work," said Benny convincingly.

Maronski smiled. "Well, I will put you on probation, and we will see. Fair enough?"

Benny nearly jumped with glee. "Yes sir! Yes."

"I will tell the foreman in charge of supplies to put you to work immediately."

"Right now?" he questioned.

"Yes. Is there something wrong?"

The tall mustached man seemed genuinely kind and had listened. Yet Benny was reluctant to tell him about the plight of his family. He stood, shifting from one foot to the other.

"Sir, I have my mother and sister with me . . ."

"With you?" interrupted Maronski. "You are not from around here?"

"No sir. I need to find a place for them to stay before I start work."

There, it was out. Maronski would have to deal with it.

Benny watched nervously as the engineer shuffled papers on his desk. He looked up at Benny.

"You say you speak several languages? Do you speak German?"

"Yes." The scrawny teenager stood with his cap in hand. "Yes sir."

"And Hebrew?"

"Yiddish, sir, but I've studied Hebrew." Instantly Benny recognized the trick. He waited, his heart pounding.

"Interesting," answered Maronski watching Benny closely. "Perhaps you will be helpful to us. We will be using some Jewish labor." He waited for Benny's response.

With a noncommittal face, Benny answered, "I'd be glad to help, sir." He thought he noticed a slight smile on the Pole's face.

"Lapinski, is it? There is a man by the name of Spira who owns a large estate not far from here. In fact, he owns several lumberyards in the area. Perhaps he can provide room and board for your relatives in exchange for work. You don't mind asking a Jew, do you?"

Without waiting for the boy's answer, Maronski began writing something on a piece of paper. "Here are the directions. Get them settled today and come to work tomorrow."

Benny smiled broadly. "Thank you, sir. Thank you." He took the paper and nearly ran from Maronski's office.

Benny looked back to see Maronski watching from the window. Did he suspect his mother and sister waited somewhere out of sight? From the window the man smiled as though he was pleased with his decision, then he turned away. Benny ran across the yard and onto the road. He could hardly wait to tell his mother and Sala the good news.

—————※—————

The brick structure, surrounded by stacks of building supplies and parked equipment, sat in the middle of the compound. A foreman stood on the office steps and barked orders to a group of men. The workers listened intently to the square-bodied man with the weathered face.

Maronski, coming out of his office, stopped for a moment to talk with his foreman who handed him a piece of paper. The large Pole glanced at the paper and then searched the crowd. When he saw Benny, he smiled and approached him.

"Find a place for your family, son?"

"Yes sir. Thank you. Mr. Spira was very nice. He will give my mother and sister room and board as long as he can." Benny was not sure how much more he should say. "I understand the project is taking place on some of his land."

"That is true, young man," answered Maronski. "Now are you ready for your duty assignment?"

"Yes sir."

"You will be carrying building supplies to the area for a few days. By the way, do you have a place to stay?"

"Mr. Spira offered to let me stay there until I could make other arrangements."

"Good. I will ask around here for a place. Perhaps there will be some room in the compound barracks."

Without another word, Maronski walked away.

Benny's first day on the job involved carrying supplies in a sling across his back. The absence of guards made the task easier and certainly more pleasant. Maronski provided both a good lunch and time to rest. With the stay at Wodzislaw and work here, there was some promise he would gain back his weight.

Perhaps I can stay here until the end of the war.

Benny allowed himself to hope that he could stay. Yet his conversation with Zalme Spira had been disconcerting. The older Jew, who housed his mother and sister, acknowledged he did not trust the Germans and wished he had gotten his family to a neutral country when he had the chance. If he did not feel safe, how could Benny believe he and his family would be? Still the opportunity to be in Maronski's employ excited him.

By the third day, Maronski's foreman assigned Benny the task of loading sand into the cement mixers. His foreman was Polish, and though he often barked his orders, he was not cruel.

Within days the SS marched Jews into the camp. When they arrived, few changes occurred, other than the larger population of workers were Poles, a few serving as guards. The difference between the Pole and Jew workers was salary -- the Poles received pay for their work; the Jews worked as slave laborers.

As the days passed, the houses took shape, and Benny learned lessons about the construction business.

Maronski often stopped where Benny worked.

"I really love the job," exclaimed Benny to Maronski one day. "I'd like to work for you until the war is over." He hoped he had not said too much.

Maronski smiled as he placed his hand on the boy's shoulder. "Nothing is impossible, Benny. My supervisors tell me that you are a good worker and efficient in every job they give you."

Benny beamed. It meant a great deal to him to get this man's praise. He watched Maronski walk away. The large Pole stopped and looked back at the youngster and said, "Benny, I certainly will do all that I can to protect you as long as it is within my power to do so."

He knows! He knows but is willing to help me!

Tears filled the boy's eyes.

"Do you think we can outlast them?" asked Sala as she turned to her confidante.

"I'm praying so," answered the youth. "We deserve to."

Benny had joined his sister for the occasional walk they managed between chores. He pulled his jacket closer to his body to brace against the fresh snow that lightly covered the fields where they walked. It was late September when they first arrived in Sedieszów. After three months of living quietly, they still expected the worst.

The two had found a fallen tree and sat down on its trunk.

"Does the silence frighten you?" she asked.

Knowing what she meant, Benny looked at her. "I would be lying if I said no. Sometimes, even during the sounds of construction, the heavy silence of impending danger lurks, and I'm distracted in my thoughts."

"I know," said Sala, almost whispering. She sighed deeply. "Benny, there are things that I have not told you."

"You don't need to, Sala."

"Sometimes I feel they weigh very heavy on my heart and need to be said."

"I know the feeling. There is a rock on my heart also. I pray that someday it will go away."

"Benny?"

"Yes?"

"They made me do terrible things. I don't think I could do them again."

He did not respond.

"They made me . . ."

"You don't have to tell me, Sala."

Suddenly the dam within Sala broke, and she talked of atrocities Benny had not even imagined. She told of being made to remove her blouse and to use it to clean toilets. Afterwards the Nazis ordered her to wipe her face with the same garment and put it on. She had seen women forced to eat human feces and wash in Nazi urine.

Benny tried not to show his horror at what his sister said. He did not meet her eye but placed his arm gently around her shoulders. Where was he when this was happening to her?

"The things they've done to my body, Benny!" Sala's voice broke into sobs.

"Shhh, shhh," whispered Benny. "Don't torture yourself, Sala. I love you, no matter what. Do you understand?"

"Benny, I'd rather die than go through that again. I feel so helpless, so small in the universe. Sometimes I compare myself to a drab, helpless little *wróbel*."

"A little bird? That's interesting." Taking his sister's hand in his, Benny smiled. "Sala, remember the family of sparrows that nested near Grandfather Lipman's farmhouse? They were dull brown and small, but fearless. They would fly away from prey with a loud warbling -- *tek, tek*. Remember?"

Sala smiled as she lay her head on her brother's shoulder. "They were survivors weren't they?"

"Yes, like us."

"You're my sparrow, Benny. Do you know that? I thank the Lord for a brother like you." She began to cry quietly.

Benny placed a hand on her cheek and smoothed away a tear. He had no answers. He was merely a teenager who loved his sister and hated what they both had to endure.

Snowflakes caressed the countryside with virginal beauty, and brother and sister, who had lost their innocence before their time, sat arm in arm. Sala's unrestrained sobs made the only sound.

It was noon when Benny knocked on Maronski's door.

"Sir, I've brought you a gift for Rosh Hashanah!" said Benny with boyish delight. There were no more secrets between the two.

Maronski looked puzzled.

"I would like to sing for you."

The large Pole grinned, gesturing for the boy to begin. Benny, immediately breaking into a hearty voice, sang a familiar Polish folk song.

The wide smile softened Maronski's weathered face. Hitting his hands together with a loud smack, he cried, "Bravo, *Śpiewak*! Bravo, singer! Benny, what a nice surprise! You have a good voice! Have you ever sung on the radio?"

Thinking his boss teased him, Benny answered, "No sir. I was very young when the war started."

"I am very pleased with the songs! As a matter of fact, I would consider it a great privilege if you came every day at lunch to sing for me. I will see that you get extra rations."

Elated with Maronski's response, Benny returned to work and doubled his output. Feeling like a human being was better than all the money in the world.

During the first weeks of January 1942, a worried Maronski called Benny into his office.

"Benny, the Germans are intensifying their efforts to round up all remaining Jews. I wanted you to be aware. I do not know how safe Spira's home is or how safe you are."

A knot formed immediately in Benny's stomach.

"What do you want me to do, sir?" he asked.

"Continue seeing your family. Be very careful, very observant. The Germans may visit any day. As long as you work for me, I will try to protect you."

Benny felt such love for this man! "Thank you, sir."

"You understand there are no guarantees."

"Yes sir. I am grateful for your kindness."

"You are welcome, Benny Lapinski."

Since Benny moved into the barracks at the work site, he had not seen his family daily. Now the Pole's words of foreboding fell heavily on his heart. He would need to make plans to visit his mother and sister soon. Little did he realize how quickly Maronski's warning would come true.

Two days later, as Benny pushed a wheelbarrow of sand to a cement mixer, he heard a loud shouting. He looked up to see the dark brown uniforms of the Waffin -- thirty or forty German SS led by several large German police dogs on leashes. Selected as Hitler's elite, they wore the *Tolenkopf* on the right collar. These SS guards, who wore the death's head insignia, were the worst of the lot, cruel and with a solitary goal -- death to the enemy.

Two German officers stood by, as SS guards screamed their orders.

"*Achtung! Achtung!*"

In the yard the laborers stood at attention and removed their hats, waiting nervously for the unknown. The Germans began to call the names of the Jewish laborers.

First, they segregated the thirty Jewish women. The selection of men followed. The guards grabbed each one roughly by the arm and shoved the Jew into line.

Advancing down the line of remaining workers, an SS officer stopped directly in front of Benny. His eyes narrowing and his hatchet jaw locking in determination, the officer stared at the youth.

Benny felt sure his heart would stop.

Abruptly the Nazi jerked the boy from the line.

"Leave the boy!" A voice sounded from the office steps. "He is Polish."

"Is that what he told you?" asked the Nazi, watching Maronski walk toward him.

"Why would you think otherwise?" said Maronski with great authority.

"I can smell him." The other Nazis laughed uproariously.

"Okay," said Maronski. "You take him."

Benny's eyes widened with disbelief.

The Pole looked into the eyes of the Nazi and pointed his finger. "When I ask for five in his place -- by tomorrow -- we will see what your commander says. I don't think he will be too pleased that you steal from my crew a person who is doing an outstanding job for the Fatherland!"

Without changing expression, the SS officer struck Maronski, first on the left cheek, next on the right. Blood gushed from the Pole's nose.

The workers caught their breath. No one moved.

Out of the corner of his eye, Benny saw another German approach. He walked with a limp.

"What is going on here?" The approaching German called out.

"The Pole engineer is protecting a filthy Jew," answered the SS guard.

"Jesse, is that right?"

Maronski turned toward Hermann, wiping the blood from his nose. "This jerk . . ."

The angry Nazi vaulted toward the Pole, but Hermann put up his hand to stop him. "Go on, Jesse."

"This scoundrel," repeated Maronski, looking into the face of the Nazi, "is trying to sabotage the work."

The Nazi, trembling, moved toward the Pole again. Hermann shot him a warning look. He stopped.

"He's trying to take one of my best workers! If I had more men like this one, your housing project would be done in half the time!"

Hermann watched closely. Finally, he motioned for the Nazis to move out with those they had selected. With a fierce stare, the angry Nazi looked back at Maronski and reluctantly marched away.

"Tell your men to return to work!" said Hermann firmly.

Benny turned to leave.

"Not you," said Hermann. "You follow me to your supervisor's office."

Puzzled, both Maronski and Benny obeyed the officer's directive.

Once inside the office, Maronski asked, "Why do you want the boy in here?"

"I want him near by, Jesse."

"I told you he is one of my best workers."

"I know what you told me. And since you have been so kind with your praise, perhaps he will consider what could happen to you if you harbor a Jew." Hermann stared directly at the boy.

Benny wanted to look at Maronski but did not dare.

"Hell, Louis, you know me better than that. We were classmates once. You know I'm just a scruffy son-of-a-bitch who likes women and hates politics."

Benny tried not to show his surprise at the classmate information.

Hermann's mouth hinted at a smile. "I have more orders for you." He handed Maronski a set of papers and waited for the Pole to read them.

"My self respect directly parallels your work, Jesse," said Hermann.

Maronski put down the orders he was reading and looked closely at Louis Hermann. His eyes met those of the German officer and held his glance, a smile spreading across his handsome face.

Hermann boldly met his stare.

Finally Maronski spoke, "Louis are you trying to tell me that your damned self-respect is more important than my ability to complete the project as I see fit?"

"It is all the same!" said Hermann, gesturing with his hands.

"Do I continue using my judgment or does everything hinge on your ego?"

Benny wondered if Maronski knew he was close to over-stepping his bounds. Perhaps he was relying on their past friendship, not the importance of Hermann with the Third Reich.

Hermann pulled up a chair to Maronski's desk and sat down opposite him. He reached for the polished box with the expensive cigars and took one. As he lighted it smoke circled around his face, the pungent odor immediately filling the small office.

"Jesse, I know your talents. After all, you graduated top in our class at university. If anyone knows the engineering of construction, you do."

Maronski smiled at Hermann's humility.

"And as I remember, you were not far behind me in university honors. I find it intriguing that you joined the German army engineering corps -- the very army that now holds my country hostage."

Hermann smiled, obviously enjoying the histrionics.

"How ironic," continued Maronski, "that you are the conqueror, giving me orders in my homeland!"

"You took on this project by my recommendation, Jesse. It will certainly make you money and put you into the good graces of your captors."

"My captors!" exclaimed Maronski. The tall, athletic man leaned forward in his chair. "Louis, I need not feel like a prisoner to do a good job! You want a large, well-built housing project for the families of the Germans stationed in the area? I will build it, but I will follow the specifications I feel appropriate." The tall Pole looked sternly at the German officer.

Benny did not move a muscle, fascinated by the discourse of the two former schoolmates.

Hermann leaned back in his chair, puffed on his cigar, and analyzed Maronski, neither breaking the silence.

At last Hermann said, "I trust you will do a good job for the Fatherland."

Maronski grinned at Hermann's "Fatherland" remark.

Benny sensed that Hermann was wrong if he thought it would persuade Maronski. He knew the Polish engineer recognized the Germans need for the construction and for Maronski's skill in directing the project.

"You will be given permission to hire more area Poles, and we will obtain more free Jewish labor for you. Schultz Construction may have some overflow of workers we can use."

"Thank you. The added workers will help," answered Maronski.

Hermann stood up as though to leave. He stepped toward Maronski. The only flaw in his otherwise perfectly uniformed and conservative demeanor was a slight limp in the left leg.

"The old leg still bothering you, Louis?" grinned Maronski. "That's what you get for getting into barroom fights. Those stab wounds don't go away easily. As I remember, that particular brawl had something to do with politics. Right?"

"That's true, my friend. Those were the days -- pretty university girls, parties and political debates."

"Yeah, politics then and Hitler's ideological business now."

Benny could not believe the Pole said it. The boy glanced at Hermann. A frown quickly spread to the German's face, but as abruptly, it faded, and he laughed.

Realizing he had almost stepped over the line, Maronski smiled. "How about a drink for old times sake?" he asked. He reached toward the stand that held a bottle of whiskey and a tray of glasses.

Before Hermann could answer, Maronski asked, "Can I send this boy back to work? We've got a deadline, here!" The Pole poured the drink and handed it to Hermann.

The German took the whiskey, drank it, and motioned for Benny to leave. "Remember what I said, boy!"

The rest of the day Benny occupied himself with his task as he tried not to think of the German's words. He felt torn between his own survival and the safety of the man who had been so kind to him.

Sleep did not come easily that night, ominous thoughts filling Benny's mind. Unable to shake a strong premonition, he rose early the next morning and made his way to the Spira estate.

Fresh snow lay on the ground.

As he approached the mansion, he noticed no smoke rising from the chimney. By this time, the fireplace should have been lit. Benny knocked on the front door. No one answered. He opened the door and entered the house.

Silence.

As he entered the living area, he saw Zalme Spira sitting in a wing chair reading from the Chumash. Tears streamed down Spira's face.

"Mr. Spira, what is it?"

The old man looked up, his face red and wet.

"Mr. Spira?"

The man motioned for the youth to sit on the stool beside him. Benny obeyed even as the knot began to form in his stomach.

"The Germans came and took my family."

"When?"

"During the night."

"My God, where is Mother . . . and Sala. . .?"

"I do not know!" cried the man. "They went for a walk yesterday afternoon -- to the village, I think."

"To the village? Why?" Benny stood up, anxious for the man's answer.

"I don't know. As far as I know, they did not return last night. They are not in the house."

Benny could not control the shaking that began deep in his body. He jumped up and ran out the door. Heading directly toward the village, he hoped to locate someone who could help him find his mother and sister. The boy found no answers at two of the homes bordering the estate.

At the third house, a man told him he saw Germans loading large groups of people into cattle cars late the day before. "Never have I seen such cruelty! It made my heart ache!"

When Benny gave him a description of Mirla and Sala, the man was not able to say if they were among the group.

The last house that bordered the Spira estate sat on the outskirts of the village, very near the train depot. A Polish woman in her sixties opened the door to Benny's knock.

"What do you want? Have you escaped from work?"

Benny, surprised by her question stammered, "No! No."

"Are you hungry?" she asked. "If you are Jewish, please do not be afraid. I will not turn you in. Perhaps I can help you."

"Thank you, but I'm looking for my family. My mother and sister work at the Spira house."

Her face darkened.

"What's wrong?"

"My husband works for Mr. Spira. I have been at his house, and I have seen your family."

"Go on."

"Son, don't you want to come inside?" The woman spoke in a hushed tone, her eyes avoiding the boy's.

"No!" cried Benny, recognizing the shift in her look.

"It is all right -- I understand." Tears began to well in her eyes. She looked at the boy. "I don't know how to tell you this . . ."

Benny waited.

"Yesterday I saw the Germans trying to separate your mother and sister. Your sister screamed, tore herself away from the German SS, and ran to her mother."

The woman stopped, pondering how to form her words.

"Yes? Yes? Go on," begged Benny.

"I . . ."

"Please, you must tell me what happened."

"The Nazi in charge drew his pistol and . . ."

Benny's breath caught in his throat. Trembling, he sat down on the porch step. The woman sat beside him and placed a hand on his shoulder.

"My son, he shot your sister, and that is not all. Your Mother started screaming loudly, her whole body writhing in great mortal pain. They told her to be quiet." The woman's voice broke and she began to sob. "The Germans -- they killed her -- with a single bullet! I am so sorry!"

Benny's body froze as the full impact of her words hit him.

"I do not want to tell you this, but I saw it with my own eyes. Never have I seen anything so brutal! As God is my witness, I would not lie to you about something like this!"

Benny stared at her blankly.

"I . . . I have to leave," he said looking away from her.

As he rose, the woman leaned forward and touched him on the shoulder.

He turned from the woman and walked slowly from the house as though mechanically manipulated by some unknown force. Benny felt the very life squeezed out of his body.

He had gone almost a hundred yards when the tears came, a deluge blinding him, almost obliterating the railroad yard directly in front of him. It lay like a ghostly scene, devoid of cattle cars and people.

Benny wiped his tears and began searching along the tracks, hoping to find something. He did not know what. Ultimately he came to the end of the rail yard. He heard only a deafening silence and saw no evidence of yesterday's occurrence, fresh snow having covered the ground.

The boy climbed onto a pile of gravel used for track beds. He stood for a moment and surveyed the landscape as far as he could see. Being seen by a German patrol was the last thing on his mind.

What is it I expect to see -- my mother and sister lying in bloody, dirty snow, their bodies ripped by cold steel, their precious blood flowing from their wounds? He sat down. *How did their faces look in death -- twisted?*

Benny shuddered. The Nazis had brought on this grotesque and perverted thought! Benny knew deep inside no medicine existed that could ever cure the sickness festering within his body.

He sat with his legs drawn to his chest and his chin resting on his folded arms. Anyone seeing the boy would have thought he was daydreaming.

He was still sitting there when Maronski found him.

TWELVE

NIGHTMARES INVADED BENNY'S SLEEP. Each time he awakened, heavy sweat drenched him. Asleep or awake he could not escape the hell. For the first time, he had grave doubts about his own salvation and questioned whether life held any meaning.

The day Maronski found him and took him to his own quarters, he broke finally. All of the emotional strain flooded into hysteria. Benny knew his very soul and heart ached with an agony that nothing could heal. He was unsure sanity would return.

He sensed others in the room with him -- a worker who took care of him during the day and the big Pole, who talked him through the phantasm that threatened him at night.

In the evening of the eighth day, Benny heard familiar sounds. An orchestra played an elegant melody, transporting him to his family's living room on Ogrodowa Street in Warsaw. He recognized the aroma of his father's pipe, and he heard the sweet sounds of Mozart's *Die Zauberflöte,* which sent soothing echoes throughout his body.

Benny sat in bed awhile trying to focus on his surroundings. At last he climbed out and walked into the next room. The Pole sat by the fireplace, his head tilted back, his eyes closed. Beside him a phonograph played.

"I will not be denied my life!"

Startled, Maronski raised his head and looked toward the voice. When he saw Benny, he smiled and motioned for him to come near the fireplace.

As Benny sat down on the hearth, Maronski took a shawl from his chair and wrapped it around the youth's shoulders.

"What was it you said just now?" asked Maronski.

"I said, 'I will not be denied my life.'"

A quick smile dimpled Maronski's cheeks and deepened the creases around his eyes. "*Dobry*! Good!" he said softly.

The fire crackled and hissed in the fireplace, the only sounds in the room. Benny watched the flames, the light revealing the gaunt face. Finally he spoke. "My grandfather Lipman once said to me that I would go through many valleys. He cautioned me not to dwell there because it would deplete my energy."

The youth looked toward Maronski. The large man smiled but did not speak.

Benny continued. "He also said that love could come through the heart of a friend. He was right. He would call you a *mensch*. Your kindness means more than I can ever say."

Embarrassed at the compliment, the Pole blushed and grinned at the boy.

"It would not be fair to my family if I gave in to men who have lost their reason. I will do all within my power to defy their cruelty."

"I know you will, Benny. I am sorry I cannot do more for you, and I am sorry about your family! You could not help it. Nobody could. None of us knows what is in store for us."

It was not until later that Benny fully understood Maronski's meaning. The Pole himself did not feel safe from molestation by the Germans. No one was safe.

It was late January 1942. Light snow and rainy days did not stop Maronski's project for the Germans. Benny put himself into a heavy work schedule. Somehow this helped the slow healing process.

It was almost noon, and Benny had just delivered siding to the project site when he saw movement in the northwest field. A horde of Germans, led by their dogs, swept down on the workers. Close to a hundred SS guards escorted a large group of prisoners -- men, women, and children.

Maronski saw them shortly after Benny. He moved quickly to the youth. "Go immediately to my office!"

Benny walked in the direction of the compound as inconspicuously as possible, but he was too late. The SS guard with whom Maronski had his earlier conflict yelled, "Halt!"

The boy did not know whether to run or stay. He decided his chances were better if he did not run.

The German walked toward Maronski shouting, "Get lost Polish pig! Stop trying to protect the Jews and you will live longer!"

"Before you take this boy, let me say something," said the Pole.

"You can say nothing that I want to hear," sneered the Nazi. "You, boy, get into line with the others!"

What Benny and Maronski had most feared was now taking place. The Pole stood by helplessly as Benny joined the line of prisoners numbering close to three hundred.

Soon they marched away from the building site. Eyes filling with tears, Benny turned to look once more at the man who had befriended him. Maronski stood motionless, a vacant, haunted look in his eyes.

The boy's honored Polish friend was the closest thing to a father and family member that Benny had left. He wondered if he would ever see him again.

The steel door slammed shut, the bolt falling noisily into place. Even the January cold could not mask the foul odors engulfing the confined quarters. By now Benny had learned what happens to the body when it has not had enough food. The stench of human gases seared his nostrils, and the foul, unclean bodies suffering from dysentery caused him to choke. It seemed forever before Benny, who was accustomed to the open air, could quiet the nausea.

Benny shared the cramped quarters of the cattle car with eighty to ninety persons, mostly boys and young men. Simply shifting one's body was difficult. The only positive thing about the insanity was that the closeness of the bodies provided warmth from the January chill.

"Where are they taking us? Does anybody know?" Benny's matter-of-fact questions startled the man standing next to him.

"I think we are going to a labor camp," he answered.

"No," said another. "They are taking us out into the woods to shoot us like animals."

A young boy, probably no more than ten, offered his explanation. "We are going to be gassed."

The boy's remark sobered Benny more than any of the others.

My God! I was near his age when this started! How much longer must we live in fear?

At first, the train seemed to move at a turtle's pace. When it finally gained momentum, it rolled with such acceleration that fear shifted from the stress of waiting to concern about the swiftness of their fate.

As long as he was alive, Benny knew there was hope. Not wanting to overlook any opportunity, he concentrated on his chances for escape. Uppermost in Benny's mind was the realization that they would soon arrive at their destination. Perhaps their arrival would dispel doubt and uncertainly.

"Awhile back when it was still daylight, I saw a road sign that read 'Oswiecim fifteen kilometers'" said the man next to Benny.

"Oswiecim? Where is that?"

"Southern Poland, not very far from the Czech border."

"Then we are heading for Auschwitz," whispered a young man next to Benny.

"How do you know?" asked Benny already knowing what it could mean.

"Because Oswiecim is the closest town to Auschwitz. I traveled to the area before the war, and recently we heard stories in our village about the camp. It is not that far from here."

An uneasy silence girdled the prisoners as the train rushed toward their destiny.

They had ridden several hours when the brakes squealed loudly and the train jerked violently to a stop. It jerked again then slowly moved backwards.

Benny turned to the man who knew about Oswiecim. "You say you know this area well?"

"Fairly well. Both the Sola and the Vistula Rivers are here. The Western Carpathian Mountains should be to the southeast of us. If that is true, the city of Kraków is about twenty kilometers, forty miles or less, east of here. It is my understanding that the Germans have occupied this area since 1939."

"I think we are moving to a sidetrack," said Benny. "Listen! What's that?"

"I hear rain."

The two looked toward the low wooden ceiling of the car and listened intently as the rain began to pelt the roof.

The train had come to a complete stop when they heard the whistle of an approaching train. Outside two SS guards yelled to each other.

Benny felt the belt tightening. He must make a move. Touching the young man with whom he talked, he urged, "I want you to help me start a commotion!"

"What do you mean?"

"If my calculations are correct, it's nighttime. We're going to use that possibility as well as the rain and the distraction of the other train to try to escape."

"Escape?"

"We have no time to discuss it! You go to that side of the car and I'll take the other side. Move toward the door yelling."

"Yelling what?"

"It doesn't matter! Start a scene! Hurry!"

Benny began shouting at the top of his lungs, pushing his way through the others to get to the door. His partner did the same. Startled and confused, the frightened occupants began screaming.

By the time Benny and his partner reached the door, the two SS guards had jerked it open. Before the guards realized what was happening, Benny and his friend had jumped into them, knocking them to the ground. Sensing a chance for escape, others in the car jumped and ran frantically through the startled guards.

Benny immediately rolled under the cattle car, and once on the other side, ran into the night. He was already a short distance away as he scrambled through the underbrush and darkness, when he heard the first shots and the SS screaming for the Jews to halt. Popping sounds, followed by the crackling explosion of machine guns, surrounded him.

Gliding his tongue over his teeth, he looked for moisture that might prevent the choking in his throat. Swallowing hard, Benny prayed not to cough. The shots were close -- surrounding and caging him. He ran on through the darkness, not able to distinguish direction in his flight from death.

The boy had crouched so long that he felt his back would break. He dared not stop. Finally Benny dropped to his hands and knees and crawled. At that moment, he felt the burning thud in his right shoulder. Still he ran. He ran until he could run no more.

Exhausted, Benny collapsed into a large, soft mound of mud. He could go no farther and pushed his body into the clump. The boy prayed the darkness would hide him from danger.

He heard the Germans stomping through the underbrush and yelling to each other in the darkness. Benny held his breath. In moments he heard heavy breathing, and he felt the rifle barrel push against his leg. He froze. It slid down his leg and into the muddy mound. Satisfied he had found only a pile of dirt, the German left as quickly as he appeared.

Benny thought he would choke before he could safely move or gasp for air. He wanted to cough, to breathe deeply. In the distance he heard the retreating SS and a new round of gunfire.

When the sounds ceased, the boy rested and deeply inhaled the night air. Cuddling close to the warm clump, he finally closed his eyes. Benny drifted into restless sleep and dreamed of African drumbeats, sand, warmth, and as much food as he could eat.

The light of day crept through the leaves of the pine trees when Benny awoke. He shivered so intensely that his teeth chattered. He had just pushed himself to a sitting position when he felt a mushy, sticky substance. The morning light revealed he had bedded with a dead man, his stomach wound gapping, pushing entrails to the outside of his body. A wave of nausea reaching his throat, Benny jerked away from the corpse. He took a deep breath, which abated momentarily the nausea.

Blood and bile of the man with whom he had spent the night mixed with Benny's own blood. Throbbing pain in his left arm weakened him. Just now, he realized bullets had struck him as he ran in his desperate attempt to escape.

Benny stumbled away from the dead man who saved his life and began the never-ending search for safety. Alone and in severe pain, he was not sure he could remain conscious.

As dawn approached, he saw the lights of several houses. With his energy sinking, he both crawled and walked until he reached the first one. When the door opened to his knock, he pitched forward into the arms of a strange man.

"What the devil?" said the man in German. That was the last thing Benny remembered.

The sun shone brightly as Benny opened his eyes. The room had a feminine feel with chintz curtains at the window and wallpaper covered with flowers. Struggling to orient himself, Benny moved to sit up, and as he did a sharp pain crossed his shoulder and moved up to his neck. Grimacing, he reached for his left arm only to find that it was in a sling. Then he remembered fleeing the train and crawling through the night. He recalled knocking on a door and hearing German words.

Oh, my God! thought Benny, trembling.

At that moment he heard muffled sounds from the next room. Carefully he crawled from the bed and inched toward the door. Now, he could hear plainly two men speaking in German.

"Hell, Franz! Of course he is a Jew!"

"He is just a boy! My God, he cannot be more than thirteen or fourteen!"

"And you are harboring the enemy!"

"And who the hell is the enemy, Jerek? Who the hell knows anymore?"

"Franz, I know you are not thinking this through. Do you not understand what could happen to you -- what could happen to me? I know the hurt is deep by the loss of your sons, and my heart aches for you, but my God, Franz, you cannot do this! What do you owe this Jew?"

"Nothing, Jerek, but he is a human being! He was on my doorstep! It is my choice, Jerek! It was not my choice my boys go fight for the Führer! I did my duty in the first war and my sons in this one. They died! I could not save them, but perhaps I can save this boy."

"Why would you want to do this, Franz?"

Benny had moved quietly to the door's edge so that he would have a better view.

"I don't know, Brother," answered the one called Franz, but I feel it here!" He struck at his heart with his fist, tears in his eyes. "My God," he continued, "I live in the shadow of this graveyard day in and day out! I can no longer deny it!"

Moving to stand beside him, Jerek placed his arm around his brother.

"Franz, I do not agree with you, and I doubt very seriously if you will get away with this, but it is your choice. You must follow your heart."

With his medical bag in hand, Jerek walked slowly to the door, his shoulders stooped. Turning to his brother he said, "If you need anything else, you know how to reach me. Franz, I love you. I want you to know that, even if we do not agree."

He closed the door softly behind him.

Benny moved as quickly as he could to crawl back under the covers.

Shortly he heard a rustling sound at his door. There stood the gray-haired man called Franz. He was holding a cup.

"Have no fear of me. I will not harm you."

There was no mistaking the kindness in the man's voice.

In German Benny asked, "What happened to me?"

"You do not remember? I found you at my door last evening. You had been shot. My brother took care of you. You are a lucky young man. I saved the bullets for you."

Crossing to the table, he picked up the three bullets and showed them to Benny. "Would you like a cup of tea?" he asked, placing the bullets back on the table.

Benny beamed at the older man. "Yes sir. I would like that."

The man handed a steaming cup of tea to the boy and asked, "Could you eat a little with me? I have not had my breakfast."

Benny nodded. "Oh, yes sir! I would be most grateful."

The man smiled and moved to a table by the door. There he picked up a tray and brought it to Benny's bed. He set it on the nightstand, and as he leaned toward the bed, he removed a large fluffy pillow that lay beside Benny. He lifted the boy gently and placed the pillow behind him.

"Thank you, sir," Benny said, astonished.

"I am afraid it is only a bit of bread and cheese, but we will not go hungry," the man said smiling. "If only my dear wife was here, we would eat like kings."

"Is she away, sir?"

The man sat down beside Benny and bowed his head.

"She died in her sleep in 1941, not long after our sons had been killed on the Eastern Front. I miss her very much."

The man's candor touched Benny. "I am sorry, sir."

The two ate in silence. The man smiled as he watched Benny devour the cheese and bread. Benny looked up to see the warmth in the man's eyes. He smiled back.

Embarrassed at his voracious appetite, the youth said, "I forget my manners. I'm sorry."

"No need to apologize, boy. I am happy to see you enjoy your meal. It has been so long since there was a young man in my house. My name is Franz."

"I'm Benny."

"You are a Jew," the man stated, looking into the boy's eyes.

Benny did not know how to answer. He said nothing.

"It does not matter. We are both human beings living in this hell. You have suffered as I. Nothing matters except that we are both here together."

For the next few days, Benny avoided being seen at the window. Franz had warned him any unnecessary movement or noise would arouse suspicion from the neighbors who could alert the Gestapo.

On the third day Benny awakened to a terrible stench. Cupping his hand over his mouth, he felt his stomach lurch, and he staggered from his bed to the window to see the source of the disgusting smell. Carefully he pulled the curtain aside, just enough to see smoke rimming the sky in the distance. He could not know that he lay in the shadows of death.

In the Birch Forest, near Camp Birkenau -- a part of the Auschwitz system -- the Germans systematically burned hundreds of gassed Jews almost daily. Before the nightmare was over 900,000 Polish Jews would perish at the Auschwitz camps.

—— ✳ ——

"Benny, take this flashlight and broom. Here are some cigarettes for you, and here are fifty marks. Wear this cap and people will think you are a porter. Do not forget to speak German."

Benny's eyes filled with tears of gratitude for this kind man who had risked so much to save him.

"You have given me another chance at life, sir -- a debt I can never adequately repay."

Franz crushed Benny to his chest, tears streaming down his weathered face. "My boy, you have brought such joy to this old heart, no repayment is necessary. I will ask the Holy Mother to keep you safe. God Bless you, boy." He kissed him tenderly on the cheek.

"I will never forget you, sir," Benny said over his shoulder as he moved into the crowd. "*Shalom*! Peace go with you!"

As calmly as possible, Benny accepted the role of train porter and watched every person that entered the train. His greatest concern was not the Germans but the conductor. Each time Benny saw him coming, the boy made a quick exit to the next car or to the men's toilet.

Nearing Kielce, the youth had a scare when the conductor yelled at him, ordering him to stop. Benny obeyed. The conductor grabbed him by the shirtfront and shook him furiously as he gave the boy a tongue lashing for not stopping. Benny's heart was in his throat, when he realized his pretense might be over.

Instead, the conductor ordered Benny to another car to clean up vomit where a man had been sick.

Benny, laughing inwardly all the way to the car, went to the unpleasant task with great delight. He was both relieved and astonished he had gotten away with his disguise. With a smile on his face, he rapidly cleaned the mess. He noticed that the sick man looked strangely at him.

Benny smiled. *I guess he thinks I'm crazy to be so gleeful about such a chore.*

When the train arrived at Kielce, Benny made a hasty departure, sure of his destination this time.

"Ah, Benny, you look refreshed."

Benny smiled and joined Maronski in front of the fireplace. "I am. Thank you for the change of clothes."

"You can thank John, one of my new foremen."

Benny sat down opposite the Pole.

"Benny, I believe in many things, but I would not have believed I would see you again. You will never know how glad I am."

"No more glad than I, sir," said Benny, sitting back in the wing chair, staring into the flames of the fireplace. "Sir?"

"Yes?"

"It's amazing, isn't it that I'm able to escape again and again?"

Maronski reached for his pipe, filled it, and drew heavily on it. The odor of the tobacco made Benny smile, and he turned to his friend.

"Did I ever tell you my father smoked that brand?"

Maronski smiled. "The same brand? He was a wise man. I love a mellow smoke." He looked closely at Benny. "Yes," he said. "I do find your escapes amazing."

The two sat silently, each lost in thought.

After a while Benny asked, "Do you believe in miracles?" Not surprised at his question considering the circumstances, Maronski pulled on the pipe and turned to the youth. "My mother always told me of such things. She was a good Catholic. God rest her soul."

"You know the Jewish faith embraces the belief that the world is good?"

Benny could tell by the look on Maronski's face that he questioned this belief.

"My grandfather Lipman says that human beings are created in the image of God. A man I knew, named Kuba, told me the same thing. They said that nothing in creation is evil in itself."

The Pole sighed deeply. "I am not a religious man, though I had a very strong Catholic upbringing. I believe in God and I believe in man's ability to rely on himself. I am sure God gave each of us that ability. Some use it better than others."

Benny looked at his friend, an immediate question coming to mind. "There's something I don't understand." He could not let go of the idea that he was very lucky in a time when all around him his fellow Jews perished.

"What is it you do not understand?"

"Why am I rescued so often? Why me?"

"Are you rescued, Benny, or do you create the circumstances that eject you from the evil? If truly nothing in creation is evil, then evil comes from man's misuse of this gift, from fear and ignorance."

Benny nodded in recognition of the idea. "I think evil must be born in the darkness of man's mind."

"Benny, you amaze me. You are such an intelligent young man and show a great deal of promise. Unlike others, you are always the optimist. You are a survivor, if I have ever seen one." He paused and smiled. "Besides, I have not forgotten the delightful songs that you once sang for me, giving me such pleasure. God cannot let anything happen to a voice like that. He must protect my own private *śpiewak*."

Benny laughed openly.

If the world had more Maronskis, it would truly be a wonderful place to live.

The two sat silently for a time as they embraced their friendship and relished their ability to communicate with each other. At length Benny rose from his chair, picked up a fireplace tool and poked at the logs. Sparks shot upward. He turned and looked at Maronski.

"Sometimes I feel so guilty," he said.

Waiting patiently for the youth to continue, Maronski pulled on his pipe.

"I'm alive and my family is not. Should I feel guilty that I don't openly cry daily for them, even though I carry the hurt deep in my heart?" Benny turned back to the fireplace and stared at the flames. "How have I kept my sanity? Will I ever be able to remove the rock from my heart? There are so many questions and so many feelings!" He turned, again, and looked at Maronski.

"I am not a philosopher, Benny, nor a rabbi. In my heart I know there is a reason. How much time do you have? I do not know. How much time does any of us have? Knowing you, you will use the time given you."

Benny looked at his friend and smiled. "You know that according to Jewish belief, we must sanctify every moment of life we have. Are you sure you aren't Jewish?"

"Hell, Benny, didn't you know Jesus Christ was a rabbi?"

The youth dabbed at the tears that filled his eyes. He knew whatever happened he would never forget the Pole who had such a big heart and who loved life to its magnitude.

"I know you said there are no more Jewish workers left here. It'll be dangerous to have me here, won't it?" asked Benny.

"You must have recuperation time. It is true we will need to protect your presence. I am going to give you a letter of introduction to one of my bricklayers. We call him Ziggy. He lives only a short distance from our construction site. I know him to be a fine man and he will assist you in any way that he can."

"I plan to go back to Warsaw, you know," said Benny.

"To Warsaw?" The frown creased Maronski's face. "Why?"

"It's the only place I know."

"But you would walk back into God knows what!"

"I know the city well. I'm determined to find someone, some way to get papers to leave Poland."

"It is your decision, Benny. I will help you anyway I can."

Benny stayed and worked for his friend in Sedieszów until late May. In June the Gestapo terrorized the remaining Jews from several towns in the area, including Sedieszów. The Germans transferred twelve thousand men, women, and children to the Rzeszów ghetto, another holding pen, bringing that total population to twenty-three thousand. Zalme Spira, the man who befriended Mirla and Sala Lipman, disappeared.

THIRTEEN

CHANCES WERE REMOTE THAT Benny would find his friend. The house he searched for on Twarda Street stood alone among the skeletons of bombed homes, one of the many images of a dying city, fallen at the hands of its invaders.

He climbed the broken steps and knocked at the door. No light shone from the windows. A knot formed in Benny's stomach as he realized the return to his home on Ogrodowa Street would mirror the exact scene -- a dark shell, once a home.

Just as Benny turned to leave, he saw in the window the outline of a face.

Anxiously, he grasped the door handle and whispered hoarsely, "Open up, Heniek, if that's you. This is Benny Lipman."

The door swung open to a figure standing silently in the shadows. Benny entered the darkened house, and the door slammed shut behind him. He stood quietly, his heart beating nervously. His mysterious host remained hidden, saying nothing. Suddenly the specter grabbed Benny by the arm and pulled him down a narrow hall and into a cavern-like room.

A kerosene lamp dimly lit the room that showed stages of demolition. As soon as they entered, the unidentified person pulled a heavy drape over the entry, blocking light to the street that could endanger the occupant's life.

When the man turned and faced Benny, the boy exclaimed, "A *kholereh*! Heniek, you scared me. I didn't know whether it was you or not!"

"May the cholera get you, too, Benny Lipman. Where did you come from? Are you a ghost?"

The tall young man with a shock of midnight black hair and dark eyes grabbed Benny and squeezed him to his chest. Benny smiled. Heniek Horowitz still had his keen sense of humor, even now.

"Come, sit, old friend. Catch me up. I'll see if I can find anything to eat."

Benny sat at a small wooden table in the center of the room while his friend searched through the cabinets. Locating a can of sardines and some stale bread, Heniek said, "I've been saving this for a rainy day. Seeing an old friend calls for celebration." He put the sardines and bread on the table and sat down opposite Benny. "Where've you been?"

"Dodging fate," answered Benny.

"I know what you mean."

"I came in on the train a few hours ago from Sedieszów."

"Sedieszów? And you came back here?" Disbelief registered on Heniek's face.

"I know," said Benny looking up from his sardine sandwich, "one could question my sanity in returning to this living graveyard."

"You're correct!"

"All I can say is no other choice was practical at the moment. This seemed like the logical place."

Benny, knowing Heniek would understand the complexity of his problem, shrugged his shoulders. "I guess I'm like a wild animal, choosing to stick with the known hiding places, in preference to the unknown."

"I understand. Were there problems on the train?"

"Not really. My friend Maronski gave me a suitcase with decent clothes, a ticket, and a winter coat."

Benny paused to take another bite of food. He remembered Maronski's words when he bid him farewell at the train station. "You will need this," he said, handing Benny the bag. Pleased by the

Pole's gesture, he also recognized the lesson in optimism. A renewed determination filled every fiber of Benny's being.

"Anyway," he continued, "I knew recapture was a danger. I knew I couldn't relax my guard. From the moment I entered the train, I moved from one car to the next until I found a less crowded one. Of course, many of the cars were marked 'Germans only.'"

"Just another degradation," responded Heniek angrily, "first class for the Germans, second for the Poles, and of course third class for the Jews if they're lucky and it's not a cattle car." Heniek looked intently at his friend. "You've come back into a hornet's nest, Benny. Did you notice much activity on the streets?"

"Yes. As a matter of fact, that's one of the reasons I didn't go to my old house tonight. That street was heavily patrolled."

"The Germans seem to have renewed their efforts. Roundups and violence come more often. Damn it!" Heniek slammed his fist on the table. "There's one Nazi who drives around with his pals, looking for prey. They club every Jew they can find and laugh as they do it."

Benny listened closely.

"Each night street blockades are set up with heavy motorcade. The Polish police help the murderers by blocking exits and aiding the Nazis in their systematic search of houses. Jews are executed, never knowing their crime."

"That activity is not new."

"My friend, it has greatly intensified. Only a few days ago Nazis went on a rampage against Jews on Karmelicka Street. Some of us thought they were taking out their anger on us for England's defiant stand against Germany."

"Did they ever not have a reason to mistreat Jews?"

Heniek did not answer. After a moment or two, he continued, "The nights are filled with fear. No one knows when his turn will come."

Benny bowed his head and shook it in sadness. He had lived in fear so long that it had become a part of him. The reality of such horrors was at times almost unbearable.

"The worst," said Heniek, through gritted teeth, "are those known as the 'Thirteen.'"

Benny looked up quickly. "The 'Thirteen'?"

"Yes, supposedly named for number 13 Leszno Street."

"Not a part of the Jewish police force?"

"No. We call them the 'Jewish Gestapo' and consider them equally merciless as their leaders. They wear green caps and arm bands, similar to those worn by the Order Service."

"What do they get from the Germans?" scoffed Benny.

"The German Intelligence employs them to work under the guise of contesting the ghetto Black Market."

"In other words, they're informers for the German Gestapo."

"Yes, and for this they get all the food they can eat. It's also rumored they are offered German citizenship."

Even after what he had seen, the story seemed incredible to Benny. "My God, to what degree of degradation will the Jew whores subject themselves? They have ordained their own execution. I truly believe that!"

"If we have our way, it will be sooner than later."

"We?"

Heniek's eyes lit up. "A resistance force is building, Benny."

"Resistance?" Benny could not hide his excitement. "Tell me about it!"

Heniek sat down at the table slowly. "After they took my parents, I thought I'd go crazy. It wasn't long after that I found a group within the ghetto organizing to find ways to limit the mental ravage of our fellow Jews. We've healed the lesions somewhat by cultural activities, underground of course -- makeshift libraries, secret radio sets to hear news from abroad -- those kinds of things."

"Is that the only way you get the news?"

"Also from clandestine presses -- *Der Oyfbroyz* or *Slowo Mlodych*. And early this year the PPR began cooperating with our movement."

"PPR?"

"*Polska Partia Robotnicza* (Polish Workers' Party). There are not many, but they are helpful. The resistance is slowly intensifying and may evolve into armed resistance."

"How are you getting arms? What are you using for money?"

Heniek laughed, "Don't worry, we have that problem solved. If you're interested, I'll take you to a meeting." Immediately Benny nodded his head in affirmation. "We use the caverns and cellars under the bombed areas for hiding places. It's a small group, and we must work cautiously. Much vitality is needed, including supplies to arm the movement. Tomorrow I will take you with me to meet some of the others."

This news was the ray of hope Benny needed but had not expected.

—————◆————

Leaving Heniek's house early the next morning, Benny walked to Ogrodowa Street. The streets were empty of the activity he had viewed the evening before. Still, he tried to appear calm and relaxed to avert detection by any roving patrols. He knew he must return home before he did anything else. He must say a final goodbye.

Benny clambered up the steps to the deserted house and pushed open the splintered door that hung by one hinge. The interior was in shambles -- bare, cracked walls, the remains of a few broken pieces of furniture, some rags and paper. The smell of decay penetrated the air.

Tears fell as Benny sadly walked through each of the rooms. It was no longer a home -- just a battered shell. Returning to the area that the family once considered the living room, he sat down on the floor and hugged his knees to his chest. He sadly surveyed the shambles. In the once beautiful fireplace lay the charred remains of a partially burned piano leg.

Past memories and the emptiness of the room flooded him with the reality of his loss. He began to sob.

When the crying finally subsided, he sat quietly, the tears still wet on his cheeks. Grandfather Lipman's voice came through the silence. *"No one dies, Benny. As long as memories prevail, they are a part of you. The world is held together by things you cannot see."*

Out of the eerie stillness that filled the shell of a room came the sounds of laughter and distorted images -- haunted memories. His father sat at the piano and played lilting sounds, while the family stood nearby singing. The aroma of his mother's cooking spread through the room.

"Come on, Benick," laughed his father, *"you sing the next verse."*

"Sing it like Jan Kiepura," said Sala. *"Remember when we heard him perform at Teatr Wielki?"*

As quickly as he had imagined the sounds, the utter stagnation of the room girdled him.

"If you can hear me," Benny said, hoping somehow his family somewhere was listening, "know that we are joined at the heart. I carry your very souls within me. They shelter me!" Benny's voice choked as he spoke. "I can't change what happened to you or what I've already lived, but I promise you, no matter how miserable my existence, I will survive. I promise you!"

The youth stood up, looked around one more time, and walked out the front door. He knew he would never return to this house.

Benny and Heniek cautiously made their way through the ghetto. Eventually they came to the escape exit that would get them to Krochmalna Street in the Polish sector.

Heniek led him into a large bombed out building, down a flight of stairs, and through winding passageways. At last they arrived at what appeared to be a manhole, a narrow opening that allowed only one person at a time to enter. Following Heniek's lead, Benny climbed down into the chasm. Heniek explained that the passage walls were adjacent to the ghetto, and that some of the passageways led directly into it. In order to avoid detection by any unfriendly eyes, the group avoided using them unless it was absolutely necessary.

The two youths came to a large cellar room in which a small group of young men had assembled. When Heniek and Benny entered the room, they saw a tall, stalwart man talking to a group of young men. He stopped when he saw Benny and Heniek. The others turned and looked curiously at Benny.

"It's all right," said Heniek. "This is Benny. He's alone, too. He escaped and returned to Warsaw. He wants to help."

Members of the small group voiced their welcome.

"Good," said the man who had been speaking. He smiled at Benny and continued his dissertation, his powerful voice filling the room.

Heniek turned to Benny and whispered, "That's Martin Idzikowski, a former organizer in the Polish PPS Party."

"The Nazis' guiding standard," continued Idzikowski "is the subjugation of a certain number of Jews every night. Militancy is the only answer. We must dedicate our movement to avert the inhumane activity."

Benny, though excited, wondered how a handful of people could succeed against the large, well-trained and equipped German army.

The speaker continued. "When Hitler made it clear in January of this year that, regardless of the outcome of the war, the annihilation of Jews would continue, the hope for survival collapsed."

The young men, looking at each other, shifted in their seats and nodded in agreement.

"Surely," interrupted Benny, questioning the Pole, "that was not reported in a newspaper for the world to see?"

"Not in a newspaper originally," responded Idzikowski, "but in the party anniversary speech acquired and secretly passed around by a Jew employed by the Germans. Now the world knows. For the first time in history, a tyrant has openly said what he will do with his captives."

"Last night proved the point, another night of slaughter," said a young man, sitting in the back of the room. "Each time the sun sets, the bullies prowl in search of prey."

"How do you suppose they choose who will die?" asked Benny.

Idzikowski looked closely at him. "Some believe there are files from which names are drawn randomly. The stress on the populace gives little hope; therefore, the Jews have a heavy heart. Their spirit is dying."

"Can't the Judenrat do something?" asked Benny.

"They represent the well-to-do," said one young man, "while the masses starve."

Another responded quickly, "Some of us think that members of the Judenrat are open to whoever bids the highest."

"You mean bribes? Not Czerniakow!" replied Benny emphatically.

"I don't know how many doubt the chairman's loyalty or patriotism," said Idzikowski, "but some feel he cannot last much longer under the pressure. His efforts to prevent favoritism in the Council, especially concerning collecting taxes, appear to be continually blocked. That's perplexing to those who cannot afford the taxes. The Germans have arrested and beaten him on at least one occasion. You can see how that dishonor does not give much hope to the Jews whether they like him or not."

Saddened Benny replied, "I only know him as a good man, a wonderful friend to my father and my family."

"Regardless," said Idzikowski, "Warsaw is a failing city."

"Why aren't more people struggling against it?" asked Benny.

"They have lost hope," responded a boy, perhaps twelve or thirteen years old. "At first, they believed if they were innocent nothing would happen to them. Now. . . ."

Benny was not much younger when the Nazi invasion first ravaged his life.

Members of the group readily volunteered their comments regarding the plight of the Jews.

"The Nazis seem to delight in a variety of killings."

"Yes. Some Jews are shot without warning, often in the back."

"Others are poisoned with lethal gas, burned, drowned . . ."

"Or electrocuted."

"The Germans appear to be clever in their creativity, even taking babies from their mother's arms and killing them in their presence."

Benny winced with a memory he had tried to forget.

"It all seems more systematic and with widespread activity. The Nazis continue to pack and seal increased numbers of prisoners, like material goods, into heavily guarded freight cars."

"Some are killed at will on the way to wherever they are taken."

Benny listened as each of the resistant members gave him information he did not want to hear.

"Benny, did you know that almost forty thousand of Lublin's young men have vanished?" asked Heniek.

"And seventeen thousand Jews are missing from Cracow," said Idzikowski. "Who knows how many other areas have been victimized. The rumor has it that some towns' populations are totally destroyed."

"No trace?" asked Benny sadly.

"None."

"And women are singled out and herded together to be shot," said Heniek. "I'm sure it gives the Huns great pleasure to destroy the future of Israel by killing its mothers."

A silence fell over the room. Though the Nazis introduced Benny to hell, hearing further reports burdened him greatly. How could he have hope for his relatives scattered throughout Poland?

"All the while they fool the outside world with their propaganda," said a man who stood leaning against the wall. "Just this month Gestapo agents surged through the ghetto to take pictures of Jews going about their Shabbat activities."

"A ploy to fool the world," sneered Heniek "See! The 'good' conquerors encourage religious activities."

"Fanfare," said Idzikowski, "while rumors spread that a camp named Treblinka, just fifty kilometers from Warsaw, is being built as an extermination center for the Warsaw deportees. Major deportation is to take place soon."

"We must quickly arm ourselves," said Heniek.

"Agreed!" cheered the group.

"If we make certain contacts, we will receive help from unexpected sources," said the Pole. "Each of you will be given an assignment. We will change our meeting place each time, in order to avoid detection. Stephan will be your contact."

A tall, Aryan-looking Jew nodded in agreement. Each member of the group received a pistol and instructions to reassemble in two days.

The idea of group resistance fascinated Benny. He had no experience, but he knew he could help in some way.

Benny departed the ghetto by one of many holes in the wall next to a bombed-out building. Eighteen kilometers (eleven miles) of walled area guaranteed a possible way to exit but could not affirm the lack of a sentry, or that the SS guards would not catch Benny. With every departure Benny risked death.

He looked now for the address of the house where a former Polish railway worker lived. His directive was to report to the man for an assignment. Idzikowski had given Benny a false passbook that listed the youth as Romek Kryzanowski, age twenty-one. Benny hoped his looks would not reveal the seven-year difference in age. Heniek had been unwilling to divulge the source of the passport.

A short, stocky man, about forty, immediately answered the door. Upon entering the house, the unidentified man led Benny to a room in the cellar. He showed the youth a machine used for duplicating Polish Zloty.

"You will be working with me to produce bills," said the man. "You understand what the money is for?" The man looked closely at the youth.

"Yes," answered Benny, "a means to raise money for arms and the movement."

The Pole accepted Benny's answer and immediately put him to work. Under the Pole's close supervision Benny learned to operate the machine. He worked hard that day and into the night turning out the bills. The plates, crafted well, produced near-perfect bills. By midnight they had turned out somewhere near 100,000 Zloty -- a good start for their smuggling activities.

Benny knew about smuggling even before he left the ghetto. It became commonplace because the Jews were starving with only the meager two kilos of bread allotted to them. This was an entire month's ration.

The Gestapo had created special watch points along the wall in an attempt to catch the smugglers. Benny knew from personal experience that illegal import activities had become a very dangerous business. Because Nazis explored the smuggling of arms, it became both a liability and an asset to the movement with which Benny was now involved.

Benny learned that a Pole, with connections to an SS officer by the name of Schweppe, made arrangements to exchange the newly printed bills for military equipment. The Pole contact orchestrated the negotiation with the officer who purchased grenades and rounds of ammunition. Someone's going to get wealthy off of this deal, thought Benny, and it won't be the movement. The German smuggler will be the fortunate one.

The deal and the first delivery occurred on the same day. Benny accompanied the Pole and another member of the group late at night to a spot on Stara Street where they exchanged money and arms.

After the pick up, members of the resistance took the goods to the first of the secret arsenals hidden in bombed-out, subterranean cellars. Attired in German uniforms and with official credentials, members of the resistance made second and third deliveries.

This is too easy, thought Benny, uncomfortable that the deliveries and storage of goods went so smoothly.

Though his instincts alerted him to the danger of complacency, he put his heart into his job for the operation. It gave him great delight to make counterfeit money to buy weapons that could save his fellow Jews and thwart the monsters destroying them.

Besides forgery, Benny accepted the assignment to solicit 250 Zloty from Jewish families who had been able to hoard at least part of their wealth. This was difficult for him. He remembered well his own family losing their wealth early in the Nazi siege. With prying and unrestrained SS a constant threat, he did not fully understand how anyone could have held on to his assets.

It's a crazy time, thought Benny -- *no standards, no rules, and no rationale. If any of us survives, our memories will tell the truth.*

Daily Benny passed by bloated and stiff corpses lying on the street ready for the black, square-boxed carts that carried stacks of bodies to unknown gravesites. The dying, with scarcely audible pleas, lay moaning on streets and sidewalks. Passers-by tried to ignore the dying and the dead, but fear locked itself into their eyes. No one wanted to admit death's presence. No one knew how to awaken from the nightmare.

Benny's positive attitude toward survival weakened during those moments when sorrow at the loss of his family and the uncertainty of his future overwhelmed him.

Oh, God, he thought as he viewed the loaded carts. *These people are better off than I am. Their worries are over.*

Destitute children sit barefoot on the pavement in the Warsaw ghetto. USHMM, courtesy of Instytut Pamieci Narodowej

It was the children that affected Benny the most. On one occasion, he was on his way to find a place to sleep when he came across some children in tattered clothes standing on a street corner begging. As they held out their little hands, their large, hollow eyes searched the face of each person walking by. Watching them, Benny's eyes glistened with tears.

He stopped directly in front of them, took a loaf of bread he had just purchased and tore it in half. He then handed one half to the children who rushed forward in a mad scramble for the treasure. As he walked away, he smiled through tears at their joy.

Suddenly he heard them screaming. Turning back to them, he saw the bread literally ripped from their hands by several adults who devoured it like animals. The little children's screams turned silent as they stood, tears streaming down their faces.

Benny tried to close his eyes to the suffering and human misery, but there were times when it was almost too much to sustain. He was only fourteen years old.

—➤ ✵ ◅—

More than six weeks had passed since Benny re-entered the ghetto. He felt useful and full of hope but was always hiding, always cautious. His routine varied greatly according to the ever-present SS patrols. Sometimes he stayed with Heniek, other times with a member of the group. Most often he slept on the ground in the Jewish cemetery. In early July the Nazis ordered the digging of a mass grave for several hundred Jews, an ominous plan to hide them among the already dead. Benny lost his cemetery lodging.

The yoke of uncertainty and terror continued to enfold the ghetto. In mid-July rumor spread of a decree allotting seventy thousand Warsaw Jews for deportation. Other rumors suggested that negotiations over the decree involved the Nazis, Chairman Czerniakow, and other officials of the Judenrat.

One rumor indicated Adam Czerniakow, head of the Warsaw Judenrat, offered ten million Zloty to invalidate the decree. At the same time, the Judenrat denied the rumors of expulsion.

Factories, scattered throughout the ghetto, created a massive forced labor camp. Jews clung to the belief that work and resettlement would save them. What else could the powerless do? Word spread that the German firms within the ghetto, which employed Jews, were in conflict with the Nazis.

Ironic, thought Benny. *While the Nazis exile and kill relatives, the Jews aid the clever Nazis in the production line for the benefit of the war.*

No one knew how distorted the rumors were. The people tended to hold on dearly to the positive ones and dispel the others. Waiting suspended life.

The feeling of impending doom was the strongest instinct. When news arrived that German General Rommel had caused a defeat of England in an African battle, nerves grew more ragged.

It became apparent that requests for Jews to register for deportation to Palestine were only a ploy to confound the Jews. In the true sense, it meant exile to death not to the "motherland."

The killing escalated. Daylight revealed distorted bodies at doorsteps. The Nazis dragged people from their sleep and shot or clubbed them. Blood tracked streets and walks. Dzielna Street prison became a holding place for pre-burial corpses and for the skeleton-like living, tagged for death.

Talk among the Jews was that SS guards forced their peers to dig their own graves with their hands then stand at the edge while the Nazis shot them. Reports confirmed rumors that the construction of Treblinka, using Jewish labor was almost finished. Fear that the camp was an extermination center for the deportees placed the Jews in a quagmire of terror. Living became agony as they waited for death.

Because speculation concerning the eventual betrayal by the SS officer selling them goods was ever-present, the small resistance group moved slowly in making money and in arms dealing. It was crucial to be as clever as the enemy was. Members of the small resistance force carefully chose storage areas for the arms and ammunition. They made all deliveries under cover of darkness. One slip would be fatal to the people and the movement.

Time was no longer on their side. From a small band of Jewish and Polish youths centered on saving as many Jews as possible, the resistance was born.

———✡———

It was July 22, 1942. Benny felt uneasy as he made his way to Heniek's house for an emergency meeting. He wore a light jacket to hide the sidearm concealed in his trousers.

Before knocking softly on Heniek's door, Benny looked both directions down the street, eyes alert to movement. A resistance member opened the door immediately. Benny made his way down the dark hallway to the kitchen where the meeting had already begun.

"How does it look on the street?" asked one of the young men.

"Dangerous," answered Benny. "I wasn't sure I'd get past the patrols."

"I called the meeting," said Idzikowski, "to make you aware of information I found posted today."

Puzzled, the group listened carefully to the Pole.

"The rumors are true. At four o'clock this afternoon the Judenrat posted a notice, announcing deportation of large numbers of people."

Silence.

"It is my understanding the Germans demanded six thousand Jews by four this afternoon. Indicators point that their goal will include a daily quota of the same number, seven days a week. Expulsion actually began at noon."

"My God!" one of the men cried.

"It is strange," continued the Pole, "Czerniakow's signature did not appear as usual on the notice. It also listed exceptions to the expulsions -- Jews working in German factories and shops, officers of the Judenrat and its agencies, Jewish police, and qualified laborers."

"How long do you suppose the exceptions will last?" scoffed Benny, disbelieving anyone would be spared.

"Who knows!"

"If we can hold out," said Stephan, "my Polish contact tells me there is a possibility of fifty recruits within a matter of days."

"We're too late!" said one of the group.

Idzikowski frowned. "We will do the best we can. I have faith the movement will grow in numbers. Let's talk about putting one of our plans into action. It would be wise to post guards at the front windows. Any volunteers for the first shift?"

Benny and Heniek responded immediately.

The two had been at their post less than an hour when Benny noticed a movement on the street in front of the house. "Heniek, look," he whispered.

"It's the Jewish Gestapo," answered Heniek. "They're coming to the door. Alert the others."

As Benny moved quickly to the back of the house, someone pounded on the door and called out, "*Efen-up*! Open up! We know you are there."

No one made a move to comply. By now the others had drawn their arms and had moved quietly into the living room, each taking a post that would enable a defense.

Again the Gestapo pounded on the door.

Noise of a vehicle screeching to a halt alerted the young men the Germans had arrived.

"German trucks and motorcars!" whispered the redhead from one of the windows.

The Germans called out orders to empty the house. When no response came, a staccato chatter of automatic weapons filled the night. The men in the house fell to the floor to seek safety. Several crawled to the windows, broke the glass and began firing.

Crouching low to the floor, Heniek moved to Benny. "Remember the small hole at the back of the kitchen wall that leads into the adjoining building?"

"Yes," answered Benny.

"I don't think I can squeeze my body through it, but you can. Save yourself so that we'll have another chance."

"Yes," said Idzikowski, above the sound of the bullets. "For all of us to resist further is foolhardy! It is more important for some to get out alive. I will send others behind you, and we will cover for you. Now go, quickly!"

Benny did not know what he should do. He knew the end was minutes away. Even as he realized this, a spray of bullets shattered the room, and Heniek pitched forward at Benny's feet. Crouching beside his friend, Benny gently rolled him over. Blood oozed from his nose and the corner of his mouth. "Heniek," he whispered, "I can't leave you."

"Benny, please go -- for me." Struggling for the words, Heniek said, "God speed, my friend." His head slumped to the side.

Without warning, one of the resistance members flung open the front door and leaped through as he fired into the night. Not wishing to be caught with a pistol, Benny threw it down and ran for the back of the house. Several others followed him to the hole in the wall. Instantaneously another burst of automatic fire shattered the front of the building.

As Benny entered the narrow passageway, he could hear one of his comrades screaming, "Come on in, you dirty devils. I'll gladly kill another of you!"

Benny crawled on his belly, barely able to move. Broken bricks cut his hands and scratched his body as he clawed and pushed his way through the rubble.

Suddenly he heard a deafening explosion, and several bricks fell onto him. Lying in the heavy dust and pieces of stone, Benny listened for further sounds. He did not know if the others had followed him in the narrow tunnel. He listened, and hearing nothing, he groveled from under the bricks and began inching along the narrow passageway. He finally reached a bombed-out cellar where he crawled in and waited.

On July 23, 1942 Nazi officials gave orders for an *Aktion*, the "Final Solution," of nine thousand, not six thousand Warsaw Jews, daily. Treblinka officially opened its gates to accept the deportees for extermination by gas. Refusing to deport further Jews, Adam Czerniakow committed suicide. As Benny foraged for food, he was discovered and shoved into a single cattle car with more than one hundred other Jews.

FOURTEEN

ORCHESTRA MUSIC RESONATED over the noise of the crowd.

Puzzled, Benny tapped an older man on the arm. "Sir, where are we?"

"Ober-Maidan," answered the man in a matter-of-fact manner.

"Where's that?"

"Don't you know? It is the transition station for trains to neutral countries."

"Who told you that?" questioned the youth in disbelief.

"German officers. We paid money for our exit visas and passports." The man looked closely at Benny and turned away. Calling back, he said, "I am sorry. I must go. They are telling us to hurry on."

"But where are we going?" called Benny.

The man did not answer, disappearing into the crowd. A woman passing by answered instead. "We are going to work on farms in the Ukraine." She smiled and pressed forward.

Brilliant floodlights illuminated the night. People carrying luggage and assisted by special train agents -- not the usual guards -- crowded the station platform. German SS stood by silently watching.

Something doesn't seem right, thought Benny.

Station signs displayed arrows, indicating directions to Warsaw, Bialystok, and other cities. A cashier's booth, cafe, and baggage room projected the "normal" feeling of a train station.

Ahead of Benny two small children, a boy and girl, stumbled and fell. Suddenly a German SS rushed up. "Come, children, we must hurry. Food and entertainment await you."

The little boy looked at him and cried, "I want to see my mother."

"And you will," answered the German. "You must hurry now."

The child resisted. "You took away my mother and father. I hate you! I won't go!"

"Your mother is waiting. Come let us go. She wants to see you."

The children did not know what to believe. The thought that they would soon see their mother encouraged them to move forward.

This situation was unlike Benny's previous experiences. As he had waited, a prisoner crammed in the cattle car, he had mulled over what he was likely to find when he reached this destination. The waiting on the train with no fresh air or water seemed an eternity. Dehydration was a constant fear. The boy was lucky the pieces of plundered cheese in his pockets had gone undiscovered when they caught him.

When he finally disembarked from the train, he had noted the long line of passenger cars carrying Jews. The car in which he had ridden was one of the few cattle cars. Special agents met the travelers with water and food.

Benny watched, curious and bewildered. A strange odor permeated the air, causing him to search his memory for the familiarity of the smell. He remembered. It was Oswiecim where he recuperated in Franz's house. A disquieting feeling engulfed him. The smiles on the faces of the German SS seemed fixed and false. Whatever was happening, the SS commands seduced the people around him. The Jews moved like robots.

Perhaps, thought Benny, *we are all being tempted into complacency.*

A small freshly raked area began where the train platform ended. Benny questioned why the tracks ended so abruptly. Where were the tracks leading to the posted destinations?

The regal music began again.

Wagner, remembered Benny. This particular melody had been part of his father's record collection. *Is it possible this is further delusion,* he thought, *the splendor of the sound making the crowd regard themselves as visitors rather than prisoners? Ridiculous!*

The young Jew could not shake the ominous feeling that the welcoming music was really an orchestration of death?

"*Achtung!*" shouted an SS corporal to the arrivals. "Leave your belongings here in the reception area, except for your valuables. Take them with you and go straight to the baths."

"Why must we leave our luggage here?" asked a woman of her husband.

Benny turned to hear his answer.

"They will let us pick it up after we have refreshed and had food," he answered.

This just doesn't make sense, Benny reasoned. *Something is very sinister.*

Benny found himself caught in the crush of people. After a short march, the group, numbering more than five hundred entered a smaller complex. Later Benny would learn it was called Deportation Square. The SS guards immediately directed them into lines of twenty to twenty-five. Segregated, the women and girls stood in one group, the men and boys in another.

"Men remain here," barked the SS corporal. "The barrack on the left is for women and children. You may leave your shoes and stockings outside the door. "Take your valuables with you, and after you have undressed, wait for further directions."

Undressed? Benny wondered why that made him feel more vulnerable. It was as though he could feel his power being stripped away with the clothes. He decided to keep them on as long as the Nazis allowed.

"Benny, Benny Lipman, is it you?"

Startled by the calling of his name, Benny turned quickly toward the sound. A tall, thin youth, dressed in dirty and tattered clothes, stood among the others waiting their turn to undress and bathe.

"Rubin? Where did you come from?"

The old school chum moved quickly to Benny's side and embraced him.

A stocky Nazi, with a fixed smirk on his face, shouted orders for the group to proceed forward, but it was a slow pace.

Quietly Benny asked his old friend, "What is this about?"

"You don't want to know."

Benny looked closely at Rubin.

"I've been working here. Sometimes the workers just disappear after a few weeks. Now I join all of you."

"What do you mean you join all of us? I have overheard some of these people say they are transferring trains; others are going to the Ukraine," remarked Benny. He paused, looking closely at Rubin. "Should I have these uneasy feelings?"

"You're correct to feel troubled. No one leaves here alive. As much as it grieves me, I must tell you that you and I won't need anything more when they take us through 'the tube.'"

"What's 'the tube'?"

"It's the path to hell. It leads to a stone structure standing at the opposite end of the compound. It's a dingy gray color, and an enormous chimney rises skyward from its roof. As you approach, you see wide concrete steps that lead to a double wooden door. Carts wait along side the building for the bodies".

"Bodies?" How do you know that?"

"I know. At first the Nazis shot or buried alive prisoners not used for labor. Recently they began gassing them."

"In that building you described?" Benny's eyes widened.

"Yes. There is a long hallway with doors leading off on each side, as you will soon see for yourself. Once there, you will smell the most horrible smell ever."

"I smell the smell! What is it you're trying to tell me Rubin?"

"They're going to cremate us! That's what Treblinka is, a death house for our people. Thousands are shipped here daily."

Benny's heart froze.

"They shave the hair of the women over there in that barrack."
Rubin pointed to the building ahead and on the left. "I have heard
some weep for the beautiful hair they've lost."

"If they're going to kill them, why would they shave their
hair?"

"Witnesses have told me that the hair is disinfected and put into
sacks and sent to Germany."

"What for?"

"To stuff mattresses."

Benny could not find words to question further.

"One person said he heard the Germans may use the hair like
yarn for making rope for technical purposes."

Bent on keeping Benny's full attention, Rubin continued his
gruesome stories. "I'm telling you, there's no way out. Chambers are
built to kill thousands of people. In the short time since completion,
several groups have been sent through. It takes no longer than twenty
minutes, sometimes shorter, to die."

Rubin's eyes suddenly filled with tears. "My God, Benny, I've
had to help take the bodies out and load them on the small carts that
take them to one of the burial pits behind the building. The whole
damn place is nothing but a conveyor-belt of factory death!"

At the rise in Rubin's voice, Benny glanced to see if any of the
guards had heard.

"Enough, Rubin!"

The look on Benny's face prompted Rubin to stop.

Abruptly the guards ordered the group, in which the boys waited,
to move toward the barrack on the right.

Rubin put a hand on Benny's arm and whispered, "If we are
to die, Benny, please, for friendship sake, let's die together. Let's
pretend we are just going on a long trip, it isn't real, and later we will
meet our families again and be happy."

Benny shuddered at Rubin's rambling and the proposed death
pact. He turned away watching closely what was happening just
ahead of them.

Men left their valuables at a small makeshift booth where an SS officer sat and several Nazis stood guard over boxes stacked nearby. Once the valuables were in the box, the Jews entered the barrack to disrobe. Benny and Rubin waited their turn. There would be no valuables from them.

Though reality showed on their pale faces, the Jews mechanically obeyed. An older man, about forty feet in front of Benny, approached the booth. When the Nazi in charge ordered him to give up his valuables, a ring remained on one finger. The German demanded the ring, while the old man, shaking his head and looking at the Nazi with pleading eyes, tugged at his finger.

The Nazi shoved the man into the table, grabbed his hand and tried to force the ring from his finger. The man cried out in pain. When the German did not succeed in removing the ring, he motioned to another guard. Quickly he moved to the old man, drew a knife from his holster, and hacked off the man's finger.

Benny's stomach lurched.

The smiling guard held the finger bearing the ring in the air for all to see then dropped it into the valuable's box on the table. The man wobbled for a moment thereupon fell to the floor in a faint. Immediately the Nazi, who ordered the disfiguring, began kicking the defenseless man.

Unexpectedly Benny's focus was diverted to a Nazi, who ordered him and Rubin forward. Benny hesitated, reluctant to take off his clothes. The fear was so debilitating he could not think nor breathe. He was trapped in a vacuum where he could hear only the beat of his own heart and the pounding in his ears.

Abruptly a tall SS guard grabbed him by the arm and pulled him out of the line. Rubin cried, "No, let him go. We're friends and want to die to . . ."

Instantly the guard shoved Rubin, sending him sprawling onto the ground. "Your friend can die later," snapped the SS over his shoulder. "Right now I have a chore for him." He reached into the line and grabbed another boy.

Benny, half-paralyzed by fright, followed the guard to the spot where the fingerless man lay lifeless in a pool of blood.

"Pick up the filthy Jew and follow me."

Before the two youths could remove the man, a Nazi sergeant approached and told the guard to bring the boys to a jeep that waited in the reception area as soon as they had completed their task.

A jeep? Benny wondered what that meant.

The SS nodded an agreement to the request and motioned the boys to pick up the dead man.

Benny stooped over and lifted the man's legs while his partner put his hands under the man's armpits. The two struggled with the man's weight. Benny tried to avoid staring at this poor creature's face, beaten beyond recognition, his mouth gnarled in a frozen scream.

The two youths followed the German through the Jews standing in line at Deportation Square and onto a curved path. At first Benny did not realize it was "the tube" Rubin had told him about. Soon they approached a fenced area stuffed with tree branches, obviously a camouflage. Once inside Benny saw the stone building his friend had described.

The Nazi led them to the east side and several hundred feet from the building. An immense pit gaped like an open mouth. Close by were other huge holes.

Rubin had been correct. Thousands of bodies lay in the pit, dumped like trash.

"Throw him in," said the Nazi.

The boys gave each other a quick glance then threw the man into the cavity. Shivering, Benny watched as the body fell with a thud on top of the heap. He wondered how he could forget that he was a part of the terrible tragedy. If he survived it -- how it would shape his attitude about life.

Prodded by the Nazi, the two youths returned to "the square" and to the military vehicle. The sergeant, who had approached their guard, sat behind the wheel with a Nazi colonel beside him.

"Get in the back," ordered the officer. "You can leave," he said to the man who had ushered the boys to the jeep. A large box crowded the back of the jeep causing the youths to hesitate climbing in.

The colonel snarled, "Find a place, swine! Aren't Jews supposed to be creative entrepreneurs?"

Benny and the other youth, squeezed into the back of the jeep, were perched precariously, one on each side of the box. As the jeep sped away from the building, the two hung tightly to the box.

When they passed through the gates, sentries snapped to attention and saluted. Reentering the area, where the Jews left their luggage, Benny saw a group of men, wearing blue kerchiefs around their necks, searching and sorting the bags. Shipping boxes nearby held transferred items. Other crewmembers raked the ground, leaving no visible evidence where luggage had been.

Shortly the vehicle came to a stop at the railroad tracks where a train prepared to depart, its engines already bellowing smoke.

"Sergeant, stay with the jeep. You two, take the box and load it on that car." He pointed to a rail car near the rear of the train. Its door stood open.

Benny jumped out of the jeep and reached back to grab one end of the box as he motioned his co-worker to take the other. The two struggled with the heavy container. When they reached the train, Benny could see that it held clothes, piled high. He suggested getting into the car and pulling the box upward while his partner pushed from the bottom. The lad agreed.

While the officer watched, Benny jumped into the railroad car. In the process of struggling with the container, the top came open, revealing valuables taken from the prisoners. As Benny pulled the box into the car, he glanced cautiously at the officer. The Nazi had walked away to seek the light from a nearby lamppost. He fumbled for something in his breast pocket and finally withdrew a piece of paper and a pen.

Benny quickly looked toward the jeep. The sergeant sat smoking, his head resting on the back of the seat, eyes closed.

Head first, Benny dove into one of the piles of clothes. He scrambled to crawl under the tallest stack toward the rear of the car. His co-worker stood silently, eyes shifting to both the driver and the officer.

Moments later the German officer yelled, "Where is your friend?"

"I don't know, Herr. I think he went under the car." He pointed at the darkness under the train.

When gunfire sounded, Benny shuddered.

"Sergeant," shouted the officer, "get over here! The train is about to pull out."

Benny could hear the sound of the sergeant's heavy boots hitting the loose gravel as he ran toward the command.

"Find that son-of-a-bitch!" yelled the officer. "Use your bayonet. Search the clothing."

The young Jew's heart pounded so loudly he thought his breathing might give him away.

Furiously the sergeant jabbed the pile of clothes across from Benny. He had just begun to jab at the pile under which the youth hid, when the train began to move slowly.

"Enough," said the colonel. "The stupid pig can't be here. How far can he go anyway? Someone else will find him."

Benny never thought the sound of a steel door slamming shut and bolting into place would sound so good! At last he took a deep breath.

The train, laden with the clothes and valuables of the Jews, pulled away from the death camp. Hidden in the cargo, young Benny silently thanked God for his escape. Saddened by the loss of the young Jew who helped him load the box, he recognized that no Jew had immunity from disaster. He knew he must be strong mentally and physically if he were to survive.

Benny escaped the tragedy of Treblinka. In July of 1943 the camp shut down after an insurrection of approximately 750 prisoners. Only seventy survived. However, more than 800,000 Jews perished there -- 300,000 were from Warsaw or the Warsaw area.

Benny did not know how far they had gone before the train stopped. He heard German voices and a clicking as the car door unlocked. His heart racing, he moved quickly to cover himself with the clothes. The conversation led Benny to believe the Nazis were removing the box of valuables. This puzzled him. Obviously Nazi scavengers not only picked a Jew's carcass clean before death; they also stole from each other.

Relief came as soon as the door slammed shut, and the train whistle blew. The youth rested finally when the train picked up speed and lumbered into the night. Benny's was yet another unknown destination.

He awakened to the daylight filtering through the slats of the small window. Benny knew that he must make plans for escape. Breaking the wooden slats that barred windows had worked before, but he must be wise in choosing the time and place to escape. He would need to prepare himself, and he needed darkness. The young Jew searched through the clothing, soon selecting a suit and shoes for himself. While he waited for night, he would work on removing the slats one by one.

The hours passed and Benny struggled with the weathered pieces of wood covering the exit. Again he used a shoe for a wedge. He worked through the day. Shortly after daylight had begun to turn to dusk, the train slowed, shunted, and gradually came to a stop. Hoping for the opportunity he needed, Benny watched closely through the small opening that he had created. It was his. The train had stopped to switch tracks, and there was no visible sign of a town or people. Eventually the train would move forward again. He must make his move now.

Benny squeezed through the opening and fell to the ground, where he rolled several times before landing in a sandpit. He lay for a moment watching and listening. Confident that he could move under the guise of nightfall, he began crawling toward the semblance of trees several feet away. Hemmed in by the protection of the forest, Benny decided to wait out the night, for accidentally stumbling into the enemy would be fatal.

He slept restlessly. When he heard a rooster crowing and the lowing of cows, he got up and headed in the direction of the sounds.

Was he already in Germany? He prayed it was not so.

Daylight was imminent when he came into a clearing where a small brick house nestled near the woods. The need for food and drink motivated Benny to risk approaching the house. As he reached the porch, a barking dog came from the side of the house. The boy and the dog watched each other with apprehension. Benny knocked on the door that posted a sign reading "Miller." The dog continued to bark but did not approach.

A woman with a pleasant face opened the door. She asked him in German if she could help him. Haltingly Benny answered in the same language, hoping to hide his nationality.

"My name is Bernard Lapinski," he said. "I've been working for a German farmer since the overrun of Poland. Now because of bad health, I am allowed to return home."

The young Jew thanked God for giving him a quick wit and the talent to speak several languages. Both already proved life saving. Confidently he smiled at the woman.

"Come in, young man." She smiled back, holding open the door for him. "Come into the kitchen. I have food from breakfast."

Benny sat at the small kitchen table while his hostess warmed cabbage, potatoes and onions, cooked with a generous portion of pork. He would not refuse the forbidden meat.

Famished, Benny ate without conversation. The woman, smiling as the boy took second helpings, sat with him. "Watching you eat makes me miss my sons," she said. "Two of them are with the Wermacht in Hungary." She paused, sadness creeping onto her face. "Our third son was killed in Poland. I miss *mein Söhnchen*." Tears filled her eyes.

Startled at the woman's sudden frankness, Benny responded, "I'm sorry, ma'am. I understand that you must miss your son. So many have lost their lives in the war. I lost my family."

The woman looked tenderly at the youth "And you are so young. Who will you go home to?"

Between mouthfuls he answered, "I have friends I will stay with. Can you help me get back to Warsaw? I have no money or directions."

"How did you get here?" she asked.

"I hitched a ride on a train."

She laughed. "Oh, a regular gypsy. Yes?"

Benny smiled at her teasing. "Not a very smart one, I'm afraid, if I've gone the wrong direction. By the way, am I in Germany?"

"No -- near the border."

That his get-away train had not crossed the border into Germany was a blessing.

"Hitching a ride on a train is something my lost son would have done," remarked Mrs. Miller. "He was a very resourceful young man, very much like you."

Benny welcomed the woman's friendliness. It had been too long since he had felt safe. In some ways she reminded him of Franz, the German man in Oswiecim.

"Why don't you stay on for a while? I cannot see that my husband would object."

"What does your husband do?" asked Benny.

"My husband works at an ammunition factory now, but he wanted to be a Storm Trooper. He applied but was not accepted."

This new information was enough to convince Benny he needed to move on. He did not wish to meet a man desirous of being a Storm Trooper. The boy knew the requirements demanded of those recruits.

After the meal, Mrs. Miller packed a feed sack full of her dead son's clothes. She gave it to Benny and offered him a ride in a horse-drawn cart to the nearest village. At the station, she bought him a ticket to Lódz, approximately eighty miles southwest of Warsaw.

As he said good-bye to Mrs. Miller, she took his hand and put twenty marks into it. "Son, I wish good luck. Let us pray the war will soon end and return us to normalcy."

"And your sons will return safely."

Unexpectedly Mrs. Miller took Benny into her arms and crushed him to her bosom.

Benny welcomed the embrace. *She is no different*, he thought, *than mothers of other nationalities.* A wave of sadness nearly overwhelmed him as he waved good-bye and faced his own reality of no mother. Regardless of the duration of the war, he had no one left to go home to.

Home? Where is home? he pondered.

Yet the youth chose to return to Warsaw once again. Where else could he go? It was the only place he knew. Perhaps there he would locate someone to help him escape this hell.

—◆ ✦ ◆—

"If I were you, boy, I would not masquerade as a Pole. If you are caught, it will go badly for you."

The Polish farmer's remark startled Benny. He did not answer.

The cart moved slowly, and the two rode in silence.

It had been an uneventful train ride to Lódz. On the outskirts of the city, Benny hitched a ride with a trucker. Then he walked a half-day before a farmer picked him up.

After the strange statement by the Pole, they had ridden in silence. Benny feared the man had intentions of turning him in.

"Of course," said the farmer, "if you think it is best to turn yourself in, you must use your own judgment. We are nearing Praga. I will have to let you off soon."

"Sir, I appreciate the ride." Benny hoped friendliness and a small lie would forestall being turned in. "I'll take your advice and turn myself in." He smiled coyly at the farmer.

"Good," responded the man, looking straight ahead. Benny could see a smirk on the farmer's face.

When they reached Praga, the farmer surprised the youth with a gift of tobacco.

Strange, thought Benny, thanking him. Watching the man pull away, he vowed to himself never, under any circumstances, would he turn himself in.

The streets of Praga seemed familiar to Benny. Canopies hung over tabled areas, exhibiting products for sale -- garden produce, dairy, and poultry goods.

The white cheese caught Benny's fancy. He decided he would buy some of it and a little bread. A Polish woman dressed in a babushka and a black, old-fashioned farm apron watched him count his money. A broad smile spread across her strong-featured face.

Without hesitation, she forced into his hands a large round slab of cheese.

This must weigh five pounds, thought Benny, grinning, *certainly not the five deko I requested.*

Benny could not explain the "why" of human behavior, but he was soon to meet another benefactor -- on Zombkowska Street. A Polish man, in his fifties, offered him water and soup as well as friendly conversation. Later the man rode with him on a streetcar into Warsaw, giving him twenty Zloty at the end of the ride.

Benny believed that the good Lord directed him to the people he should meet. This eased the pain of meeting those with evil intentions.

—➤ ✳ ◀—

Benny had tried to re-enter the ghetto, but the numerous patrols dissuaded him. Finally he decided to try to find help in the Polish sector, first appearing at the door of the man for whom he made money for the ghetto resistance. No one answered his knock, and the house looked deserted.

Soon afterward he remembered Antek Krazynski. Mr. Krazynski was the Gentile who had worked for Aaron Lipman as a handyman at the shop. Later the family employed him as the shabbesgoy who shut off the Lipman house lights and fires so they would not have to break the Sabbath laws. The Krazynskis had been guests at the Lipman home for many meals. Jana Krazynski often sat with Mirla, passing the time. Their son, Stanley, was Sala's age, though the two were not friends.

In late 1938 the Krazynski family promised Aaron he could count on them for help if anything happened to the Jews in Poland. Before the Germans had a chance to confiscate the Lipman business, Aaron had hidden approximately twenty-five thousand dollars worth of material with Antek Krazynski. He hoped to keep it from the Germans.

Though the Krazynskis secreted the materials, they told the Lipmans they could not endanger their own family by harboring them. Later Benny had approached the Krazynskis for the goods, needing them for food bartering. They told him the Germans had confiscated the materials.

When Benny reached the Krazynski house, it was beginning to rain, a cool pre-fall wetness that sometimes preceded September and October in Warsaw. Nightfall crowded the daylight, giving him little chance of finding shelter. In the distance, thunder growled and lightning flickered.

Mrs. Krazynski opened the door to Benny's knock, a puzzled look crossing her face.

"Don't you remember me? I'm Benny Lipman."

She looked closely at the youth. With recognition, her face flushed. Hesitantly she invited him in and asked about his family.

"I am so sorry to hear your news," she said. "We did not realize those sorts of things were occurring."

How could she not know what was happening to the Jews in the ghetto? "I felt sure I could count on your family for help. I have nowhere to go. Could you put me up for one or two nights?"

A long pause validated his earlier sense of her reluctance.

Finally she answered, "We will wait for my husband to come home." Her eyes shifted from his. "He works as a janitor at the Okecie Air Force Base -- in the SS office."

As they conversed, the front door opened.

"Here is my son," she said nervously. "You remember him? Stanley, do you remember the Lipman boy, Benny?"

Studying Benny, Stanley grunted a greeting as he passed him and moved toward the back of the house.

"Would you like to have something to eat?"

"If it is not too much trouble, Mrs. Krazynski. Thank you." Benny could never seem to get his fill of food.

When Antek Krazynski arrived home and saw Benny, his eyes widened with surprise. Regaining his composure, he stuttered a greeting, grabbing Benny's hand.

"Benny, how are you? And your family? How is your father?"

Before Benny could answer, Krazynski said, "It's nice to see you. Do you want something to eat?"

"He has already had some soup and bread," said his wife.

"Soup? He needs something more substantial than that." Krazynski reached for a whiskey bottle and started to pour drinks.

"Not for me, sir," responded Benny waving away the glass. He did not want his wits dimmed by liquor.

"Will you spend the night?" Jana Krazynski gave her husband a quick look. "We will see in the morning how we can help. My wife and I cannot keep you here more than one night because our neighbors might see and call the Germans."

Benny nodded. He understood.

"It is getting late. Let me show you to a space in the attic. I am afraid it is all we have."

Too tired to worry about the condition of the area where he slept, Benny bid the family goodnight and followed Krazynski up the narrow staircase to the attic.

Benny fell asleep quickly, but was startled shortly afterward by loud voices. The angry sounds worried him. He moved from the pallet to the door, but he still could not hear clearly. Quietly he slipped down the stairs to the attic doorway. The Krazynski's bedroom door was halfway open.

The voices were those of the two older Krazynskis.

"Antek, we cannot harbor a Jew," said Mrs. Krazynski.

"What should we do?"

"Since Benny is the only one left of his family . . ."

"He didn't say that."

"Antek, the Germans will discover we exchanged the hidden material for money."

"I have an idea . . ."

The door closed unexpectedly, muting sounds and the rest of Antek Krazynski's suggestion.

Benny moved quietly into the attic, the half statement causing chills along his spine. Should he leave now or wait for morning? He risked waiting, but he could not sleep. What if the old man planned to kill him? Surely his wife would not let him. Maybe the fear that the Germans will see them as harboring a Jew will overcome a wise decision.

Benny decided he would leave at the first opportunity.

As he tried to reclaim sleep, he remembered the kindness his parents had bestowed on this family. Aaron had given Antek two suits a year, worth more than the money he could have given him for his general handyman duties, both at the house and the shop. The wife and son received clothes as well. It was so like Benny's mother and father to share with employees as well as strangers. Surely they would not allow harm to come to the son of a man who had been so generous with them.

When Benny entered the kitchen the next morning, Antek sat at the kitchen table, a half-empty whisky bottle in front of him. He looked up as the youth entered the room but said nothing.

"Good morning," stammered Benny, surveying the room.

Antek took a drink from the bottle, brown liquid running from the corners of his mouth. His wife ducked her head, nervously adjusting the cook stove. Neither spoke.

Stanley was nowhere in sight.

"Thank you for your hospitality," said Benny as he moved toward the door. "I will be on my way."

Surprised, Antek put down his bottle and moved quickly to the window. Pulling aside the curtain, he glanced outside. "Offer the boy some milk, Mama," he said.

The woman rushed to obey, still not meeting Benny's eyes.

"No, thank you," said Benny, worried now.

When he headed for the door, Antek moved abruptly from the window, reaching out his hand. "Stay, stay awhile longer."

"No," responded Benny, jerking away from him. He moved quickly to the door, tears moistening his eyes.

As he opened the door and stepped on the porch, he saw Stanley coming toward the house gesturing wildly to two Jewish policemen who accompanied him.

Benny, scrambling down the steps, ran in the opposite direction of the oncoming police.

"There he is!" yelled Stanley, pointing at Benny.

"Halt!" shouted a policeman.

Benny kept running. He had not gone more than two blocks, when he ran into a German patrol that quickly surrounded him.

Benny, like a trapped animal, began to shove and push his way from the ambush. Immediately one of the SS guards knocked the boy to the ground and began kicking him.

Soon the Jewish police entered the fray, and the Germans, joking about the Jews taking care of their kind, stood back and watched.

As Benny looked up into their leering faces, searching their eyes for reason, the Jewish police hit him again and again.

My God, my own people have prostituted their souls to the Germans. That was the last thing Benny remembered.

Only four to six months after Benny's recapture outside the Krazynski home, the psychological resistance, begun by the small group of Jews and Poles battling the dishonor and disfranchisement of the Jewish people, escalated to an armed uprising. It was a battle for self-preservation.

Defiant members of the revolt placed placards on the ghetto walls, and in Muranowska Square raised two flags from the top of a building -- a flag of Poland; the other, a blue and white Jewish national symbol. The resisting force called for aid from their fellow Jews. The response was weak.

Compared to the massive German force -- three times larger -- the resistance was small. The Germans torched the ghetto -- building by building -- chasing Jews from bunker to bunker. Sometimes they used gas grenades or search dogs to find them, and by May 16,1944 they had captured or killed 56,065. Only a few Jews held out in undiscovered bunkers until August.

The uprising lasted forty-two days, and when it ended, the ghetto stood like a graveyard.

FIFTEEN

THE SHRILL WHISTLE RIPPED INTO the dawn and extinguished the quiet time when he was alone with his dreams. Benny dreaded these moments when he first awoke. It was inconceivable that the still-exhausted body must struggle to move again into the roll-call line. Waiting were the few ounces of bread and the cup of thin, watery soup -- certainly not enough sustenance for the bone crunching work that faced him.

In the time warp that physical abuse, hard work, and lack of food provided, he could not calculate how long it had been since he arrived at the Lublin area.

---●※●---

The day Benny returned to Lublin -- the fall of 1942 -- he knew that history had a way of repeating itself. K. L. Majdanek stood in the open field, where in 1940 the boy had lived with other laborers in quickly constructed barracks.

Benny could not forget the forced march and the runners who had died, the fake rabbi, the transfer to the river project, and the deaths of Moses and Jacob.

After arriving at the Lublin station in 1942, the prisoners had marched the mile and a quarter to Majdanek, guided by the usual verbal and physical abuse. The fright of the women and children

243

created a noise that added to the pandemonium. When people stumbled and fell, Nazis freely clubbed them with their rifle butts.

The 675-acre camp loomed before them -- double rows of electrified barbed-wire fence surrounding the camp. From high towers, sentries holding machine guns viewed the recruits. Large numbers of Alsatian dogs stood by SS guards.

Within a year the camp would be complete with its additions of foreboding chimneys and additional gas chambers. Completed, the camp would hold six sections of twenty-four barracks, housing sometimes more than three hundred persons. Benny would become a part of that work force to build a crematorium that by the end of the war would have burned a large number of the estimated 1,500,000 prisoners killed at Majdanek.

When Benny returned in October 1942, gassing cells, torture, starvation, and shooting were the means of death. The bodies, piled high in bonfire fashion, burned in nearby clearings. Just before his arrival, 350 women and children had been gassed and burned. Shortly after his arrival, five thousand Russian war prisoners were taken to a nearby former stone quarry and shot.

Prisoners at forced labor at the Majdanek concentration camp. USHMM, courtesy of Instytut Pamieci Narodowej

Eventually Benny and the other prisoners marching in from Lublin formed groups of one hundred twenty to one hundred fifty. If he had not seen it with his own eyes, Benny would not have believed the size of this roundup. He guessed it totaled somewhere between four and five thousand people. Idzikowski had been right. The Germans had escalated the daily deportation of Jews to work or to death camps.

Serious doubts clouded Benny's belief that he could once again suspend sentence and execution. Always seeking means to prolong his life, he remained observant of his surroundings. His sole salvation was forefront in his mind.

As the camp gates opened for the recruits, some prisoners had rushed up to them, begging.

"Please, give us bread!"

"Give up your food, if you have it. You will die anyway."

Everywhere eyes registered want and hunger.

Prisoners carried stretchers with lifeless, skeleton-like bodies. Trucks, with special platforms hauled by tractors, transported stacks of dead people. The stench of decay pervaded the compound. Other prisoners walked hunched over, picking up papers with sticks, nails driven into the ends. They looked like scarecrows in their oversized striped uniforms and shaven heads. Some captives stood listlessly, rags hanging from their feeble bodies, skin tinged blue with cold, their teeth chattering. Still others squatted by makeshift campfires scattered about the compound.

Benny and the other new prisoners had marched quickly by the inmates. With great military efficiency, the German SS in charge of the march ordered the captives to halt in front of the camp commandant. The SS guard saluted and left after giving the officer a full report. Soon the commandant departed, leaving the prisoners standing at attention in the cold.

The boring military procedure continued over a period of two hours. Benny considered he had become an expert at the foolish game of waiting. He was one of the fortunate who wore a coat.

Finally the commandant made his second appearance, and the old familiar selection began. A nervous tension riffled through the prisoners.

With the first sign of confusion among the crowd, Benny eased his way toward the favored right line.

"Halt!" called an observant SS guard.

Benny's heart beat staccato in his chest.

"Move out of line! Follow me!"

The young Jew obeyed, following the SS guard to a concrete building nearby. A sign indicated it was the camp headquarters. Benny stood quietly while the guard gave a report of Benny's misconduct.

A large man sat behind a desk and stared at Benny. No expression crossed the man's face as the guard talked.

When the guard finished reporting, he clicked his heels, turned sharply, and walked out of the room.

Benny looked fully at the man. When the Nazi rose, he stood like a giant, towering over the boy. The German never said a word, but his stare made Benny's skin crawl.

The Nazi moved from behind his desk and walked up to the youth. He stood close to Benny, almost touching him.

Silence.

Benny held his breath.

With the hint of a smirk, the man punched him in the stomach. In excruciating pain, Benny fell to the floor. When he struggled to get up, the bully hit him again, knocking the wind out of him.

On the floor, Benny lay gasping. He felt his lungs would burst.

All the while the big man never uttered a word.

Next he seized the boy by the neck and jerked him into a standing position. Dazed, Benny watched the ugly set of the man's jowls and the intense anger reflected in his eyes.

"You no good dirty Jew, I will give you a lesson that will make the gas cell seem like a school party! I will make a man of you, Jude!"

Without warning he hit Benny in the face. Before Benny could fall, the man caught him, lifting him by the seat of his pants and the nape of his neck. Stomping through the office and across the compound, the Nazi carried the boy like a sack of feed into a nearby barracks. Maliciously, he threw Benny into one of the bunks.

"Tomorrow is mine, Jude," he promised as he walked out of the barracks.

All night Benny lay awake. He knew that Nazis had a peculiar memory for keeping their vows, especially vengeful ones.

Early the next morning, the man entered the barracks, pulled Benny out of the bunk and ordered the boy to follow him. Later he would be thankful he slept with his coat on.

The cold morning air made his swollen and bloodshot eyes sting. He could barely make out the outline of the gray building that housed the gas cells. Shuddering, he could not discern between fear and cold.

They stopped at a spot where snow had accumulated. The Nazi ordered Benny to remove his shoes. Instantly the boy knew the punishment, and a wave of fresh fear overtook him. He followed the orders.

Standing barefoot in the snow Benny lost track of time. He fought tears, his feet throbbing. Soon numbness set in. Now he struggled with the thought of frostbite and loss of parts of his feet.

Somehow he kept his sanity by trying to forget his own predicament, by visualizing warmth and safety. When trucks rolled by with their cargoes of death, human bodies piled high, he thanked God he was not among them.

The morning sun brought some warmth, but the young Jew wondered if he would live to see another sun.

As late afternoon shadows began, reprieve came from his icy platform. His feet were numb. Accompanied by the staunch-faced Nazi and with great difficulty, he stumbled back to the barracks.

Exhausted, Benny fell into the bunk. He rubbed his feet with the hope to stir them back to life. When they slowly began to thaw, the deep gnawing ache threatened to make him nauseous. Although the pain tormented him, Benny welcomed feeling.

Just as the youth finally dozed off, he was startled by cold water splashed in his face. The large Nazi brute towered over Benny. With his usual sinister smile, he once again issued the detestable orders.

Outside Benny removed his shoes and stood in the snow. For three days the torture continued -- the numbness, and soon afterward the thawing, followed by numbness. Each time he returned to the snow, Benny thought it might be his last. The vicious game the Germans played provoked the young Jew to wonder if his mind would succumb before his body.

On the fourth day, when the Nazi tormentor came for him, Benny begged, "For the love of God, don't make me stand in the snow again!"

No answer was forthcoming. Instead the German pushed him toward the camp commandant's office. It was a brief meeting.

"We are satisfied that you have learned a lesson," said the commandant from behind his desk. "Now we are giving you the opportunity to work for the Fatherland. Work hard and rewards will come your way."

Benny glanced at the giant who had been his constant torturer the last few days. The man stared straight ahead, no show of emotion on his face.

Benny welcomed the reprieve from death, though he realized how close he had come to accepting his fate. When he reflected later on this turn of events, he wondered if fortitude made him a prime candidate for hard labor. He had no idea what the labor was to be.

The new job was a gruesome task. All day Benny's work crew of six fellows carried the dead. The carrion, mostly naked skeletons, died either from disease, starvation, or beatings. Neither age nor gender prevailed. Usually two workers carried a single body, one lifting the corpse by the arms, the other by the legs. Sometimes each carried a carcass over his back.

Benny carried his load with as much dignity as he could muster. The stench almost overwhelmed him, but the greatest burden lay in his sadness for the once human baggage, naked for the world to see, flesh stretched tightly across bones, mouth gaping, hollow cavities where once eyes could see.

Day after day they carried their freight to the back of a large building where they dumped it. Benny tried to block from his mind what the SS guards did with the bodies. Each time the smoke bellowed in the distance, Benny wondered which cargo it was. He felt he would never again smell fresh air or clean himself of the soot that drifted across them all.

Once, following the last work detail of the day, Benny turned to an older fellow worker and asked, "What do you think they do with the bones that remain?"

The man hesitated before he answered, "Son, I've heard stories." He paused. "Do you really want to talk about this?"

"Yes," answered Benny, prepared for the worst.

The man looked to see if the guards could hear. Then he whispered, "Fertilizer is made . . ."

"What?"

"Shhh," cautioned the man.

"You don't know!" accused Benny.

"Yes, I do and worse -- combs and soap and . . ."

"Stop!"

"And what's more," insisted the man. "It is our fate also."

Benny stared at the man. "Not mine," he vowed as he walked away quickly. *Not mine!*

Tears began to slide down his face even before he reached the barracks. Benny did not want to believe the man. Yet confirmations of other acts haunted him. Where had Benny heard that women's hair stuffed pillows and mattresses and even interlaced technical wiring? He remembered. It was Rubin at Treblinka.

From somewhere deep inside him, Benny knew he must not dwell on this. Instead he must have a goal that would sustain him. *Did the others die because they had no hope? I will not let that happen!* Benny pledged that each time he slipped into morbid thinking, he would replace it with expectations of life. Perhaps that would be his salvation.

The whistle shrieked again, displacing Benny's thoughts of his return to Majdanek. Soon the winter of 1943 would give way to spring, and he had survived each day of the last months by clinging to his goal. In two months he would be fifteen years old. He crawled out of the bunk, his frail body aching as he made his way to the roll call line.

It was customary -- roll call and a meager meal. Those missing from the line-up met their fate. Nazis dragged them from their sick beds and shot them in the presence of the others. The Germans were good at intimidation.

As usual the cold pierced Benny's body, and the wind chilled him throughout. His tattered clothes and worn-thin shoes did not ward off the unrelenting winter. A threadbare, oversized coat was a small blessing.

He sensed it immediately. Something was different today. The Nazis began selecting and ordering certain prisoners to assemble in the reception area. Pointing at their choices, they moved quickly through the lines. One picked Benny. Along with fifteen other youths, he joined a group of five hundred. They waited for their orders.

Using a cart holding large kettles, the Germans began dispensing dark bread and bean and potato soup. Benny could not believe his good luck. Too early he had broken his promise to himself and assumed the worst. His hopes rose. The Germans would not give a Last Supper to the condemned.

If Europe's greatest chefs had prepared the food, it would not have tasted better. Not only did it warm Benny's chilled body, but it also fed his mind with confidence.

The assembled did not know the Germans had broadened their labor force scope. They needed workers to make much needed ammunition for the German army. Benny was one of the chosen. He and the others would leave the completion of the five furnaces at Majdanek to others.

As they marched out of the camp toward the train tracks, Benny whispered to one of his compatriots, "Friend, it looks like we aren't bait for the gas cells, at least for a while."

The man mustered a weak smile and nodded, "Perhaps. You cannot trust these butchers. If it is not gas, it will be by other means."

Though Benny considered the remark sobering, he decided to ignore it. Having chosen protection from the bitter cold in the center of the group, he marched in silence as he left Majdanek.

—◆ ✧ ◆—

The truck pulled up to a large compound fenced with barbed wire. Almost a year earlier, in August 1942, the Germans had organized *Zwangsarbeitslager-Judenlager*, the Skarzysko-Kamienna forced-labor camp, into three smaller camp factories adjacent to an ammunition plant. Two SS guards opened the gates, and the truck pulled into Werke A, the largest of the three camps.

The sun left distinct shadows on the snow-covered ground as the men piled out of the truck and formed the inevitable lines. After a short march past a line of barracks, the group arrived at a five-story concrete building. Along its side sat a one-story frame structure attached to the large building by a narrow corridor. Several Jewish, Polish, and German guards waited for them.

"You will work for the Fatherland," said a blond officer. "You should be proud to be chosen. Work hard and you will be rewarded. Heil, Hitler."

It was always the same promise. When the assembled, standing with their caps in hand, did not respond, the Polish deputies and Jewish police modeled their reply, "Heil, Hitler." They encouraged the new group to repeat it.

Hesitantly Benny and the others gave the verbal salute to the Führer. They were afraid not to.

Before being allowed to join the work detail, Benny and the others reported to a building across from the foundry where the Germans ordered the men to submerge themselves in a big barrel filled with disinfectant. The treatment to kill suspected body lice lasted only a short time. Afterwards a barber gave each a close-cropped haircut. A shower followed, groups of fifteen and twenty sharing only a few stalls. No one complained about the rough soap that produced little lather. The shower was an unexpected treat.

In the afternoon, the Jews assembled to tour the foundry. Amazed at the size of the machines, Benny missed nothing as he walked through the area. When he ventured to speak with some of the Polish and Jewish machine operators, they all agreed that working conditions were not too bad. When the workers spoke of Werke B and C, they noted drastic contrasts, especially with C. Some noted it was a demotion leading to death to be transferred there. Those who could not keep up the workload in C eventually ended up before the firing squad or died from exhaustion, like worn out machinery.

At the first opportunity, Benny sought out someone who could give him information. As he walked around the compound, Benny saw that conditions were better than he had experienced. Men stood talking and smiling. Some cooked over campfires, peeling potatoes and placing them in a large pot. Food seemed fairly plentiful -- apples, dark and white bread and even candy bars. He would soon learn that one must be clever in order to obtain food.

As he roamed the area, Benny came upon an old man in tattered clothing. His bowed head epitomized the plight of the Jews, and the boy's heart went out to him.

"Hello," said Benny to the man. "My name is Benny."

Startled, the man looked closely at the boy. A slow smile spread across his wrinkled face.

"Tell me about this place," said Benny.

"You know we are in the Polish state of Kielce?"

"Yes. Tell me about the labor camp."

"There are three Werke, identified as A, B, and C. The Jews were sent here in 1942."

"How long have you been here?"

"I have been here a long time. I am from Sandomiez and have not seen either my wife or my eight children since the beginning of the war."

"Oh. . . ."

"It is difficult here. The meager food supply is not enough to live on and not enough to die from. I clean the streets and garbage containers. Garbage may become your best friend."

"I understand." Benny, too, had eaten discarded food.

The man moved closer to the youth and whispered cautiously, "Your biggest concern is how long you will remain in Werke A. A large number of the people who come here are transferred to other camps. Pray that you get to stay here."

"Why?"

"The working conditions in this camp are much easier than in the other two camps. The general manager of the factory system is a German officer by the name of Hines. Each Werke has its own commandant who answers to him."

"What about the Jewish police?"

"Each camp has a Jewish elder or president. Beware of them. Free Poles are paid as workers or deputies. Some very vicious ones act as factory supervisors."

"Where do most of the Jews come from?"

"Mostly Poland, though some come from Czechoslovakia, Austria and the Netherlands, even Germany." He placed a hand on Benny's arm. "I must go now. Perhaps we will meet again." Tears moistened his eyes. "Thank you for giving me the opportunity to talk to you."

"*Shalom.*"

"Peace go with you, young man."

Benny watched the man walk away, saddened that life had reached such a state that a friendly talk could be so gratifying to a person.

Hoping to find a friendly face, Benny roamed farther. To his surprise he saw a man he had seen several times in the village of Wodzislaw, the home of his grandparents. He knew him only as Libel. Libel was earnestly trading some saccharine with a fellow prisoner.

"I know you from Wodzislaw," said Benny.

The man stared at him, annoyed at the disruption. He did not answer and continued the barter. Finally satisfied, the two traders parted.

Libel turned to Benny. "Money talks."

"But where did you get the money?"

"I'm sorry, but you are on your own." Ignoring Benny, Libel walked away without further comment.

Benny called after the man. "I'm hungry. Please, can't you give me some bread?"

Libel did not turn nor acknowledge Benny's plea. It was a hard lesson for Benny. Prisoners, forced into the animal lifestyle of the camps, learned to focus in a singular fashion to save their own skins. It was very different from the instruction Benny had gained from his humanitarian parents. He remembered vividly Mirla's beggar proposition.

"Aaron, it's time we did something for those people on the street."

Nine-year-old Benny, who sat at the breakfast table with his family, looked to his father for an answer.

"What is that, dear?" smiled Aaron.

"Do beggars still greet you each morning outside your office?"

"Yes indeed. And they are always so appreciative of what I give them."

"Then let's give them more," said Mirla.

Benny and his sister watched the smile that spread on Aaron's face. They knew he would not deny their mother any request. Brother and sister nudged each other, waiting for their mother's suggestion.

"I think we should make it a regular occasion to have a few of them for dinner each Friday evening, that is, if they are comfortable with the offer of celebrating Shabbat with us."

Before Aaron could answer, Benny asked excitedly, "Please, may Sala and I be there?"

"Of course you will be there," answered his mother. "It will be our traditional religious celebration."

Aaron laughed loudly. "It appears the decision has already been made," he said, winking at Benny. "I will attend to it. It was a wonderful suggestion, Mirla."

Benny looked forward to "beggar's night." Usually five or six appeared for dinner. Mostly the guests were men, but occasionally a woman was among them. They all sat around the huge Lipman dining table, eating and talking. They talked of their dreams for success or how they survived the situations facing them daily.

Those were happy times for Benny. The "beggar dinners" lasted until the war broke out. Then the Lipmans became paupers too.

Now as Benny reflected on that experience, he believed it may have been one of the best of his life. He learned courage from those men and women. He would draw on that and find a way to make money or barter for his physical existence, just as he had before.

Later he approached the men peeling potatoes. After they refused him the skins, he searched a garbage pail near the kitchen. He found what he was looking for -- discarded peelings.

If it's going to be each man for himself, then so be it.

He ate the prize find, glad to have this small source of food.

He was to have a further dividend. That evening when the Jewish police entered the barracks for a head count, an SS guard followed and ordered the prisoners to a nearby distribution area. There they received pajka, a piece of square-shaped bread. Benny, determined to chew his portion slowly, savored the oatmeal and potato bread as long as possible.

Each evening men and women laborers lined up together for the pint of pasty, thick potato soup. Under normal conditions, swine ate the substance, but to Benny it was a treat, even if it was insufficient to quell his hunger.

Days passed and still he searched for the answer to more food. It seemed that all those around him had money to buy luxury items such as oranges, apples, and other treats. His mouth watered for even one of these prizes. Later he learned that Polish workers in the camp brought in the many items for sale.

One evening, shortly after his internment, Benny slipped back into line for a second helping. As he reached the front of the line, a Jewish policeman recognized him, and taking a heavy metal ladle used to portion out the soup, he hit Benny on the head.

Benny jumped back, his skin stinging from the blow. When he reacted angrily, the man admonished the boy.

"What are you thinking, boy? Think about where you are!"

"I just wanted more food. I need more food," reasoned the youth.

"Well, if you are found doing that again, your wants will get you Werke C!"

Although he had heard disparaging remarks about Werke C, Benny did not fully understand. He did reason he would have to be more sleuth-like to get what he needed.

The Jewish police aroused the workers early each morning and ordered them to assemble outside. They marched a short distance from their quarters to an area marked "Werke A," a foundry where laborers extricated long, hot metal bars from the furnaces. Both Poles and Jews worked in the foundry -- the Poles since before the war. The Jews helped stack the cooled iron bars in neat tiers.

Benny decided it was wise to make friends with the Poles. One of them worked alongside Benny and told him that conditions differed in the foundry in regard to the workers. The Polish workers made about 150 Zloty per week while the Jews made nothing, similar to the German control of Maronski's project.

"The best that you and your people can expect is a little larger portion at mealtime. That is all."

One day Benny took the opportunity to approach a Polish worker who was eating lunch. Eyeing the food, Benny asked, "Would you like to hear a song?"

Surprised, the man nodded in affirmation. Benny burst into melody, an old Polish ballad often sung in the small villages. Smiling and clapping, other Poles circled around the two.

Once Benny finished the first song, he started another, plaintive and sad. When he finished, his voice choked with emotion.

Immediately the crowd chorused, "Bravo, *śpiewak!*"

One man stepped forward with a ham sandwich. Others, following suit, offered coffee and soup. For the first time in a while, Benny felt that life had some meaning. A final gift was a piece of homemade cake, a real luxury for the young Jew.

One of the Poles informed Benny that, even if he transferred to another of the area camps, he could come back to Werke A on Sundays for a shower along with the other prisoners. He asked if

Benny would share his songs again. Pleased at both the request and information about a weekly shower, Benny readily agreed. Many of the Poles voiced their good wishes and their desire to hear him sing again.

"Have faith," said one man, "Your status as a human has been summarily removed from you and your people. I pray you will soon regain it."

Overwhelmed by sudden emotion, Benny's eyes glistened with tears.

The deepening shadows of evening hung across the heavens when one hundred laborers marched the five miles from Werke A to Werke B. Uniformed Jewish police carrying nightsticks heavily guarded them.

Benny did not know why he was among the transfers from Werke A. Looking at the perimeters of the camp, Benny could assess that the two camps were carbon copies. Two Jewish police guarded the giant gate to the outer compound. From there they walked into a wooded area that held long wooden barracks. Inside he discovered the truth. Tarpaper covering the interior walls provided little warmth, and three-tiered, bare wooden bunks provided sleeping arrangements.

Benny's new barrack companions, skin stretched tightly across their gaunt faces and frames, looked hollowed-eyed at the recruit. Benny looked back. No one spoke. The boy decided he could accomplish nothing by allowing himself the luxury of pity. Instead he would do everything possible to cheat death.

Tired, he stretched out on his board bunk and fell asleep. Too soon the Jewish police roused the prisoners for work.

It was nine o'clock in the evening when the police ordered them to prepare for work. Surprised at the hour, the recruits looked at each other for answers but said nothing and followed orders to line up. An SS guard separated them into groups, and they marched out the gate into the night.

Herr Scheck stood in front of the workers.

"Someone will show you how to use the machine to which you are assigned. Pay close attention. Your staying in good stead with me depends on it." His face showed no emotion. He stood tall and straight -- every bit the stature of a factory commandant.

Soon Benny's group entered the factory where giant machines beat out a deafening roar. A Polish foreman took Benny to a square-shaped machine with a big wheel on top and several smaller wheels behind. He learned its function was to trim machine gun bullets.

The foreman ordered an emaciated laborer to instruct the youth. Benny questioned how well this stumbling, frail instructor, who limped toward him, could give directions.

Surprisingly, the crippled man showed Benny how to operate the machine and how to remove the excess material. It was precise work. Benny did not want to admit it, but the procedure baffled him. He had not been at the machine long when a Polish foreman came to check Benny's work. Benny waited anxiously for the man to say something. The foreman turned and left. When Benny saw him returning with Herr Scheck, he knew the verdict.

"Come with me, Jude," demanded Scheck.

Benny followed the Nazi into an adjacent office. Once inside, the German closed the door.

"Do you have any idea what you have done? You have committed sabotage against the German Government."

Damn!

"Bullets are ruined because you cut off too much material." The commandant looked sternly at Benny. "You have a doubt you have done this?"

Benny nervously shifted his stance. How could he explain it was his first attempt?

"You have committed a serious offense. You must pay for it -- the hard way."

Benny could guess what was in store for him. He had been the victim of the German object lessons before. The youth stood quietly, waiting.

Scheck took a rubber handle wooden stick out of his desk. He stood for a moment looking at Benny, slapping the stick on the palm of his hand. Then he said, "Lay across that chair." He pointed to a chair near the desk.

Benny followed the orders.

The first hit nearly knocked him from the chair. He gritted his teeth as the officer continued beating him, counting off twenty-five lashes. Each hit vibrated through his thin body. His stomach began to roll, and he felt faint. He fell to the floor.

"Get up, dog!" yelled the German.

Before Benny could comply with his request, Scheck lifted him by the seat of his pants and planted a booted foot into his back, sending the youth crashing into a plate glass door. As his weight hit the door, knocking it open, glass shattered across the room. Benny fell through the opening and slammed against a machine in the next room. As he hit, a trap door flew open and oil sprayed out, covering him in black slime.

Scheck stood, livid with rage, his fists clenched.

"Guard!" he screamed. "Get this Jew swine out of here!"

As the guard shoved Benny out of the room, the officer turned to him and said, "I want you back in this office the same time tomorrow night. Understand, Jude?"

Benny nodded his head in affirmation.

For two nights, Benny returned to the office for his punishment in failing to master the machine.

Eventually Scheck had his fill. He assigned Benny the job of cleaning the machines. The beatings had weakened him, but he was able to do the easier task. Benny did not know why the man had not killed him.

The work schedule put the laborers in the factory from ten o'clock at night until seven thirty the next morning. Each day found Benny more exhausted and rapidly losing weight on the meager diet. Even though he needed the daytime rest, he realized he must soon find more food. He would try to barter his vocal talent again.

He found his first audience in the women's barracks. Overjoyed to have a respite from their daily drudgeries, the women clapped eagerly at the youth's performance. Soon several Jewish police from the next barrack joined them. When they first entered the room, Benny stopped singing, but one of the policemen waved him on.

Benny sang for thirty minutes before he stopped, exhausted. Immediately the women shared a small amount of rations they could afford. A Jewish policeman took him to the provision room and gave him a large loaf of bread. It seemed the Jewish police were the only people in Werke B who were not hungry. Benny had found a source for survival.

Encouraged that he could find extra food, he volunteered for a daytime kitchen cleaning detail. There were nine of them who received an extra ration of soup for this duty.

Benny made every effort to keep up his strength. On several occasions the SS guards invaded the compound and picked out the weakest to transfer to Werke C. The prisoners believed that those transferred to the dreaded camp faced death from exhaustion or shooting.

"Werke C will make your blood run cold and death appear as a delight rather than a dread," remarked an inmate.

This was a statement, not an explanation.

The idea that they were all on a treadmill to systematic death was a belief difficult to ignore. If Benny learned nothing else from his experiences, he recognized how important it was to stay healthy enough to work. He was learning something else. At all cost, he should avoid Werke C.

SIXTEEN

STARING AT THE NEW prisoners the enslaved stood like finely carved sculptures. Their near naked, decaying bodies formed a backdrop for their graveyard surroundings. Occasionally one moved -- a bony mouth or sunken eye, both mute.

The late day sun polished the scene already coated with yellow. The jaundiced hue blanketed everything -- the living skeletons, the trees, the ground, and the buildings.

Even as he walked through the yawning gate, Benny displaced his brief terror with curiosity. So this was Werke C.

Benny found the source of the yellow hell soon after arriving at "C." Picric was a powder from which explosives were made, and it contaminated everything. Shortly, Benny too, would become polluted.

Was it Kuba or Maronski who philosophized that each person had the responsibility of finding answers to his or her problems? If that were true, the boy's place in time was now, and he would have to find some way to fulfill the tasks set before him in this new arena.

Grieving silently for his youth, Benny felt very old and tired. He knew the lessons from his past and the love of his family were a source of his strength -- among the few things for which he could be thankful.

"That which does not kill me makes me stronger." It was a quote he remembered. *Father would be proud I did not forget my lessons. My God, I've learned so many new ones.* Benny was to soon learn many more.

An average of twenty-six Jews died each day in the camp from picric poisoning, brutality, starvation, or from the epidemics that struck all three Werke camps -- dysentery and typhus.

Finding food was the first task facing Benny. When he learned he would need his own utensil at "C" or there would be no food, he began searching immediately. He looked first in his assigned barrack. The futile search led him to other barracks. This is how he stumbled upon the women's quarters. He opened the door without knocking.

"What do you want?" snapped a woman who sat half-dressed on a bunk near the door.

"I'm looking for a container for my food."

"Well, you will not find it here. You should not be here."

Benny stood for a moment looking at her nakedness.

"What are you gawking at?"

Blushing, Benny averted his eyes, surveying the room for a can. Just as he spied one on the floor several bunks away, she said matter-of-factly, "Do you want to touch me?"

Startled, Benny jerked his head toward her. He stared at the white, firm breast, not yet sagging from overwork and lack of food. Surprised by the sudden feeling in his groin, he turned away and bolted toward the container, grabbed it and ran out the door.

She yelled after him, "Don't take that! That is not yours!"

Benny ran as fast as he could. In time he forgot the naked woman, but not before he pondered the thought he might die a virgin.

Each morning Benny rushed out of the barracks, eagerly awaiting his portion of food -- a small piece of bread that he ravenously devoured. The prisoners would not eat again until supper, brought to them by horse-drawn wagons carrying barrels of soup. Fellow prisoners served them the thin watery soup from the giant cauldrons that sat on the cart. Always, the line was too long and the serving too slow.

A Jewish policeman by the name of Solomon was in charge of the food detail, and he often chastised his fellow Jews who stood eagerly awaiting the food. Some prayed that Solomon's mean spirit would turn into a miracle that would heap them with a shower of food. Their prayers were not answered.

Hunger pains gnawed relentlessly at Benny. He knew he would have to gamble again by singing for food supplements and would need to be alert for opportunities.

On the second day of their arrival, the chief foreman introduced the prisoners to the labor expectations at Werke C. As they entered the main plant, an SS officer, wearing a uniform coated with yellow dust, approached. Herr Witzle was short and stocky, and his facial expression never changed. A constant frown wrinkled his forehead and his mouth turned down at the corners.

If I had his assignment among the yellow people, thought Benny, *I would be unhappy too.*

The officer showed each of the crew their assignments. In one area of Hala Thirteen, people worked before benches that held trays of picric. Hammering at the malformed chunks, they smashed them into fine powder for reuse.

Benny immediately received his first assignment. He was responsible for loading cylinders with the picric acid passed down by women who first weighed it on a small scale. Afterwards, one of the women called out to a numbered press operator who took the powder and pressed it into containers. "One" was Benny's operator number.

Soon a woman called out, "Number One, the powder is ready."

Benny knew that as the presser, he had a difficult task. If the woman weighed the powder incorrectly, it could explode while he was stuffing the container. If the load were defective, it was pulled from the pile and passed to a worker for hammering into fine powder for restoring. This took time, and if improperly packed, the mine could detonate. The danger was twofold -- improper weighing and packing, and the Germans treating either mistake as sabotage.

Benny tried to keep his hand from shaking as he accepted the tray of powder. He funneled the weighed amount into a container and pressed it with a wooden ram. Then he passed the mine on to another man who inserted the detonating pin. After every insertion of the rod, Benny withdrew it and passed it to another worker sitting behind him, who dismantled and cleaned it. No residue power could remain on the rod.

The completed mines measured two by four inches. Long flat packing boxes held as many as five hundred of the explosives.

Each day Benny dreaded the wake up whistle. The workday began at seven in the morning and ended at seven at night. The unwelcome morning whistle, blown by a member of the Jewish police, always seemed to come too early. The Jews lined up for roll call even if they were sick, or the Jewish police dealt harshly with them.

Already Benny tasted the bitter acid of the yellow dust. The dry yellow powder that pervaded everything, including the skin, also made the mouth bitter and acrid. In a short time Benny's skin started to change color.

Near Benny's barracks stood a wooden hut that served as a washroom. Latrine-type washbowls with faucets, providing cold water for washing, ran the length of one wall. Though he washed many times, Benny could not rid himself of the yellow dust from his face and hands. Already the nasty taste made him sick at his stomach.

The Sunday after his arrival in Werke C, he and the other prisoners marched down the state highway to Werke A for showers. After he showered, Benny sought out his Polish friends.

"Ah," smiled one. "*Śpiewak* is here. The singer is here."

The others gathered around.

Benny chose a love ballad, one of his favorites. He took a deep breath and began to sing. His voice, no longer the strong treble of a younger boy, had beginnings of a more masculine baritone.

"Softly through the night my songs entreat you. Come to me beloved."

When he finished, he sang still another and yet another, each received enthusiastically by the workers. When he had finished they rewarded him with bread and soup as well as sweets. His heart felt lighter. Too soon he had to say good-bye.

As he prepared to leave, several of the Poles invited him to visit their homes after the war. Benny could only hope for such a wonderful thing.

When the prisoners left the foundry, they saw a group of people gathered under one of the trees that bordered the street. A lifeless and bloated man hung by his neck. A sign pinned to his chest read, "This could happen to you, if you try to escape."

So Werke A is not immune to adverse rewards.

The message had a reverse effect on the young Jew. It motivated him to endure the humiliation and death surrounding him. He was proud of the man who had the courage to try the escape.

Each of the lessons Benny learned was bitter -- from death to the deceit of his fellow Jews. Foraging for food one day led him to a barrack set back away from the others. As he approached he could smell the aroma of food. Since no sign forbade him to enter, he went in. The barrack, arranged much like a house, appeared to have individual rooms. The order and cleanliness surprised Benny. He knocked on one of the doors. Immediately a big man answered.

"What in hell do you want? Don't you know where you belong?"

Startled by such hostility, Benny believed he must have entered German quarters. He jumped back as the man raised his booted leg to kick him.

"Get away and stay away," he yelled. "Go back where you belong."

Benny left quickly, learning later that the man was Stephan Eisenberg, a Jew and the brother-in-law of the head of the camp's internal administration.

Again, a prostituted Jew, thought Benny.

The youth returned to his own barrack even hungrier than before, exhaustion overtaking him as he fell onto the bunk. His nostrils burned with the stench of human decay. The anger welled in him, and he resolved not to be one of those loaded on the death truck that came weekly for the bodies.

———◆※◆———

Herr Witzle grabbed Benny by the collar, dragged him outside, and immediately summoned the Polish foreman Boczkowski.

"He is all yours."

"You lazy bastard. You'll do a days work today if you have never done one before in your miserable life. *Potepiac*! Damn filthy Jews!" He picked up a wooden mallet that lay nearby.

Benny tried to fend off the first hit, but it found its mark on the side of his head. With each blow Boczkowski spewed forth a gusher of hate and pent-up emotions of an embittered man. Whether imagined or real, he unleashed his feelings toward Jews. Benny was his scapegoat.

The hits came again and again. Soon the pain was too much and Benny lost consciousness.

Benny would learn later that two prisoners took him to the camp sick room, a designated area in the far corner of the camp. No doctor attended. The boy lapsed between consciousness and unconsciousness for about forty-eight hours. He knew little of what was happening around him. His first recollection was the stench of human excretion. It almost overwhelmed him. Living skeletons with heartbeats lay in their own filth, their cots sitting side by side. A man that lay close by spoke to Benny in a raspy voice.

"Son, get out of here as soon as you can. The truck is due."

Benny did not respond.

"If you do not recover quickly, you will be put before a firing squad."

Benny sensed the true reality of this information but was in no position to do anything. He could barely move, let alone walk out of the place.

By the end of the day, the truck had not arrived, and the man who had given information was unconscious. The more Benny thought about what he had said, the more he struggled with movement. Even as he tried to ease himself from the bunk, the intense pain caused oblivion.

It was near dawn when Benny awoke. Determined to leave the sick room and using the side of the neighboring cot as a brace, he pushed his body over the side. He managed to slide onto the floor, pain shooting through his body as he landed.

A sense of urgency pushed Benny beyond his endurance. Glancing around the room, he looked for a hiding place. There was none, except under a cot.

He dragged his aching body along the floor and eased it under a cot farthermost from the door. Underneath lay a dead man curled into a ball and lying in a pool of human refuse. Benny's stomach rolled. Fighting the nausea, he set his mind to pushing past the man toward the small floor space at the head of the bed. Painfully he pushed his body toward the wall where he pulled his knees to his chest and lay quietly, afraid to breathe.

Just before sundown, he heard the screeching of brakes. Shortly two SS Ukrainians bursting into the room hollered for all to fall out. This was futile, as most patients could not move. The two forcefully dragged the men from their bunks and loaded them into the truck. One Ukrainian, with flashlight in hand, began searching under the cots, starting with those near the door.

Benny held his breath. As the beams of light hit his dead companion, the Ukrainian grabbed the corpse by the feet and pulled him out. Within minutes the door slammed shut, and Benny heard the truck's wheels spinning in the loose gravel. The dead man had hidden the Ukrainian's view, sparing Benny's life. Fearful of moving, the boy spent the night under the cot. The sick room had already begun filling again with dying men when he left at dawn.

Though weak and hardly able to move, Benny was determined to return to the barrack. He had already learned that Camp Commandant Scheck had little patience with those who could not perform their work. Major Hines, a six-foot-six giant in his seventies and director of all the camps, had less patience. Often prisoners referred to him as the meanest and most sadistic man in any of the compounds.

Benny was hungry, and he needed sustenance to return to work. He hoped he could find the much needed food in the Jewish police barracks.

Eisenberg opened the door to Benny's knocking. "What the hell? You survived the sick room and the truck pick up?"

Benny could not believe the disdain in the Jew's voice. Any Jew should have seen that he had survived the sick room as a victory. Benny was too idealistic.

Eisenberg reached to his belt for his nightstick. Not finding it, he shook his fist at the young Jew. "You are supposed to be dead! Why are you here? Get out of here you yellow cur! Get out!" He struck at him.

Benny recoiled, the fist barely missing him. "Are you trying to do what the Germans could not?"

The older Jew stopped and stared at Benny. Grabbing him by the scruff of the neck, he dragged the boy from the barrack. The man took him to the prisoners' quarters and literally threw Benny onto the nearest bunk.

"You stay here. There will be no food for you for two days -- my orders!"

Benny lay quietly, tears welling in his eyes. How could he ever understand the Jew traitors?

Benny was fortunate that two of his bunkmates overheard, and at great risk sneaked food to him. It was common practice for each prisoner to live in his own self-made isolation and fight for his own life. To do this, it was necessary to shut out the surrounding horrors. This humane act encouraged Benny more than the food he received.

From the very beginning of his stay at Werke C, the morning meal consisted of a slab of bread, and the evening meal was the customary ration of soup. It was not enough. Shortly after his arrival in camp, Benny worked sorting bullets and putting them in cases for shipment. One day as they disassembled from the march line to return to their individual barracks, Benny noticed a section of the camp he had not yet explored. A sign on the building read "*Verboten.* Under Penalty of Death."

The sign did not dissuade him. He walked to the door.

A rotund middle-aged man dressed in long johns opened the door.

"You stupid son-of-a-bitch, don't you know you can be shot for coming here?"

"Who is it, Franc?"

The man turned and answered, "Some stupid Jude, Sergeant. You want me to take care of him?"

"Leave him to me."

Benny stood quietly. Should he stay or run?

Suddenly the man loomed before him, staring at him, his forehead furrowed. His shoulders were broad as a lumberjack's, and his neck bulged from his shirt. A large hand rested on the door edge. His eyes were dark and a black mustache framed smirking, fleshy lips. A sergeant insignia labeled his left sleeve.

Benny lied. "I was told I could find the camp president here."

The man stared at him. "What do you want with the camp president?"

"Uh . . ." Benny's mind raced for an answer. "He wanted me to sing for him."

"To do what?" the startled man answered in Ukrainian.

"Yes sir," Benny answered in the same language. "I sing to get food." Benny smiled at the man's surprise.

"You speak Ukrainian?" the sergeant asked.

"Why don't I sing you a song in Ukrainian?" Benny boldly stepped inside the door.

Several men sitting in the area looked at him with disbelief. The sergeant stepped aside. "Let's see what you can do, Jude."

Benny sang a Ukrainian song, followed by a tender German ballad. It was the same song that had enraptured the Poles at Werke A. As he sang "Serenade," his audience listened quietly. When he finished, they slapped their hands on their thighs and shouted "bravo." Pleased by their reaction, he sang another song.

Too soon the large man, who had opened the door, told him he must leave, and he handed him a small bag of food and a little money. At the door, the man whispered, "You should not return. I am not sure you know where you are. We will find the opportunity for you to entertain again. All right?"

Benny smiled broadly. "Thank you," he said.

It was not until two days later that Benny discovered his almost fatal mistake. Taranov, the man who allowed him into the forbidden barrack, was an executioner, a sergeant in charge of the firing squad. The barrack housed the Werkeschutz, the Ukrainian factory police in charge of camp security. Under the influence of Nazi ideology and anti-Semitic views, the Ukrainian battalion operated within the framework of the German army.

Now as Benny remembered the experience, he wondered if it was time to find another opportunity to sing for the Ukrainians. His own hesitation led him to believe he should wait. He must not let hunger drive him to make a fatal mistake.

On the return to Hala Thirteen, Benny made a grievous error by exploding one of the mines that had too much powder. Herr Witzle ordered him outside and chastised him for this act of treason. "Boc, you take over," he commanded, looking at the foreman who stood with his arms crossed, ready for his turn.

Boczkowski, the Polish foreman, grabbed Benny by the collar and yelled, "You filthy Jew cur. Your action is treason against the Third Reich! It happens again and Herr Witzle will have the pleasure of shooting you. If he doesn't do it, I will!"

Unnerved, Benny listened obediently. He had heard about Boc, and it was not good news.

"Get back to work. Get over to the shed and get a hammer to pound the blocks you ruined, and make it snappy!"

Benny, obeying immediately, sat at the worktable, and began hammering the defective mine into powder.

But Boc would not give up. "Lazy bastard!" he screamed. I hope I have the pleasure to kill you myself." Benny hammered, while the tirade continued. Finally Boc found another prey.

After this incident, Benny was determined to find a way to escape, but now food was his objective. After the encounter with Boc, the boy decided to employ his usual method of securing extra rations. As the group marched by the camp kitchen, Benny quickly slipped out of rank and headed for the back of the building where he waited until they were out of sight.

When he entered the kitchen, he saw several men and women preparing food. Without asking, Benny began singing a lively Polish ballad. Immediately all heads turned in the direction of the voice. They saw a frail-looking youth with a strong and melodious voice. So caught up in the moment of surprise, the workers stopped their chores and listened, their faces beaming. By the time Benny had finished, some approached him and patted him on the shoulder; others placed food in his pail securely tied at his waist.

Pleased, Benny chose a corner in the kitchen, sat down, and immediately devoured the contents of the pail. When Benny turned to leave, one of the women motioned him to her side. Smiling broadly, she refilled his pail, then turned back to her chores. Benny, savoring the act of kindness, stood for a moment. He then turned and left.

Weakened and nervous about accidentally causing an explosion, Benny returned to work after the beating incident. Soon after his return, a younger boy named Choc, who worked near him, made the fatal mistake of firing a mine. Though he only ruined the powder, Herr Witzke came quickly to the scene and removed the boy.

Choc never returned. Benny later learned Witzle took the boy to a wooded area a distance away and executed him for his third act of sabotage against the Germans.

Unnerved by the incident, Benny did less than an adequate performance on the job, yet they did not kill him. Witzle did not want him. He sent him to work for Boc, but he did not want him either.

Shifted from job to job, Benny never knew what to expect. He believed the worker shortage and his perseverance kept him alive, but why had it not Choc?

At Hala Twenty-seven he worked in the paraffin section where laborers dipped mines in various color wax baths, packed them, and transported them to Werke C for transfer to the battlefront. A cruel foreman, assisted by a boy of thirteen too big for his age and sadistic, made Benny's life hell.

In still another factory section, Benny helped ladle mines and grenades onto a large flatbed wagon. Sometimes he sorted bullets. Finally the Germans sent him back to Hala Thirteen and assigned him his old job.

In a short time, he made his third mistake. He accidentally exploded a defective mine.

Herr Witzle was soon on the scene. Solomon, the Jewish policeman, pointed to Benny. Witzle's eyes narrowed. "So you are the wimp Jude cockroach that bothers Solomon. The policeman must be losing his touch. Come here, Jude!"

Benny, following his command, stood directly in front of Witzle and looked him in the eye.

Witzle's lip pursed inward and anger flickered in his green eyes. "Damn, Jew," he said. "Are you trying to stare me down? I'm going to take care of you personally. You are a leech. We squash leeches."

Benny decided he would dare him no further. He lowered his eyes and waited nervously for the dreaded beating.

Witzle, red-faced and sputtering, ordered Benny to follow him.

The two walked away from the camp and into a wooded area. Finally the German stopped, pointed at a tree, and ordered Benny to stand against it. Benny did as he was told. As Benny stood facing the German, Witzle drew his pistol from his holster and aimed it at the youth.

"Wait," said Benny in German.

Stunned, the officer stopped.

"Please hear me out, sir."

"What the hell can you possibly say that will prevent me from shooting you?" His eyes snapped, both angry and surprised by the boy's audacity as well as his knowledge of the German language.

"Sir, I belong to a family whose clan numbers eighty-five," sputtered Benny. "Would you allow me the great privilege of being the only one who remains alive?"

The astonished German was speechless.

"Just think what that would mean. You would have saved the one remaining member of such a large clan."

"I don't believe this," said the German. "Who the hell do you think you are?"

Benny paused only a moment. Boldly he lied, "I'm a singer of great renown. Haven't you heard of me?"

"You!" mocked the officer. "You are just a runt Jew!"

Uncompromising, Benny continued, "I'll tell you what, sir. How about I sing you one of your favorite songs in German? How long has it been since you've heard one?" Benny rambled on. "You will be my last audience." Benny tried very hard to prevent the fear from showing on his face.

Witzle looked at Benny as though he were crazy. He cocked his gun. Then slowly a smile began at the corner of his mouth, and he lowered the pistol. "Why not!" he said. "Sing, you little scoundrel, it will be your last song."

Benny caught his breath, and taking advantage of the turn of events, he immediately burst into a melody. Deep in the woods and facing death, the young Jew reached into his soul and belted the verse in robust German style. His voice pierced the air with rich and mellow tone.

The Nazi's eyes widened at the brazen young Jew's talent. Still holding the cocked pistol, the officer stood stoical.

As soon as Benny finished one song, he started another without asking. The new one was lusty, not a song a dying man would sing.

While he sang, Benny noticed a slight change in the man's facial expression. With a spurt of new energy, Benny sang vigorously.

Slowly the German replaced the pistol's safety and lowered the hand piece to his side.

At last Benny risked silence.

"I'll be damned," said the German. "You have the most colossal nerve I've ever seen." He shook his head in disbelief, a grin forming at the corners of his mouth. "I'll be damned! How can I ever live down this moment, if I let you live?"

Benny said nothing. The German could not know that his prey was so exhausted he could not have sung another note.

"This will plague me the rest of my life." The German continued to argue his thoughts out loud. "Killing is a particular hobby of mine, and you have cheated me of the pleasure."

Benny believed the man talked to convince himself -- not to educate the youth.

Without warning, the German walked toward Benny, slapped him across the face and said, "Get back to work Jude."

Benny did not dare thank the man. He risked insulting him. The youth walked toward the camp, his heart racing, and his mind spinning with anxiety that the man would change his mind and shoot him in the back.

That night, as Benny lay awake in his bunk, he thanked God for helping him cheat death once more.

The Lord loves me!

When he could, Benny rested on his bunk and allowed his eyes to grow accustomed to the daylight darkness. Even the sun was not exempt from the yellow dusk.

The barracks stank with the foul odors of dirty human beings. Two tiered bunks in long, continuous rows slept twenty people. The familiar round iron stove stood in the middle of the room. Trying to ward off the early spring chill, the feeble with their frail bodies waging the battle for life, hovered around the hot stove.

Each day brought new horrors. Often Benny found a bunkmate lying cold with an uncanny, haunted expression on his face. Soon the once living creature would be carted away to the grave pit. Many who still breathed waited for the peace of the cool earth. The threat of death loomed constantly. Some let it demoralize them; others struggled for a shred of hope, as they often reached into depths that might not have been considered under other circumstances.

Benny knew he had entered hell when he saw a fellow prisoner bite into the hand of a dying bunkmate. Desperate, the man had turned into a cannibal.

Shortly after he arrived at Werke C, Benny awakened during the night after hearing strange sounds. Fearful that it was another cruel attempt by the Jewish police or the Germans to interrupt the sleep of the tired prisoners, he became instantly alert for danger. He lay quietly, listening. He rolled to his stomach and glanced toward the sounds. Light from a security pole, just outside one of windows, dimly lit the room. Across the aisle, in the semi-darkness, he saw two men, their arms wrapped around each other. They breathed heavily. Although Benny had turned only slightly, his movement disturbed them, and they both looked at him. The light through the slatted window shone directly into their eyes. Both stared at Benny, their hollow eyes and thin faces silently begging the young boy to ignore them. They knew the consequences if the Germans found out.

Self-gratification among the prisoners was deterred by overwork, lack of nourishment, degradation, and fear of being caught. Mostly they sought solitude for their own private thoughts.

When Benny rolled quietly to his back, he lay quietly, remembering a history lesson about Pompeii, evidence of coupling etched into the concrete remains, a last moment in the search for comfort amid the disaster. How could he not have compassion for those who revert to their primal instinct for survival? He was only a young boy caught up in the perpetuity of instantaneous death, drowning in the devastation of day-to-day fear.

Finally Benny fell asleep.

Benny became obsessed with living, more now than ever. Determined to outlive the horrors, he began to think of the day that he would write a book, telling the world about the injustice to mankind. Perhaps he could be a great teacher, like his friend Czerniakow, and instruct young people in the art of preserving human dignity.

Often his mind drifted into the realms of the great music he knew. He allowed the memory of the rhythm to takeover his body and mind. It soothed him even in the worst of times. He thought of his family, not their deaths but their lives, the joyous times spent together. Benny felt that time consumed him and stalled his life, both at the same moment. Yet he knew his course could be altered if he held onto hope and dismissed the feelings of futility.

His days were the same routine. Regardless of the job and with only the slightest provocation, the on-duty foremen beat him. Because of the various beatings and accidental explosions, his eyes and ears bothered him. The kitchen women felt pity for him and often sneaked him food, sometimes potato peelings. This probably saved his life. His weight dropped below one hundred pounds, and his clothes hung in rags on his frail body.

He wore the clothing issued while he was at Werke A, over a year ago. He welcomed the too-large and already threadbare clothes. None of the prisoners questioned the source of the clothes supply although they suspected it was that of dead Jews.

Occasionally a prisoner found valuables sown within the garment. This inspired Benny to rip open a pair of shoes he so badly needed. Finding nothing, he searched for something to hold the tattered shoes together. He was lucky to find a few pieces of wire.

The rumor among the prisoners was that the Germans sold much of the better clothing to the Poles, and the Jewish police and camp president confiscated the best of the remaining garments.

Benny fought the constant battle for his self-respect. Singing gave him not only food but also value as a human being. In this effort, he was an individual and not just one of the animals the Nazi's strove to dominate.

There were few moments of solitude. Constantly the Germans, the Polish foremen, or the Jewish police pushed him beyond his endurance. At every opportunity, the young Jew wove threads of human dignity and ego into his life, all precious moments from his past.

Benny knew he was often dependent on the moods of the guards or foremen, and he strove to use this to his advantage. He refused to slip into apathy. Even in moments when he knew the wrong decision could cost him his life, he fought his fear, for being non-committal could be just as devastating.

SEVENTEEN

IT WAS ONLY A MATTER OF TIME before the guards noticed his absence. Fever ravaged his body, sapping his strength, every muscle aching.

While Jewish policemen yelled their orders, outside work lines assembled. Solomon entered the barrack and searched under each of the bunks. He found Benny cowering under his bed.

"You dirty yellow scoundrel, why didn't you line up for work?"

He reached under the bed and dragged Benny toward him.

"You will pay dearly, you little son-of-a-bitch!"

Solomon shook the youth viciously, all the while yelling at him. "You place us in a very bad spot when you do not report for work. You should be hung, you bastard!"

Finally Solomon let him drop to the floor where the youth lay lifelessly.

When Benny awoke, he was in the sick room. He knew he was very ill. His head ached severely, and his high temperature caused moments of delirium. He fought the delusions, fearing his malady was the dreaded infectious typhus, created in mite-and-louse-infested quarters. Others fought the sometimes-fatal disease. There was no doctor, no medicine.

He wanted nothing to eat. He was cold, probably from the high fever. Clothes did not protect him. He had none. After his clothes had worn out, he covered his body and feet with double-layered paper bags in which supplies had been packed. Often his skin burned from the residue of the grenade powder. When his paper clothes became wet, he made new ones. Benny wondered what his fashion designer father would say.

I wish I could hear him tease me.

Covertly one of his barracks mates slipped him soup. Forcing himself to eat, Benny struggled to recover. If he gave in to the depression, pain, and lack of appetite that threatened to consume him, it would be fatal.

He did not know when the truck would come. Fear hovered over him for two days as he lay in the sick room. On the third day, Solomon entered.

"Get out of your bunk, Lipman. Fall in line for work detail."

Benny, his eyes pleading, looked at the man. Even an animal would be given consideration under the circumstances.

"You have screwed off long enough," scolded the Jewish policeman. "Get back to work."

When Benny did not move, Solomon grabbed a board from one of the bunks and aimed it at Benny's face. The blow split Benny's upper lip, blood spurting from the gap. Shortly the red gore covered his chin and neck.

It has a strange taste, thought Benny, as he looked into the eyes of his fellow Jew.

"Yellow Jew boy, get your ass out of that bunk! Get to work before I really do a job on you!"

Anger rushed through Benny and gave him renewed strength he did not know he had. He got up slowly and stumbled toward the door.

They assigned him the task of loading boxes of picric at Hala Twelve. Somehow he got through the day, his lip still oozing blood. As they marched back to the barracks, thoughts of escape crowded Benny's mind.

Though his fever subsided, and he did not have the dreaded rash that sometimes followed the outbreak of typhus, he still struggled with his appetite. Needing sustenance, he continued to force himself to eat.

By the time supper was over and he had returned to his quarters, it had begun to rain. Soon after his barrack mates had bedded for the night, Benny made his way to the rear of the barracks and slipped outside unnoticed. He crept through the dark night to the sick room that occupied a rear corner of the camp. The fence wires, passing close by the shack, carried no electricity. Listening for unfriendly noise, Benny moved cautiously.

The sounds of footsteps nearby frightened him. Perhaps the Jewish police or the Germans had already discovered his intentions. When he realized he was apparently alone and undetected, he moved quickly into the sick room and grabbed the very board with which Solomon hit him earlier. The poor sick souls never knew he was there.

It was now raining hard. He thanked God for the cover. The soggy paper bag clothing clung to his bony frame.

Using the board, he dug into the mud just below the fence line. Later he would remember thinking that the Germans were careless not to protect this obvious patch of wire and secluded area.

The digging was easier than expected. Soon he was on his knees, crawling under the wire. The moment he felt safe to stand and walk, he moved in the direction of the railroad tracks.

Suddenly a siren screeched, startling him. It did not seem to come from the direction of Werke C. Puzzled, he fell to the ground and remained very still. Several minutes later, he heard the chatter of machine gun fire, followed by screams. Then all he heard was the rain patting the leaves and ground.

Benny remained on the ground for an hour before he dared move. As he crawled along, his hand touched a wire, more than likely a telephone cable knocked down by the storm. He sensed that, if he followed it, it would lead to the railroad tracks. Using it as a guide, he moved forward. He had not gone far when his hand touched something that he recognized as a human head. He jerked his hand away. No sound came, no movement. He moved forward again. Several yards further he came across the bodies of two more victims, and at the tracks even more, an apparent German massacre.

Benny moved guardedly across the tracks and entered the woods. By now the rain had stopped. Curled under a bush, he stayed all night.

—➤ ✦ ◄—

His experiences from previous escapes served him in good stead. Moving in systematic fashion and always being alert to his surroundings had proven to be the best method of escape.

Through a clearing he saw a small farmhouse. With daylight approaching, the yellow paper-clad figure would be very obvious. He must take a chance that those who lived there would help him.

When he knocked on the door, a middle-aged woman opened it and gasped, "Jesus and Mary! Janek! Janek, come quick! We have a Devil in our house."

Dobry! *Good! She's Polish! Oh, thank God, she is Polish!*

"Please let me in!"

"No! I cannot! You are one of the yellow people. You cannot come in here."

Benny knelt on the porch before her.

"Please!" he begged. "Hear me out. I will not hurt you."

By this time her husband had joined her. He stared at the yellow creature dressed in a wet paper bag that threatened to fall from his body at any moment. The man motioned impatiently for Benny to come inside the house.

"What do you have to say?" the man asked.

"Please sir," pleaded Benny. "I only ask for some old clothes to decently cover my body, then I'll go."

"Clothes will not keep you from being recognized and returned to camp."

"With clothes I may have a chance to escape these inhuman madmen!"

The man's face softened. "Sit down, boy," he said as he asked his wife to get some old clothes. "Bring him something to eat," he called after her.

Benny rested only thirty minutes in their home. It was obvious they were nervous he was there, and he did not wish harm to come to them. He thanked them and walked back into the woods.

Freedom was brief. Benny had gone, perhaps a hundred yards, when two Ukrainian soldiers approached, rifles pointed. He could not run. Where would he go?

Benny remembered something the Ukrainian Taranov had said after Benny had entertained him with song. "I cannot promise, but if you are in trouble, try to let me know." Benny had not taken him seriously. As he recollected, the sergeant had been drinking heavily when he made the remark.

It was worth a try. Benny said, "I know your Sergeant Taranov. Take me to him."

Astonished, the two men looked at each other. "The Devil is the only person you will see, Jew!" said one of the men. Slapping their thighs, they both laughed.

They were right.

When they reached camp, the Jewish police placed Benny under heavy guard. That evening Eisenberg brought Benny the news that hanging would be his punishment -- the following afternoon at two o'clock. The henchman chosen was one of the Jewish police who had previously performed such tasks for the Germans.

Desperate for an idea that would give him a way out of the situation, Benny spent a sleepless night. The boy had nothing to lose. He had noticed earlier that loose gravel layered the foundation of the barracks and the tarpaper siding that extended from the wooden wall to the ground lifted easily.

Perhaps I can bury myself in the loose gravel.

Before dawn, he peered outside. One guard stood watch at the front of the barracks. Benny quietly moved to the rear of the building. Stealthily he pushed open one of the windows and slid down the side of the barrack to the ground.

Down on his knees, he lifted the siding, scraping away the gravel to make an opening large enough to crawl into. Soon the hole accommodated him, and he crawled under the building. Benny reached back to smooth the disturbed area and prayed the tarpaper flap would also hide the evidence of digging.

Under the building he scooped the gravel in around him. He would rest there until morning, and then he would make a decision what to do.

Early the next morning, the Jewish police discovered Benny was missing. Chaos broke out in the camp. Both Jewish police and SS guards searched the camp. Scheck, the factory supervisor of Werke C, and Hines, the camp commandant of all three camps, were on hand. The appointed hour for execution came, but Benny was not there.

Livid with rage, Hines ordered a full-scale search outside the camp.

Benny remained secluded for a day and a half. As he grew weaker from lack of water and food, he sensed he would die under the building. He decided to risk going outside.

It was not long before he was in the arms of the Jewish police and presented to Eisenberg. Benny begged the Jew to help him escape.

Eisenberg looked contemptuously at the youth. "If you think we wish to lose our heads for the likes of you, you are mistaken. I'm surprised they've let you live this long."

Benny wondered the same thing, and he had expected Eisenberg's answer. He hoped it would be over quickly and not a tortured, prolonged death.

When the guard shoved Benny into the room, two men faced each other across a large desk.

Neither acknowledged the boy or the guard standing just inside the door. The two argued heatedly.

"He is one of the sneakiest bastards I have ever known!" shouted Scheck facing the man behind the desk. "He has lived too long as it is!"

"I agree," answered Hines from his seated position. "However, the point to be made is that I am general manager here, and I will choose the means of death for the filthy Jew."

Scheck's face turned red with anger, the veins on his neck protruding above his collar. "But I am the manager in charge of factory C laborers! I should be the one to make this decision! I will lose face before the workers, if I do not make it! I promised the Jews that I would administer the lesson if someone tried to escape. I told them, after his flight, they might think Lipman a hero, but I would show them he was a dog and would die like one!"

"I . . . I," mocked Hines. "And I was the one who had the sense to order the full scale search Herr Scheck, not you! You were lax in this matter!"

Furious Scheck answered, "You cannot say I was lax! I directed the Jewish police to search the moment they discovered the bastard missing!"

"And it was Eisenberg who called it to my attention. He obviously did not have faith in you to handle it correctly!"

"Herr Hines, you are defending a Jew! Eisenberg may help administrate the internal affairs of the camp, but he is a Jew!" Scheck's voice was more than edged with anger.

With eyes narrowed and jaw set, Hines shouted, "Don't you dare reprimand me! We may be equal rank, but I remind you that I am commandant of the entire camp! Is that quite clear? I will make the decision!"

Scheck glared at his fellow officer. His eyes censuring Benny, he stormed through the door and slammed it behind him.

Hines' entire body was shaking with the anger that consumed him. He turned to the guard. "Bring the damn Jew over here, now!"

The aide shoved Benny toward the officer.

"I will take over now," said Hines to the aide. "It will be my pleasure to handle this alone."

The aide saluted and stood aside as Hines grabbed Benny by the neck, and forced him through the door.

When Benny and Hines entered the vacant compound, the sun had dropped in the western sky, leaving streaks of red color mingled with yellow. Prisoners in the distance waited for their meager night meal, while guards stood nearby.

Herr Hines and Benny marched briskly toward the edge of the camp toward an area known as the firing squad range.

Benny's mind raced with questions. Why had he not shot him on the spot? Would it be a fast, efficient bullet with the firing squad? Could he defer the sentence? He marched in silence.

At length they reached the camp gate. Hines motioned for one of the guards to follow. As they walked past the firing squad area, a confused Benny did not know what to expect. Outside the complex, they walked toward a Panzer truck that sat about seventy-five yards from the main gate. Hines motioned the guard to climb behind the wheel.

The truck had the usual cab, but the rear was small and square. It had a metal body with only a rear door.

Oh, my God! Benny knew immediately what was in store for him. This was the mobile gas cell used to asphyxiate prisoners in route. The small area held few, limiting its use.

Paralyzed, Benny suddenly pulled against Hines' grip.

"You filthy Jew," he said, lifting the latch and opening the door. "Get in!"

When Benny hesitated, Hines literally picked him up by the neck and the seat of the pants and threw him into the truck. Visibly shaking with anger, Hines slammed the door.

Blood rose to Benny's pounding temples. He could not breathe. The darkness was so thick he could not see his hand before him.

The truck started to move. As the truck picked up speed, Benny wondered how long it would take the poisonous carbon monoxide gas to start flowing into the unit.

The boy stood, reaching toward the walls he could not see. His hands touched one. It was smooth, cool. With a rage Benny charged the wall. He threw his small body into the darkness, feeling no pain as he lunged, first one direction, then the other.

Without warning, he fell into an abyss. He hit the ground hard. Stunned, he lay in the middle of the road as the truck sped away, the open door swinging back and forth. In Hines' angry mood he had slammed the door so hard the latch popped up, hanging precariously in place. Benny's quick and forceful movement had dislodged the unsecured door.

His heart racing, Benny lay motionless. Then carefully he glanced back at the compound, now three to four hundred yards away.

When the young Jew could catch his breath, he crawled on his belly toward the woods. From the edge of the brush he saw the truck finally disappear down the road. By now it was almost dark.

"Oh, Lord," said Benny, "thank you for this miracle." The young Jew smiled broadly when he imagined Hines' satisfaction at having finished him off.

Benny walked as fast as he could without collapsing.

At length, he found a place under a brush and exhausted fell asleep. He did not know how long he slept. When he awoke, the sun had risen, and he was starving. His teeth gritted as the pangs of hunger gnawed at his insides.

Benny was afraid to move from hiding. He reached up to the branches of the bush that covered him and began to pick the leaves. He ate them, regurgitated, and ate again. He lost all track of time.

"My God! I am an old man, but never have I seen such a horrible sight in my life!"

The youth, speechless, stood at the man's door. His eyes held a wild look, his emaciated body barely able to stand.

"I could pass sixty-nine and seventy and still not have seen anything like this!"

Benny stood silently. He did not know whether or not to be thankful the man spoke in Polish.

"Don't worry, my yellow child, come in, I will not betray you to the Germans. I am too old a man to be inhumane to my fellow man."

Benny stumbled as he reached out to the man. Placing his arm around the youth's shoulders, the man guided him inside.

After the young Jew had eaten, he washed himself and put on the clothes the old man gave him. As he rested, he finally gained enough strength to carry on a conversation with his host.

"Your kindness, sir, overwhelms me." Benny's voice was almost inaudible.

Listening carefully, the man leaned toward the boy and encouraged him to speak.

"Now I know how a little dog feels when he receives a kind word from his master."

The man's eyes glistened as he answered Benny. "It is hard to imagine that we are in such times that a few kind words could save a human soul."

For several days the farmer not only fed Benny food for his ailing body but also fed his spirit. Benny felt as a long lost son might. The man waited on him by feeding him well and making sure he had plenty of rest.

Fearful of being too easily recognized as one of the yellow people, Benny left at night. He carried with him a leather bag filled with food.

At the door the man kissed him on the forehead.

"Go with God's blessing, Benny. I will pray for you."

Benny could not believe he had traveled full circle. He was back in Warsaw. Why had he returned again? Even if he survived, he would never be able to explain it. He was just a youngster caught up in an incubus, trying to find a way out.

Luckily, after he left the farmer's house, he hitched a secret ride on the back of a horse-drawn wagon loaded with hay. When they arrived in Kielce, it was nighttime. Benny cautiously crawled from under the hay and sneaked, under cover of darkness, to the railway station. There, he climbed into one of the empty cattle cars headed for Warsaw.

While it was still nightfall, he walked toward the ghetto. When he reached Targowa Street in the Polish sector, he searched for a deserted building he knew. He slept until next evening when he headed for the ghetto. He entered through one of the familiar bombed areas. Everything had changed. The streets were empty of activity.

When he reached Stawki Street, he had been in the ghetto less than an hour.

He did not know they were upon him until he heard the shouts. "You, stop!"

No! I've had no chance! No, God! Please!

He glanced to see if there was a hiding place. There was none. Members of the dreaded "Thirteen" had captured the infamous escapee. Immediately the Jewish Gestapo turned him over to the Germans -- but not before they beat him.

Like an uninvited stranger, a vacuum of darkness enveloped him. Pain consumed his thoughts. It was difficult to breathe, and he could not think -- his senses blunted. At the compound, he stood quietly while the Nazis read a complete dossier on his escapes.

"You think the show is over, Lipman! It is just beginning for you, pig! We want you to live. You've become a game for us."

It had been a simple statement, but they made him wait all day, worrying. Before long, it began. At first the Germans beat him like a punching bag. He hit the floor, and he crawled on all fours. They hit him again. Struggling to rise, he fell backward with the next blow. When they had their fill of this sport, they turned to another.

They tied him, naked, to a pole, his belly flush against the rod. A black handkerchief covered his eyes. He could not see what was coming. That was their plan. When the heated iron poker touched his skin, he screamed in agony. Repeatedly, they applied the poker. Nothing seemed to matter anymore except the pain. It controlled him, pulling him deeper and deeper into the abyss of defeat, drowning his hope, his faith.

Then he thought he heard a violin. It wept a sweet melody, its elegance and balance soothing his pain.

When the Germans brought Benny back to Werke C, they made the prisoners, the Jewish police, and Jewish camp president watch.

They drove the young Jew like a donkey with a rope around his neck. He stumbled, almost falling but continued his march into the camp.

It was difficult to recognize Benny. His eyes swelled shut and fresh burn marks covered his legs, thighs, and the bottom of his feet. His emaciated body and bloated stomach showed signs of starvation.

Benny struggled to stay upright, to remain dignified.

His fellow prisoners looked as though they had seen a ghost. They watched silently as the youth fought to walk as a human and not be dragged as an animal.

Benny had become an enigma not only to the Nazis but also to his fellows.

As he marched past them, Benny heard Eisenberg. "My God in heaven! It is a walking miracle! You will live forever!"

Ironically Eisenberg would not.

If one had looked closely, they could have seen each and every prisoner square his shoulders with hope. A smile formed on many lips. If they could have applauded for Benny, they would have. Admiration lit their eyes.

EIGHTEEN

THROUGH THE NIGHT the sound of planes droned overhead. Listening, Benny lay quietly. They did not sound like German planes, but how would he know? Perhaps it was a false hope that these planes carried the liberators.

Benny had been a prisoner in the yellow hellhole for more than a year. To maintain hope was a constant struggle. Exhaustion was a faithful companion. He ached in every sinew of his frail body. Benny's skin stretched tautly over his bones, and he constantly fought the edema that swelled his feet and legs, making walking torturous. The threat of the reoccurrence of the dreaded typhus hung over his head. The lice were constant. He could not remember when he last brushed his teeth or had a warm shower, and he continued to make his own clothes from paper bags.

The young Jew just wanted it all to end. Right now, any kind of freedom would be welcome. Rumors from the Polish foreman, who came in daily to work, indicated that the Russians had liberated Lublin in mid-summer 1943.

Why were they taking so long to get to Skarzysko-Kamienna?

Hundreds of prisoners disappeared from within the camp in late 1943 and early 1944. Always, they marched in the same direction to the nearby woods. No one talked about the gunshots echoing from the forest, and no one wanted to think about what could have befallen the marchers.

Benny wondered why he lived while others died.

Though each day was a struggle just to survive, Benny remained determined to live.

As the prisoners lined up for roll call, Benny heard urgency in the voices of the SS guards. The hostages stood waiting for the daily lecture while more planes passed overhead. Soon the sounds of bombs exploded from the direction of Skarszysko-Kamienna.

Benny felt a great surge of hope. It soared in his heart as a wild bird released from captivity.

The optimism seemed contagious. No Jewish police or president of the camp was in attendance. The German guards appeared nervous, and the Polish foremen seemed disoriented.

The SS officer in charge stepped before the group. "You will all be dead before the liberators arrive." His voice was calm and matter-of-fact. "Your Jewish camp president and the police aides are dead."

The stillness sucked at Benny. It was almost as though he and the other prisoners had stopped breathing.

"They died, fleeing." The officer's mouth formed a sneer, a look the prisoners knew well. "Loyal to their brotherhood -- to the end." He laughed boisterously.

Immediately a reading of names began. Obviously the Russians were near.

Why don't they just shoot us here? Benny knew the answer to his own question. It would seem chaotic, not systematic enough for the Germans.

"Jacobs, right; Chenowski, left."

Oh, no! thought Benny. Chenowski was a good man. The Polish foreman exemplified acts of human kindness to the Jews on many occasions.

When Chenowski protested, a nearby guard smashed his head with a rifle butt.

"Get rid of this crazy devil," ordered the German officer.

The injured foreman took a step forward. "I'll kill you murderers. It makes no difference to me if I am killed here or at the firing squad."

As the six-feet-four Pole lunged toward the guard who hit him, the officer drew his pistol, aimed it at the Pole, and pulled the trigger. The bullet found its mark. The Pole, still on his feet, stumbled forward with great determination as the blood covered his face. He reached out and grabbed the officer by the front of his uniform and tossed him against two of the guards. The rapid succession of three shots broke the stillness, plowing into the giant's back. He arched backwards, slowly turned then fell with a thud. He lay staring upward with vacant eyes, dirt and blood covering his face.

The calling of names continued as though nothing had happened.

"Lipman to the left."

There it was. Benny walked quietly out of the ranks and took his place with the other condemned persons, twenty-five in this round. The group marched out the gate and into the forest.

Numbness controlled Benny's mind and body.

Before long they reached their destination. It was the same scene Benny had witnessed at Treblinka when he helped carry the old man. A huge pit gaped, holding hundreds of decaying bodies.

An SS guard ordered them to strip completely.

Benny followed the orders. It was easy to remove the sack he called clothes. It was less easy to remove the wrapping he called shoes from his swollen and bloody feet.

When the guard told the prisoners to climb into the pit, Benny followed the others down the embankment. As he struggled with the unleveled ground, he slipped, reaching out to balance himself. In so doing he touched the decaying body of a fellow prisoner. He did not cringe. He silently uttered a prayer, hopeful someone would do the same for him. Benny stumbled forward with bare feet crossing over some still warm and bleeding bodies.

He looked toward the sky. *Beloved family, I know I promised I would survive to tell your story. I tried! I tried so hard! I am so weary. Please forgive me for failing.*

The only sounds heard were those of the SS guards shouting to the Jews. "*Los! Los!*"

Standing naked in his potential grave, Benny felt surprisingly calm almost peaceful.

"Benny," called the voice.

Benny bowed his head and waited.

"Benny Lipman," came the voice, again.

The youth, puzzled at how real his imagination had become, looked up toward the machine gun post. The sun blinded him. A figure, waving its arm, stood there.

"*Śpiewak*, come out of the pit," called the man.

Benny recognized the voice. It was Taranov, the German Ukrainian. The youth was sure he had mistaken the order. Once again, motioning him out of the pit, Sergeant Taranov called to him.

Suddenly alert, Benny scrambled up the embankment. The Ukrainian handed the boy a German army blanket to cover himself and instructed him to return to camp.

"There will be no more firing squad details. This is the last. Tomorrow the remainder of the camp will be transferred to Czestochowa. Walk away and do not look back."

Benny started to speak. The Ukrainian turned away.

The youth walked slowly back to camp. For the first time he had no words for the emotions he felt.

In July, the Germans evacuated the remaining prisoners at Werke C. On August 1, 1944 Werke A, B, and C closed forever to prisoner labor. The number of Jews who perished at Skarzysko-Kamienna numbered between eighteen and twenty-three thousand.

The train's cattle cars, loaded with Werke C's remaining prisoners, arrived at Czestochowa the day after they left Skarszysko-Kamienna. They first arrived at Hassag, an ammunition factory, one of the four units in the camp. The prisoners stood in line while the Germans segregated them into groups of one hundred and assigned them quarters.

By the next day Benny's group had arrived at Rakow, another of the units. An instant observation of the condition at this camp gave Benny heart. The prisoners looked healthy and they seemed relatively cheerful under the circumstances.

Benny could not believe how clean the air smelled and how green the grass and trees looked. He would have described the verdant surroundings as a velvet landscape. To the sixteen-year-old they were gifts from God.

Rakow, located close to the foundries and train loading platforms, was fifteen kilometers from the arrival point. As the prisoners approached the entry to the camp, Benny saw only two guards at the gate, both Jewish police, dressed in civilian attire.

The camp president and fellow laborers welcomed the recruits.

Rakow was definitely going to be more pleasant than Werke C.

As Benny familiarized himself with the camp, he learned that most of the prisoners had spent the entire war there. Most came from the liquidation of the Jewish Ghetto in Czestochowa.

The prisoners worked hard, but for once received a livable ration of food. The "yellow people" received extra rations of soup and used clothing. Benny finally had a pair of shoes with laces. He would thread them onto his feet when the swelling disappeared and the burns had completely healed.

The quarters also improved. The wooden bunks had straw mattresses. Even with infested bed bugs, they were luxurious.

Benny wanted desperately to do well in his new job. If he could only remain here until the end of the war, he believed he would survive. His assignment consisted of helping the man who caught the molten steel flowing from a big oven. After it cooled, the laborers converted it into wire used for nails and other such items.

Benny used a long hook to grab the hot steel. He coiled it, and upon completion of the operation, snipped the end. Then the process began again.

The young Jew welcomed the lonely night shift where an even-tempered Austrian German served as his foreman. Gone were the usual beatings Benny had become accustomed to.

Again Benny made friends with the Polish workers and extended his singing career. By the end of the first week, Benny had met most of the Polish people in the camp, one man befriending him and inviting him to visit his home after the war. The friendships were a needed boost to the morale of the tired and disillusioned youth. Once more his confidence began to climb.

As the days grew into weeks, Benny's frail body filled out, he regained much of the weight he had lost, and the swelling from the edema disappeared.

Thoughts of escape did not enter his mind. Why would he want to escape from a place that helped him regain his health? Each day that he survived kindled his spirit.

"As I speak, the Russians are converging on Czestochowa."

The prisoners looked at the German officer in disbelief. Liberation was only hours away. Smiles forming on their faces, the men seemed to stand more erect. At that moment, they heard the announcement.

"All Jewish prisoners will assemble for transportation to another camp. The rest of you should return to work."

Benny had been at Rakow only four short months.

One of the Poles standing near Benny whispered, "Why don't you hide in one of the canal pipes until the Russians arrive? I could help you."

Surprised at the suggestion, Benny's mind rejected the idea. To be killed now by the Germans for hiding from them would be terrible. Benny was having trouble analyzing the situation. After these years of instant decisions, he now seemed unable to make a valid one.

Soon Benny heard the sound of heavy cannon fire, and the word spread quickly that the Russians had already liberated Warta, one of the sister camps.

Now the Germans hurried them. They marched quickly toward Hassag, fifteen kilometers away, and the railroad tracks. Confusion surrounded them as they arrived at the tracks, a short distance from Czestochowa.

Once again, the Jews were loaded onto the familiar cattle cars. Before the train could leave, a man in Benny's car broke through the slatted window and jumped to freedom.

Benny watched as he ran toward the Russians, their tanks and motorcycles now in full view. Benny prayed that the cannons pointing toward the tracks did not destroy the train in which he rode.

The door slammed, and the train shunted, slowly pulling out of the station. Even as the train pulled away, Benny could not put the doubt out of his mind. Why had he not seized the opportunity to jump and run or make the decision to hide in the canal?

Am I becoming a coward? Have I given up hope of freedom? Did I make the wrong decision to go with the Germans?

Resignation showed on the faces of the Jews, packed once again in a cattle car. They were once more pawns in the calculated German deception? Would it ever end?

It was late fall 1944, and Benny not only shivered from the night air but also from the realization of his grievous error not to try an escape.

Rakow and the other Czestochowa camps closed January 16, 1945.

To Benny, Buchenwald was only a name, but education would be swift.

The trip to Camp Buchenwald in central Germany had taken two weeks. The Jews lived in horrible conditions. They pleaded at every opportunity for toilet facilities. Denied this, they had no choice but to designate a corner of the crowded car for these purposes. Before long the odors of urine and feces became unbearable. Soon the acrid scent of vomit joined the other stench.

Infrequently the train stopped for food and water. Many of the prisoners were too ill to take the nourishment. At one stop, the

Germans gave the occupants a small bag of turnips that they ate like cattle, dirt and all.

By the time they reached their destination, the stench in the car was so overwhelming that the SS officer, who opened the door screeched, "Who is responsible for this animal behavior?"

No one answered. Immediately SS guards ordered ten passengers to the side of the track and shot them on the spot.

When they mustered and provided their names for roll call, forty people answered, one hundred cattle car occupants reduced to sixty persons, excluding the ten murdered in cold blood. The others had died of exposure and starvation.

Benny knew it was starting all over again. The desperation in the faces of the half-starved and emaciated faces that milled around the camp gate was an all-too-familiar sight. The poor souls begged for food. Why they believed the recruits would have such luxuries, Benny did not know.

The new prisoners marched through the big gate with its giant guard tower and attentive machine gunners. Buchenwald was a large camp with buildings designated for specific activities -- quarters for prisoners and guards, hospital, medical experimentation, body disposal plant and ammunition factory, among others.

Inside the camp a Capo, wearing red trousers, a tight black jacket, and a yellow armband with a black swastika, assisted the SS guards. The Capos, on occasion, administered beatings.

The middle-aged Jew, appointed Capo by the Germans, ordered the recruits into a huge concrete building. They entered in groups of fifty to seventy-five as the Capo taunted them with his whip.

Benny's fearful thoughts must have shown in his facial expression, for a man working in the area said, "Son, do not worry. The Germans here in this camp have stopped their killings by gassing. Now, they burn only the dead. However, it is difficult to stay alive here."

Benny wanted to believe him about the gas cells, but his statement did little to quell the youth's fear. Because of his indecision to try an escape, Benny's confidence had dwindled. He felt helpless.

Once inside the building, they lined up at tables marked with numbers. There, they received issues of clothing -- a striped shirt, underwear, shoes, and a coat -- used items from the crematorium victims.

Their next stop was a large concrete room where they waited in a long line to have their heads shaved. Then, the Capo ordered prisoners to submerge in a delousing solution before being allowed to dress in clothing given to them.

Benny's clothes were three times too large, but he was thankful to have them. If they were giving them clothes, perhaps they were not going to gas them.

The prisoners regrouped outside and marched to their new barracks. Benny wore on his trousers the stamped number "115918."

He found at Buchenwald an international mix of prisoners -- French, Czech, Hungarian, Rumanian, Ukrainian, English, Polish and Russian. Here he met those who had openly spoken against Hitler's actions. One was a general who had made the grievous error of disagreeing with the Fürhrer. Rarely was a German political prisoner treated harshly.

The triple-decked bunk on which Benny slept was twelve feet long by twelve inches wide. Two feet spaced the base and the next bunk. The long bunk shelves that extended the length of the room slept sixteen people on each level. Benny guessed a single barracks housed fifteen hundred persons. The rumor circulating among the prisoners was that Buchenwald's population numbered close to fifty thousand.

During the first weeks it seemed to Benny that the German goal was to work the prisoners to death. Often the labor was futile. They worked in freezing temperatures. One of the jobs consisted of marching outside the gate to a hillside that had five-story buildings, which housed German officers and soldiers' families. The prisoners spent the morning picking up large stones. In the afternoon they replaced them in their original spot. Captives were also used to build roads and to construct gallows.

Buchenwald prisoners at forced labor doing road construction.
USHMM, courtesy of Instytut Pamieci Narodowej

SS officers supervising the erection of a gallows in the forest near Buchenwald
concentration camp. USHMM, courtesy of Robert A. Schmuhl

Benny's assignment often changed. On several occasions his task consisted of carrying bodies to the crematorium for burning. He knew this job well. Records would later show that disposal capacity often reached four hundred bodies within a ten-hour day. Six coal-burning furnaces held three bodies at a time, reducing the bodies to ash and thus destroying evidence.

Food was scarce. Hoping to sing for food, Benny sometimes sneaked into other sections of the camp. It was on one of these trips that he met a French Jew who had been a prominent figure in the French government before Hitler's take-over of Europe. He also met a French socialist. It was Benny's understanding that both later died at Buchenwald. No Jew was exempt from the Nazi wrath.

During one of Benny's treks for food, he found himself face-to-face with Adolph Eichman's dog. Eichman, Director of Jewish Affairs, had come to inspect the camp. The prisoners stood at attention as Eichman reviewed them. Curiosity got the best of Benny. He leaned forward in order to get at look at the man who had committed so many crimes against the Jews. It was a bad error in judgment. The officer accompanying Eichman noticed Benny and reported him to his chief.

Eichman immediately gave orders to his huge German Shepherd dog. "Rudolph, bite the Jude!" He pointed to Benny.

Effortlessly the dog bounded toward the youth and grabbed his left leg. He ripped not only the boy's pants but also a hunk of his calf. Benny did not dare scream though the pain was excruciating.

With a smirk on his face, Eichman called his dog to his side. The damage to Benny's leg was severe, a scar the young Jew would carry the rest of his life.

Benny had been at Buchenwald a little more than three months when the sky blackened with Allied planes. Insignias on the wings indicated they were English and American. They passed over Buchenwald to another target.

The prisoners could feel the vibrations for miles as the planes dropped their cargo. That night the sky lit from the fires of the destruction. The very next day the Germans transported some of the laborers to the bombed city to clean up debris. Benny was one of those.

—————※————

The Nazis killed between seven and eight thousand prisoners before they hurriedly evacuated 28,250 from Buchenwald on April 6, 1945. Benny was among the evacuated Jews. On April 11, the SS fled, and the Americans liberated the camp.

—————※————

The Germans marched the evacuees to a small camp a short distance from Coldiz, a village nestling in the hills near Leipzig. This was Benny's next home.

In his heart Benny knew the Germans wanted to get them to a place where they could make further use of their captives. He believed that the longer he lived the better chance he had to survive. The boy felt lucky to march away from Buchenwald.

The prisoners immediately assumed tasks. Benny's was cleaning the sewers under the watchful eye of twenty German Wermacht, who replaced the SS guards in finalizing the Jew problem. Even though he did not trust the German soldiers, Benny welcomed the reprieve from the Nazis' ugly tempers. The laborers worked hard and ate poorly, but the soldiers did not physically abuse them.

Fed poorly at Buchenwald, Benny ate more sparingly at Coldiz. Without proper nourishment, he shed rapidly the weight gained at Rakow.

Soon after they arrived, the droning of allied planes overhead intensified. Sirens daily caused the workers to take cover in the basement of a warehouse. The whole building shook as the bombs exploded.

Benny prayed silently that he would cheat death. To die at the hands of his liberators would have been the rudest kind of irony.

The bombs fell all around them, day and night.

The Wermacht assembled the prisoners in the camp yard, and the supervising officer announced, "The American forces are only miles away. You will march to another area. Be prepared to leave." He turned and walked away. His men followed. The prisoners were left standing at attention.

Clouds filled the sky causing a dark overcast. Soon the air was filled with a fine mist, followed shortly by a downpour. The prisoners -- six abreast, drenched, and shivering -- stood at attention. As they obeyed the admonishment to remain still or be shot, they waited for the Germans to bark orders to march.

None came. Standing in the rear of the group, Benny saw the Wermacht sneak into the woods. His eyes widened.

Are the Germans running?

No one else seemed to notice. As he stood still, he secretly watched. A single Wermacht soldier stood near the barracks.

The downpour continued.

In the distance, Benny heard the Allied planes and sounds of gunfire. He made a decision. He stepped out of line and boldly looked around the yard.

Startled, the prisoner next to him whispered, "Be careful, you idiot, you will get us all shot."

The rain had slowed, but the skies still held foreboding clouds that shadowed the land. Benny walked out in front of the group.

Paralyzed by the youth's audacity, no one else moved.

Benny inspected the length of the barbed-wire fence in all directions. He noticed that the German soldier looked at him but did not move. The boy was surprised.

The young Jew moved slowly toward the yard gate. A few prisoners dared to turn their heads to watch him.

"Halt!" yelled the soldier finally, but he did not move.

Benny reached the gate. A chain held it to the corner post.

The German yelled again but still did not move from his position. He drew his pistol.

Just as Benny reached for the chain, a clasp of thunder startled him, sending him backward into the mud. He sat there for a moment, looking at the Wermacht, who still pointed the pistol at him. He turned toward the prisoners who stood wide-eyed. Then Benny struggled to his feet and reached out to touch the gate marked "*Verboten.*"

He looked again at the soldier who still stood like a statue, staring, still holding the pistol.

Benny jerked at the chain and pulled it as if his meager strength equaled Goliath's. It did. The chain snapped. Old and rusty, it had only duped the prisoners.

Amazed, the young Jew smiled, the first real smile in a long while. With as much strength as he could muster, he flung open the large gate and walked out onto the muddy trail called a road. He did not look back. He plodded slowly, methodically.

Benny had walked a distance down the road when he turned and looked back at the compound. Only a few of the prisoners had moved. The others stood frozen to the spot, even though the soldier had vanished.

The rain lessened, until it stopped altogether, and the sun teased as sprays of light filtered through the conifer branches and cascaded delicate patterns over the spring greenery. It now fully embraced Benny. He lifted his face toward it, taking in its warmth.

Although he was only a fraction in the broad sweep of the countryside, Benny felt he was larger than life itself. He had prevailed. He was a part of humanity. Nothing could stop him now. Nothing ever again would be so challenging and so senseless.

The farther away from the camp he walked, the more erect his gait. At last, he could hear the day sounds. Benny began to hum, quietly at first. Then a lively ballad rang out as he lifted his face toward the sky, his feet and legs marching rhythmically to his own melody.

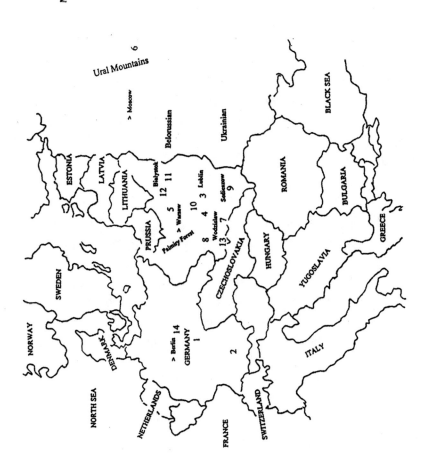

World War II
Europe
Benny Lipman's Travels

Map is a sketch with approximate distances and depicts the primary places referred to in the narrative.

1. Buchenwald
2. Dachau
3. Lubin-Majdanek
4. Skarzysko-Kamienna
5. Treblinka
6. Sverdlovsk (Russian Labor Camp)
7. maternal grandparents
8. paternal grandparents (rural area)
9. Maronski
10. Wisla River
11. Bug River
12. Narew River
13. Oswiecim
14. Leipzig (Coldiz nearby)

EPILOGUE

WHEN BENNY LIPMAN LEFT COLDIZ, he had lived in captivity for six years. The seventeen-year-old wandered the countryside, often dodging retreating Germans and eating grass, the only source of food. Benny saw a young Jew, someone he knew in Werke C, die from overeating. At intervals, German farm families, believing he was Polish, took him in.

He moved from village to village along the Polish and German border until he reached a town called Weswald. There he was able to obtain identification papers that would validate his disguise as a Pole. With these papers, he also received free food stamps and lodging.

Looking for work, he traveled to other villages where he met a young girl visiting a Polish farmer. Benny thought she was Polish, too, and her beauty smote him. She promised her father would give him a job, but they would have to travel farther into the Germany. He agreed to the risk.

Benny could not believe his bad luck when he met her father. He was wearing an SS uniform. Surprisingly, the German officer offered Benny a job, one in which he could use his knowledge of languages. He accepted. When he was given an assignment to "get rid of some Jews" locked in two railroad cars, Benny had to do some quick thinking. With the aid of the girl, he stole the father's key, and at nightfall Benny slipped out of the house unnoticed and freed the

Jews. After he had secured them with several farm families, he ran away.

While he worked in a refugee camp, Benny met his future wife, a survivor of Auschwitz. In 1946 they married. Their first child, a girl, was born before they immigrated into the United States in 1949. Shortly after arriving in the States, their son was born.

Benny did not become an astronomer; he did sing in a synagogue, once. He worked in an Ohio automobile factory, then as a part-time baker and a hat blocker.

Later he moved his family to the eastern seaboard where he settled down and became a meat cutter for a chain grocery store. After thirty years he retired.

There are four grandchildren -- two boys and two girls. Ironically, his son teaches music in a university setting, and his grandsons and one granddaughter play the violin. His daughter is a teacher.

In 1991 Benny suffered a massive heart attack. The resolute Jew drove himself to the hospital where he later received a pacemaker.

He visited Poland in 1994 for the first time since moving to the United States. When Benny went to the gates of Skarzysko-Kamienna, where he had loaded explosives, a sentry refused to let him in and denied that a labor camp ever existed there.

He visited Warsaw but could not find his childhood home. In Wodzislaw he visited the local library and found ancestral records, the only material things left of his family.

In 1995 Benny collapsed on a sidewalk in the city where he lived. A Polish lady in a near-by shop rushed to his aid. She was able to resuscitate him; however, after his arrival at the hospital, Benny lapsed into a comma and little hope was given for his survival. He awakened on the second day, jerked the medical wires from his body, and pulled free from the wrist restraints -- determined he would not be restricted. When the orderly returned and tried to reattach the straps, Benny sat up and decked the man, knocking him to the floor. Again Benny was the escapee.

With this book, Benny hoped to "lift the rock from my heart." He deeply believed that complacency allows bigotry and murder of innocent people to escalate, and that the moral lessons of the World

War II Holocaust are relevant not only historically but also in today's violent and racist world. Menachem Begin, the Prime Minister of Israel, wrote to Benny about his courage and survival: "What you have done is important for every generation so that your story -- which is the universal Jewish story -- will never be forgotten."

Benny Lipman believed that the instinct to survive lies dormant in each of us. Perhaps his story will help some of us find it.

An Adage:
If one spreads breadcrumbs on a fresh grave,
Sparrows will come and carry the crumbs into the sky
as though carrying the deceased soul to heaven.

In Memory

Bernard (Benny) Lipman
1928-2000

Aaron and Mirla Lipman
Sala Lipman
Lajbis and Mirke Lainveinber
Zalme Duvet and Cerke Lipman